Ernst Windisch

Concise Irish Grammar

With Pieces for Reading

Ernst Windisch

Concise Irish Grammar
With Pieces for Reading

ISBN/EAN: 9783337526023

Printed in Europe, USA, Canada, Australia, Japan

Cover: Foto ©Paul-Georg Meister /pixelio.de

More available books at **www.hansebooks.com**

A
CONCISE IRISH GRAMMAR

WITH

PIECES FOR READING,

BY

ERNST WINDISCH,
PROFESSOR OF SANSKRIT IN THE UNIVERSITY OF LEIPZIG.

TRANSLATED FROM THE GERMAN

BY

NORMAN MOORE, M.D.
ST CATHARINE'S COLLEGE, CAMBRIDGE;
FELLOW OF THE ROYAL COLLEGE OF PHYSICIANS.

EDITED FOR THE SYNDICS OF THE UNIVERSITY PRESS.

CAMBRIDGE:
AT THE UNIVERSITY PRESS.
1882

TRANSLATOR'S PREFACE.

I WAS at work upon an edition of the fragment of the Irish version of the Historia Britonum in Leabhar na Huidri when the Kurzgefasste Irische Grammatik of Professor Windisch appeared, and I found it so clear and well arranged a guide to the verbal forms of Irish that I wrote to ask the author's leave to translate the Grammar into English. Prof. Windisch, at once liberally gave me permission to make the translation, and has been so good as to send me several corrections which he has made since his book was published. These alterations with those given in his preface are put in their places throughout the Grammar. The whole responsibility for the translation is mine, but he has read each sheet as it passed through the press.

The earliest printed Grammar of the Irish language is by a Franciscan, Francis O'Molloy. It is in Latin, is entitled Grammatica Latino-Hibernica, and was printed at Rome in 1677. Since this publication several Irish Grammars have appeared; of which the best known are:

E. Lhwyd: (prefixed to his Irish-English Dictionary). Oxford, 1707.
Hugh Boy Mac Curtin: Elements of the Irish Language. London, 1728; Paris, 1732.
Andrew Donlevy: Elements (appended to his Catechism). Paris, 1742 and many subsequent editions.
Vallancey: Irish Grammar. 1773 and 1782.
Wm. Halliday: Uraicecht na Gaedilge. Dublin, 1808; 2nd ed. 1812.

Wm. Neilson (and Patrick Lynch): Introduction to the Irish Language. Dublin, 1808.

Paul O'Brien: Practical Grammar of the Irish Language. Dublin, 1809.

John O'Connell: Instructions for Reading Irish. Cork, 1813.

Patrick Lynch (another): Introduction. Dublin, 1815.

E. O'Reilly: Compendious Irish Grammar. Dublin, 1817.

James Scurry: An Introduction to the Irish Language. Waterford, 1820.

Owen Connellan: Practical Grammar. Dublin, 1844.

John O'Donovan: Grammar of the Irish Language. Dublin, 1845.

J. C. Zeuss: Grammatica Celtica. Berlin, 1853.

———— ed. Ebel. Berlin, 1871.

John H. Molloy: A Grammar of the Irish Language. Dublin, 1865.

These publications, of several of which a full account may be found in the preface to O'Donovan's Irish Grammar and in James Scurry's Review of Irish Grammars and Dictionaries (Transactions of the Royal Irish Academy, Vol. xv.) may be considered as, in different ways, works of authority with perhaps the exception of the compilations of Lhwyd, Vallancey, Halliday and O'Reilly. Two brief and useful Grammars based upon that of O'Donovan are:

Charles H. H. Wright: Grammar of the Modern Irish Language. Dublin, 1855.

P. W. Joyce: School Irish Grammar. Dublin, 1879.

The Grammars of O'Donovan and of Zeuss are those which are of most importance by far to students of Irish.

O'Donovan, who was born at Atateemore, Co. Kilkenny, in 1809, was well versed in the existing idiom of his mother tongue. In connexion with the Ordnance Survey he had travelled into every part of Ireland, and was thus acquainted with all the dialects prevalent in his day. He edited many volumes of Irish texts and transcribed a vast number of MSS., so that he also acquired an extended knowledge of the vocabulary and grammatical forms of mediæval Irish. The materials for a study of the most ancient form of Irish (Old-Irish) are not copious in Ireland, and it was in the language of the early period that his knowledge was least profound. His Grammar will always be valuable as a storehouse of trustworthy information on Modern Irish in the widest sense of the term.

The Grammatica Celtica of Zeuss, besides its merit as a work of general philological learning, is a mine of wealth for the ancient form of Irish. It is of course much more than a collection of material. Its arrangement, and its demonstration of the relations of the Celtic languages to one another and of their vocabulary and grammatical forms to the Indo-European and especially to the Classical forms, placed the study of Irish upon a basis of observation from which the history of the language and the explanation of the difficulties of the literature may be surely elucidated.

Others, among the grammatical treatises enumerated above, are of value as illustrations of the dialect of several parts of Ireland: thus Mac Curtin wrote of Clare; Neilson and Lynch, of Down; O'Brien, of Meath; O'Connell, of Kerry; Lynch, of Limerick; Scurry, of Kilkenny; Connellan, of Sligo; John H. Molloy, of Galway. The last in a lesser degree is of the same kind of value as O'Donovan. The author having conversed in Irish with men from all parts of Ireland, noted their local idioms, and has given the examples in his Grammar.

The dialects of Modern Irish were not without their representatives in earlier periods of the language, though how far back is not yet known, and a study of their peculiarities will in many cases give the explanation of otherwise inexplicable varieties in MSS.

Zeuss may be considered the founder of the study of

Old Irish. Whitley Stokes has, since the time of Zeuss, added most to this branch of the subject, and will, I hope, long continue the Bentley of Celtic studies. I may add, that Mr Stokes encouraged me in the present translation. Fearganainm O'Domhnallain and William Wotton, both of St Catharine's College, in past centuries did some work which deserves recollection, but Mr Henry Bradshaw of King's College will always be regarded as the real founder of Celtic studies at Cambridge, and this translation, like so many more important publications, has received kindly help from him.

Prof. Windisch's work is the first exclusive Grammar of Irish in which the subject is begun on an Old Irish basis and treated in the method of modern philology, with the rudiments of which it presupposes an acquaintance. It gives a concise view of the knowledge of Old Irish as it stands after the labours of Zeuss and of Stokes with those of Windisch himself, of Hennessy, Ascoli, Ebel, Nigra and others.

NORMAN MOORE.

The College,
St Bartholomew's Hospital, London.
October, 1882.

PREFACE.

THIS concise Irish Grammar was (1879) separated for practical reasons from a larger work, Irische Texte mit Wörterbuch, which has since been published. The Grammar forms a separate book and is furnished with some pieces for reading which are not contained in the larger work. If this Grammar prove of use in facilitating and encouraging the highly interesting study of the Old Irish language and literature, it will have attained its object, for I have not attempted to give in it an exhaustive or a comparative grammar of the Irish language. This last, with the reference to the rest of the Celtic languages, I have reserved for my part of the Grammatiken-bibliothek suggested by Breitkopf and Härtel.

In order, however, to bring this difficult language within easier reach of the beginner I have treated the phonology comparatively, at least so far as seemed advisable for beginners. The discussion in detail of difficult questions, the most modern problems of comparative phonology and the statement of all the etymologies known to me lay wide of my practical object. Repetition of the same words in the examples has been as far as possible avoided.

The form of the language which I have chiefly had in

view is Old Irish, and of my sources of information the famous Grammatica Celtica of J. Caspar Zeuss stands in the first line. Its second edition (Berlin, 1871) owing to the faithful work of Hermann Ebel is greatly improved, supplemented and usefully arranged. Ebel's Keltische Studien, which are scattered through nearly all the volumes of the Beiträge zur Vergleichenden Sprachforschung, have greatly contributed to the improvement of this second edition. The numerous books and papers of Whitley Stokes afford an abundance of further materials and in the Verb I have been deeply indebted to his treatises in the vIth and vIIth volumes of the Beiträge zur Vergleichenden Sprachforschung and to the passages from the Milan codex in his Goidelica (2nd ed., London, 1872). In his Commentary on the Irish glosses, A Mediæval Tract on Latin Declension (Dublin, 1860), paradigms are interspersed besides numerous etymologies and phonetic observations. His annotations on O'Donovan's translation of Cormac's Glossary (Calcutta, 1868) also contain many valuable philological observations. His Remarks on the Celtic additions to Curtius' Greek Etymology (Calcutta, 1874), enlarged 1875, and in the main repeated in the vIIIth volume of the Beiträge zur Vergleichenden Sprachforschung must be further considered in phonetic reference. In this last treatise some laws of substitution of sounds are set forth, which I do not think firmly established. I have made use of the first part of G. I. Ascoli's long looked-for complete edition of the Milan glosses (Archivio Glottologico Italiano, Vol. v.)[1]. As my own papers on Celtic subjects, written after my contributions to the fourth edition of Curtius' Grundzüge der Griechischen Etymologie, are printed in several publications I have here given a list of them:

[1] The second part appeared in 1882.

Preface.

(1.) Loss and appearance of *P* in the Celtic languages—Beiträge zur Vergl. Sprachf. VIII. 1—48.

(2.) The Irish T-preterite. Beiträge zur V. S. VIII. 442—470.

(3.) The reduplicated perfect in Irish—Zeitschrift für Vergl. Sprachf. XXIII. 201—266.

(4.) The Irish Infinitive—Bezzenberger's Beiträge zur Kunde der Indog. Spr. II. 72 et seq.

(5.) The Irish laws of termination—Paul and Braune's Beiträge zur Gesch. d. deutsch Spr. IV. 204—270.

The first of the above papers has been examined and criticized in the IId vol. of H. Gaidoz' Revue Celtique, by Wh. Stokes, J. Rhys, and H. d'Arbois de Jubainville. I received a second part of H. Zimmer's Celtic Studies in the XXIVth volume of the Zeitschr. für Vergl. Sprachf. after this Grammar, including the addenda, was already in print. I mention this because the equation of the Irish *re, le* with the Sanskrit *ṛi* and notes regarding the accent in Irish are found there on which Zimmer promises an elaborate treatise.

Literary authority is not given for every single word and form, for most of them are readily discoverable in the above-mentioned works. In addition it ought to be mentioned that lexicographic works and indexes have been promised from more than one quarter in the near future. In a case where difficulties of every kind have had to be combated it is only natural that some questions should have received less attention than others. With regard to the separation of grammatical forms which are written in one word in most MSS. I have not always been consistent. I have nevertheless attained fixed principles on the subject, the enunciation of which I have reserved till the publication of the introduction to my Irische Texte. Still many examples are no doubt printed together in this book, partly in error, partly from uncertainty, which would be better separated. The inconsequence of Irish orthography in MSS. is well known: a great part of it is due to the fact that the scribes sometimes retained the ancient written form and sometimes followed the changed pronunciation of their own time. I have given the forms as I found them and have only allowed myself a certain uniformity in the paradigms.

Old Irish is the language of the VIIIth and IXth centuries, as it is found in the glosses of the MSS. of Milan, S. Gall, Würzburg, Karlsruhe, Turin, &c. In the Appendix of the Grammatica Celtica specimens of them are to be seen. The Turin glosses have been published in extenso by C. Nigra (Paris, 1869), and by Stokes in the Goidelica. In the latter are numerous shorter Old Irish glosses gleaned from other MSS. together with the Irish annotations of the Book of Armagh, a MS. of the IXth century. The Codex of S. Gall (gleanings from which are edited in Nigra's Reliquie Celtiche, Turin, 1872) is to be published in full by Ascoli after the Milan Codex. [Le Chiose Irlandesi del Codice di San Gallo. Archiv. Glott. Ital. Vol. VI., 1880. In the meantime a collection of the Old Irish glosses in the minor manuscripts, but including those of the Würzburg and the two Karlsruhe manuscripts, was published by H. Zimmer, Glossæ Hibernicæ Berol. 1881.]

The Xth and XIth centuries are scarcely represented by more important MSS. [The Irish of the Stowe Missal is attributed by Wh. Stokes to the XIth or XIIth century. Ztsch. f. Vergl. Spof. XXVI., p. 298.] The oldest Middle Irish MSS. begin about the year 1100. To this period belongs the Leabhar na huidre (Royal Irish Academy), Dublin, published in facsimile 1870. The Liber Hymnorum well known through Stokes' Goidelica is somewhat later. The Book of Leinster belonging to the XIIth century will also be published in facsimile (published 1880) and from the somewhat later MSS. the Leabhar Breac was published in 1876 in two volumes by the Royal Irish Academy. My Irische Texte contains interesting texts taken from these sources. Mr Whitley Stokes who looked over the first two sheets in proof noted that x, y, z were not mentioned in § 1. The Irish x (excluding borrowed words) is only found for cs when these sounds occur in sequence, owing to the suppression of a vowel, e.g. in *foxal* metaplasmus for *fo-co-sal* Latin salio (cf. § 336). Y only occurs in borrowed words as *ymmon* = Latin hymnus. Z is less still a true Irish sound, yet compare *baitzisi* baptizavit eum Goid^2 p. 87, line 1 (Book of Armagh). On § 11 Stokes suggests that the Irish *di* answers to the Cymric *ai* and the Irish *ói* to the Cymric *u*. It seems to me that this distinction which I had myself remarked cannot be carried through. On § 57 Stokes notes some words with *iu* in initial sound in which he thinks that the *i* represents an original *j*, e.g. *iug—śuide* tribunal Sg. 50^a (Z^2 855) *iúrad* factum est (Book of Armagh) the last allied to the Old Gaulish ειωρου fecit.

ERNST WINDISCH.

Leipzig,
December 22, 1878.

TABLE OF CONTENTS.

	PAGES
I. Phonology, § 1—108	1—32

Alphabet and Pronunciation, § 1—5.

Vowels, § 6—28; Infection, § 16—24; Shortening of long Vowels, § 25; Suppression of Vowels, § 26; Variation of Vowels, § 27; Sequence of Vowels, § 28.

Consonants, § 29—77; Aspiration, § 59—68; Assimilation, § 69—73; Compensatory lengthening, § 74—77.

Intercalation of Vowels, § 78; Metathesis, § 79—80; Contraction, § 81—85.

Terminal sound, § 86—106; Aspiration, § 91—96; Eclipsis, § 97—101.

Prosthesis, § 107—108; Apheresis, § 108^b—108^c.

II. Declension, § 109—170 . . . . . . 33—45

I a Stems in *a*, § 110—114; I b Stems in *ia*, § 115—120; II Stems in *i*, § 121—125; III Stems in *u*, § 126—133; IV a Dental stems, § 134—143; IV b Guttural stems, § 144—148; IV c The terms of relationship in *r*, § 149—151; IV d Masculine and feminine stems in *n* and *nn*, IV e Neuters in *man, mann*, IV f Neuters in *as* and other stems in *s*, § 164—167; Isolated and hitherto inexplicable stems, § 168—170.

III. The Article, § 171—180 . . . . . . 46—48

IV. Comparison, § 181—188 . . . . . . 49—50

V. Adverbs, § 189 51

VI. Pronouns, § 190—228 . . . . . . 52—61

Demonstrative, § 190—198; Personal, § 199—206; Possessive, § 207—210; Self, § 211; Relative, § 212—214; Interrogative, § 215—219; Indefinite, § 220—228.

VII. Numerals, § 229—236 . . . . . . 62—64

Cardinal, § 229—232; Ordinal, § 233; Numeral substantives, § 234; Multiplicative, § 235; Distributive, § 236.

VIII. Prepositions § 237—247^b . . . . . 65—68

Prepositions in composition, § 241—247.

xvi *Table of Contents.*

		PAGES
IX.	VERBS, § 248—389	69—119

Conjugations, § 248; Tenses, § 249—250; Verbal particles, § 251; Passive and Deponent Verbs, § 253; Absolute and Conjoined forms, § 254.

Active voice, § 255—311 . . . . 71—92

Present (1. Indicative, 2. Conjunctive, 3. Imperative, 4. Second Present, 5. Present of habit), § 255—264ᶜ, 6. T-past, § 265—268; 7. S-past, § 269—274; 8 and 9. Reduplicated future with Conditional, § 275—281; 10 and 11. B-future with Conditional, § 282—284; 12 and 13. S-future with Conditional, § 285—289; 14. Perfect, § 290—303; Other tense forms, § 304—311.

Passive voice, § 312—332 . . . . . . 92—99

Present (1. Ind., 2. Conj., 3. Imperat., 4. Second Present), § 312—314; 5 and 6. Reduplicated Future with Conditional, § 315—317; 7 and 8. B-future with Conditional, § 318—319; 9 and 10. S-future with Conditional, § 320—323; Past, § 324—328; The 1st and 2nd Persons in the Passive, § 329—332.

Deponent, § 333—352 . . . . 99—106

1. Indicative, 2. Conjunctive Present, § 333—337; 3. S-past, § 338—340; 4. B-future, § 341—342; 5. S-future, § 343—345; 6. Reduplicated Future, § 346; 7. Perfect, § 347—350; *ro fetar*, § 351; Deponent forms in Modern Irish, § 352.

Participles, § 353—362 . . . . 106—109

1. Perfect Passive participle, § 353—359; 2. Participium recessitatis, § 360.

Infinitive, § 363—382 . . . . 110—116

Verb substantive, § 383—389 . . . . . . 116—119

1. *as*, § 384—385; 2. *std*, § 386—387; 3. *vel*, § 388; 4. *Bhú*, § 389.

X. PARTICLES, § 390—403 . . . . 120—124

1. Negative, § 390, 391; 2. Question and Answer, § 392—393; 3. Conjunctions, § 394—400; 4. Particles used as prefixes, § 401—403.

Addenda (on the position of the long accent, value in quantity, accent and so forth) . . . . . 125—128

PIECES FOR READING . . . . 129—141

DICTIONARY . . . . 143—166

I.

PHONOLOGY.

1. THE Old Irish alphabet consists of the following letters: *a b c (ch) d e f (ph) g h i l m n o p r s t (th) u*, with the long vowels, *á é í ó ú*, the true diphthongs *ía, ái áe, ói óe, úa, au*, and the improper diphthongs enumerated § 18 et seq. *x* is sometimes met with as another form of writing *cs*. *y* and *z* occur only in borrowed words.

The Old Irish writing is a peculiar form of the Roman character, and is in use to this day.

2. In Modern Irish the consonants *d t g c l r n s*, whether preceding or following a broad vowel (*a o u*), have the broad pronunciation corresponding to that in German, after or before a slender vowel a liquid pronunciation. *S* in this case has the sound of the English *sh*. In like manner *ch* is differently pronounced as the German *ch* in *ach* and *ich*.

3. The sounded spirants *gh dh bh mh* show the same difference in pronunciation, but are not distinguished till the later writings from the unaspirated *g d b m* (§ 68).

dh has in Modern Irish the pronunciation of *gh:* both sounds before or after a broad vowel resemble the spirant in the German word Magen, and both before or after a slender vowel sound like the German *j*: as terminal sounds they become silent.

bh before or after a broad vowel sounds like the German *w*, before or after a slender vowel like the English *v*. In median sound between short broad vowels it becomes vocalized into *u*.

mh has the same pronunciation but with a nasal sound. Both *bh* and *mh* in initial sound are always pronounced in Munster like the English *v*. (O'Donovan, Grammar, pp. 46, 51.)

4. *th* is pronounced in Modern Irish like *h*, as also is *ṡ* or *sh* (§ 91); *ph* like the German *f; f* is silent.

Even in Old Irish *lathe*, day, is found contracted to *laa, lá,* and the aspirated *s* and *f* are left out in writing: *senaig* for *sesnaig*, the perfect of *snigim; sith-laith* for *sith-flaith*, Fiacc's Hymn 19; *ind atsine* for *fatsine*, 22; *a ridadart* for *fridadart*, 32.

5. The transition of *c t p g d b m s f* into *ch th ph gh dh bh mh ṡ f* is called aspiration. The typographical marks of aspiration in Old Irish are for *c* and *t*, an *h* following (*ch*), or an Old Greek rough breathing placed over the letter; for *s* and *f*, a dot (*ṡ*). In Modern Irish aspiration is uniformly indicated by a dot placed over the letter (*ċ*).

Vowel Sounds.

6. *a o (u) e i* are the short *a*-vowel sounds: *alt*, educavit, Latin *alo; canim*, I sing, Latin *cano; saigim*, adeo, Gothic *sokja; ocht*, eight, Latin *octo; roth*, wheel, Latin *rota; muir*, genitive *mora*, sea, Latin *mare* (§ 18); *ech*, horse, Latin *equus; celim*, I conceal, Gothic *hila; berim*, Latin *fero; med*, mead, Greek μέθυ; *dligim*, debeo, Gothic *dulgs*, guilt; *midiur*, judico, Greek μέδομαι; *mil*, honey, Latin *mel*. On *e* and *o* standing for original *i* and *u* see § 21.

7. *i* occurs particularly often before *nd, nn, mb, mm, ng, ns : ind-rúth*, incursus, Old Gaulish *Ande-ritum; imb, imm*, Greek ἀμφί; *imb*, butter, Latin *unguentum*, Sanskrit *añjana* (according to Stokes); *inga*, nail, Latin *unguis; imbliu*, genitive *imlenn*, navel, Greek ὀμφαλός; *lingim*, I leap; *cingim*, I stride; *mí*, genitive *mís*, month, Latin *mensis* (§ 74).

8. *á* (*ó*) *í* are the long *a* vowel sounds: *máthir*, mother, Latin *mater;* *ru rádi*, locutus est, Gothic *rodjan;* *imrádi*, cogitat, Gothic *ga-redan;* *gnáth*, solitus, Greek γνωτός; *már* and *mór*, great; *rí*, genitive *ríg*, king, Latin *rex;* *lín*, number; *línaim*, I fill, Latin *plenus*, Greek πλη-; *dínu*, lamb, Greek θή-σατο; *fír*, true, Latin *verus*, Old High German *wár;* *míl*, beast, Greek μῆλον.

9. *é* in the *a* series originated through compensatory lengthening (§ 74): *cét*, hundred, Cymric *cant*, Latin *centum;* *sét*, path, Cymric, *hynt*, Gothic *sinths;* *éc*, death, Cornish *ancou*, Latin *nex;* *écad*, hook, Latin *uncus*, curved.

10. *i* and *u* answer to the Indo-Germanic *i* and *u* (see § 21): *fid*, tree, Old High German *witu*, wood; *biad*, victus, Greek βίοτος; *sruth*, stream, Sanskrit root *sru*. In originally monosyllabic words *u* becomes *o*: *no*, verbal particle especially in the present, Greek νυ, Gothic *nu;* *so-*, Sanskrit *su-;* *do-*, Sanskrit *dus-*, Greek δυς.

11. *é* and the thence derived *ia* (compare the borrowed word *fíal* = Latin *velum*), and *ái*, *ói*, commonly *áe*, *óe*, are the diphthongs of the *i*-series (Indo-Germanic *ai*, Sanskrit *e*): *adféded*, narrabat, *ad-fíadat*, narrant, Sanskrit *veda;* *dériad*, bigae, Old Gaulish *reda*, Old High German *reita* currus. *áe* and *óe* interchange in one and the same word: *óen* and *áen*, one, Latin *unus;* *loeg*, calf, Gothic *laikan;* *clóen*, iniquus, Gothic *hlains*, Latin *clivus*, hillock, *declinare*. It is only in terminal sound that the *ē* of diphthong origin is still further attenuated to *ī*: *dí*, two, feminine = Sanskrit *dve* (compare the Lithuanian *tĕ-dvi*, nominative dual feminine, these both). In *scian*, knife, *trian*, third, *triar*, three persons, *ia* is not of diphthong origin, but the *a* belongs to the suffix. On *biad* and many others see § 82.

12. *ó* and the thence derived *úa* (compare the borrowed word *glúass*, explanatio = glossa) answer to the Indo-Germanic

au (Sanskrit *o*); *lóche*, genitive *lóchet*, lightning, Gothic *liuhath;* *túath*, people, Gothic *thiuda;* *ócht*, *úacht*, cold, Lithuanian *áuszti*, to become cold; *óthad*, *úathad*, singularitas, Gothic *authida*, solitariness. On *ó*, *úa* due to compensatory lengthening see § 74, *ó* = *á*, § 8.

13. *au* is rare and interchanges with *ó;* *au* and *ó*, ear, Gothic *auso*, Latin *auris;* *nau*, genitive *nóe*, ship, Greek ναῦς, Latin *navis;* *gau*, *gó*, *gú*, mendacium, falsum. In *aue*, *oa*, *ua*, grandchild, *au* has perhaps originated from *av*, Latin *avus* (?).

14. *ú* answers to a *ū* of other languages in *rún*, secret, Old High German *rûna;* *dún*, stronghold, Old Norse *tûn;* *dúil*, elementum, Sanskrit *dhūli*, dust(?); *mún*, urine, Sanskrit *mūtra;* *iar cúl*, behind (post tergum), Latin *cūlus*. In other cases it has probably been derived at a later period through vocalization of *v* and contraction: *núe*, new, Sanskrit *navya*, Gothic *niujis;* *clú*, renown, Sanskrit *çravas;* *súil*, eye, Cymric *haul* and Gothic *sauil*, sun.

15. *í* answers rarely to a long *i* of other languages: *lí*, color, splendor, Latin *livor;* *críthid*, emax, Sanskrit root *krī* (Irish *crenim*), I buy, Sanskrit *krīṇāmi*. In most words the etymology of which is certain *í* may be traced to an original *ā* (§ 8). In single cases *í* has been created by compensatory lengthening (§ 74), or by contraction from *ja*, *je* (§ 57).

INFECTION.

16. The clearness of vowels is disturbed by the influence which the vowels of neighbouring syllables exercise upon one another. The modern Irish rule, "*caol le caol, leathan le leathan*" (slender with slender, broad with broad), exists even in Old Irish, though less consistently carried out in writing.

Infection. 5

Generally the vowel of the following syllable decides the modification or "infectio" (Zeuss) of the vowel of the preceding syllable. But there are exceptions, *e.g. máthair*, mother, *bráthair*, brother; Old Irish *máthir, bráthir*. *e* and *i*, of whatever origin, are slender vowels.

17. Infection by slender vowels is the commonest form. In Old Irish, however, it is only without any exception noted in writing, when the infixed *i* or *e* as vowel of the last syllable after the radical vowel has disappeared (§ 88).

18. The slender vowel either stands (always in the form of an *i*) with the vowel of the preceding syllable or wholly supplants that vowel. Thus arises a series of improper diphthongs and triphthongs.

From *a* is *ai (oi, ei): mac*, son, voc. *a maic* (for pre-historic *maqu-e*).

From *a* is *i: beothu*, life, gen. *bethad*, dat. sg. *bethid* (for pre-historic *bivatat-i*).

From *a* is *ui: cechan*, cecini, third sg. *cechuin* (for pre-hist. *cecan-e*).

From *á* is *ái: fáith*, vates (for pre-hist. *vāt-is*).

From *e* is *ei: no beir*, fert (for pre-hist. *ber-it*).

From *e* is *i: dliged*, law, gen. *dligid* (for pre-hist. *dliget-i*).

From *é* (§ 9) is (*ēi*) *eói, eúi: sét*, path, gen. *seúit* (for pre-hist. *sent-i*).

From *é* is *éi: féith*, sinew, vein (for pre-hist. *vēt-is*).

From *ia* is *éi, íai: fíach*, debitum, nom. pl. *féich* (for pre-hist. *vēc-i*).

From *o* is *ui: muir*, sea (for pre-hist. *mor-i*).

From *o* is *ói: slóg*, crowd, nom. pl. *slóig* (for pre-hist. *slōg-i*).

From *úa* is *úai: túath*, folk, dat. sg. *túaith* (for pre-hist. *tōt-i*).

From *ú* is *úi: rún*, secret, acc. sg. *rúin* (for pre-hist. *rūn-in*).

From *óe* is *ói: nóeb*, holy, nom. pl. *nóib* (for pre-hist. *noib-i*).

From *áe* is *ái: cáech*, blind, nom. pl. *cáich* (for pre-hist. *caic-i*).

19. The particle *ro* owing to the reduplicative syllable often becomes *roi:* Old Irish *ad-roi-gegrannatar*, persecuti sunt. This *oi* often remained after the reduplicative syllable had ceased to be used. It was then no longer correctly understood, and on this account came to be treated as the genuine diphthong *ói: ro leblaing*, he leaped, *roiblaing, roeblaing, raeblaing*. In the same way, perhaps, the later *caom-nacatar*, potuerunt, is related through *coem- coim-nactar* to *com-nenactar*.

20. If the infixed vowel is still present, the orthography varies in Old Irish: *aged* or *aiged*, face; *gude* or *guide*, prayer; *imrádi* or *imrádidi*, cogitat; *gréne* or *gréine*, gen. of *grían*, sun; *ingine*, gen. of *ingen*, daughter.

21. By *a* (*o*) the *i* and *u* of the preceding syllable are transformed to *e* and *o*: *fer*, Latin *vir* (for pre-hist. *vir-as*); *fetar*, scio (root *vid*); *cloth*, famous, for pre-hist. *clut-as*, Grk. κλυτός; *bond*, sole of foot, for pre-hist. *bund-as*, Lat. *fundus; sotho*, gen. sg. of *suth*, fetus (root *su*). By *a* the *é* (derived from *ai*) of the preceding syllable is changed to *ía: pían* = Lat. *poena*, but gen. *péne* (borrowed word); *íasc*, piscis, from pre-hist. *pēsc-as*, gen. *éisc; críathar*, cribrum, for pre-hist. *crētr-a* (fem.); *ad-féded*, narrabat, *ad-fíadat*, narrant (root *vid*). It is rare for *i* to have become *ia*, owing to an introduced *a: míastar*, judicabit, *midiur*, judico.

22. *u* (*o*) of whatever origin often joins in Old Irish as *u* or *o* the vowel of the preceding syllable or assimilates that vowel to itself. Thus arise the false diphthongs *au, iu, eo, éu: fiur* dat. sg. of *fer* vir, for prehist. *vir-u; do-biur* and *do-bur* I give, for prehist. *-ber-u; cenéul, ceníul* dat. of *cenél* kind, for prehist. *cenetl-u; imb-rádud* cogitatio, for prehist. *rādiat-us; ulc* dat. of *olc* malum, for prehist. *olc-u; eochu* acc. pl. of *ech* equus; *laigiu* and (after suppression of the *i*, § 26) *lugu*

minor. Sometimes also other vowels as *a e i o é* are influenced: *laeochu* acc. pl. of *laech* hero.

23. Infection by *u* is often absent in Old Irish: *bith* world, for prehist. *bit-us*, Old Gaulish *Bitu-riges ; rith* run, for prehist. *rit-us ; fid* tree, for prehist. *vid-us*, Old High German *witu ; il* much, for prehist. *pil-u*, Gothic *filu ;* especially in the infinitive in *ad* of the II conjug. e.g. *carad* to love, for an original *carajat-us*. With *fiss* knowledge, for prehist. *vidt-us*, stands the compound *cubus* conscientia, that is *con-fius*.

24. It is only in the later language that *io, ío, ea,* and *éa* (*éu*) (for the Old Irish *i, í, e* and the *é* of § 9) are added to the improper diphthongs of Old Irish, in cases where a broad vowel actually follows or once followed those vowels. Modern Irish *each*, steed; *fear*, man; *céad* or *céud*, hundred; *bioth*, world; *fíor*, true; *feargach*, angry; for Old Irish, *ech, fer, cét, bith, fír, fergach*.

Other Changes of the Vowels.

25. Long vowels in the (unaccentuated) suffix-syllables of words of more than one syllable become shortened: *bethad* gen. sg. of *beothu* life, for prehistoric *bivatat-as*, answers to the Greek βιότητος; *túatha*, nom. pl. of *túath* people, answers to the Gothic *thiudos*. In forms such as *berit*, ferunt, for prehist. *berant-i;* the *n* perhaps disappeared without compensatory lengthening. In composition even long radical syllables become shortened; *céimm* gradus, *to-chaimm, -chim* the march: in the same way *air-mitiu* honor proves the existence of a simple *métiu, Latin mentio. As the long accent is often left out in manuscripts, or is indistinguishable in them, it is not safe without further evidence to reckon on the shortness of a vowel from the absence of the long accent.

26. The short or shortened vowels of median syllables of words of three or more syllables may be suppressed: *cunutgim*

I build, for *con-ud-tegim*, Latin tego, tectum; *etir-dibnim* interimo, for *di-benim*, Homeric πέφνε; *cechnatar* cecinerunt, for *cecanatar*; *toipnitar* pepulerunt, for *do-sefannatar* (*do-sephainn* pepulit); *tuistiu* generatio with *do-fui-semar* generatur for *do-fo-sitiu* (see § 45 and § 25); *fo-dáli* distribuit, 3 pl. *ni fodlat* non discernunt.

27. On the other hand there is a certain inconsistency of the vowels in another direction: besides *air-dirc*, *ir-dirc*, conspicuus, are also found *ar-*, *aur-*, *ur-dirc*; in the same way besides *air-lam* ready, also *aur-*, *ur-lam* and so forth. In suffix syllables *o*, *a*, *u* interchange especially before *r*, *l*, *n*, *m*, Conchobor, Conchobur; *corcor*, *corcar*, *corcur*, purple; *forcital*, *forcitul*, precept; *dénom*, *dénam*, *dénum* to do, and so on.

28. An inclination for certain vowel-sequences distinct from the "infectio" § 16, founded either upon assimilation or dissimilation, is also found. It is most obvious in the transformation of foreign words; *u-a* as *cubad* = Latin *cubitum*; *rustach* = Latin *rusticus*; *umal* = Latin *humilis*; *cubachail* = Latin *cubiculum*; *putar* = Latin *putor*; *slupar* = Latin *stupor*; *e-a* as *ennach* = Latin *innocens*; *credal* = Latin *credulus*; *espartain* = Latin *vespertina*. Thus is explained e.g. nom. *drui*, gen. *druad* in the face of n. *file*, gen. *filed* (§ 134). In other cases *i-u* or *e-o* show a certain affinity to one another: *lebor* or *libur* = Latin *liber*; *circul* or *cercol* = Latin *circulus*: and in genuine Irish words: *biu* or *beo* living, *do-biur* I give, *con-riug* I tie, but *ateoch* I pray; *don fiur* to the man, but *dond eoch* to the horse; *firu* viros, but *eocho* equos; *dogniu* facio, but *do-gneo* faciam, and many others.

CONSONANTS.

29. The Old Irish *c* (*ch* § 59) answers to the two Indo-Germanic *k* sounds; *cú* hound, Sanskrit çvā; *crabud* faith, Skr. *vi-çrambha* trust; *do-ro-chair* cecidit, *ir-chre* interitus, Skr. root çar break to pieces; *cruim* worm, Skr. *kṛimi*; *crenim* I

buy, Skr. *krīṇāmi;* *techim* I run, flee, Skr. root *tak, takta* shooting thither, Lithuan. *tekù* flow, run. As to Irish *c* for *g* see § 67.

30. *g* answers to the Indo-Germanic *g* and *gh*: *ro-génar* natus sum, Grk. γέγνημαι; *liaig* physician, Gothic *leikeis;* *gáir* shout, *to-gairm* call, *for-con-gur* præcipio, Grk. γῆρυς, Skr. *gir* voice, root *gar, gṛiṇāti* to call; *gegon* vulneravi, Skr. *jaghana;* *agur* timeo, Grk. ἄχομαι; *lígim* I lick, *ligur* tongue, Grk. λείχω. (As to Irish *g* for *c, ch* see § 62.)

31. *b* also often corresponds to an Indo-Germanic *g*; *ben* woman, Grk. γυνή; *biu, béo* living, Grk. βίος, Skr. *jīva;* *broo, bró* millstone, gen. *broon*, Skr. *grāvan;* *at-bail* he dies, Old Saxon *qual* he died; *bo* cow, Greek βοῦς, Skr. *gaus*.

32. *t* (*th* § 59) corresponds to a radical *t*; *temel* darkness, Skr. *tamas;* *tám* death, *tathaim* died, Skr. root *tam, tāmyati* to lose breath, pass away; *traig* foot, Grk. τρέχω; *torand* thunder, Cymr. *taran*, Lat. *tonitru;* *túath* people, Goth. *thiuda*. As to Irish *t* for *d* see § 67.

33. *d* answers to the Indo-Germanic *d* and *dh*; *deich* ten, Latin *decem;* *sude* seat, Skr. *sadas;* *bodar* deaf, Skr. *badhira;* *dínu* lamb, Grk. θήσατο; *rúad* ruddy, Goth. *rauds;* *dúil* elementum, Skr. *dhūli* dust (?). As to Irish *d* for original *t, th* see § 60.

34. *b* answers to the Indo-Germanic *bh*: *bói* fuit, Skr. root *bhū;* *bláth* blossom, Gothic *bloma*. As to *b* for original *g* see § 31, *br*, *bl* for *mr*, *ml* see § 41, *b* for *v* § 45.

35. *p* as a single sound appears with the exception of some words of obscure origin (*e.g. patu* hare) in borrowed words only: *apstal*, Latin *apostolus;* *pían*, Latin *poena:* *prím-*, Latin *primus*. In Irish words *p* sometimes stands for *b*, in order to indicate the unaspirated pronunciation of the media. Thus after *r* and *l*: *com-arpi*, coheredes; *Alpa* and *Alba*, North Britain. In composition *p* occurs where an assimilation of a terminal dental and an initial *b* has taken place; *adopart* obtulit for *aith-od-bart;*

topur fons for *do-od-bur*. In terminal sound *p* stands for *b* in mutilated forms of *bíu* I am; *rop* for *ro-ba*, but also *roptár* for *ro-batar*. The Irish *p* never answers to an Indo-Germanic *p*.

36. The Indo-Germanic *p* has disappeared in Irish: *athir*, father, Latin *pater;* *lár*, floor, Anglo-Sax. *flôr; ibim*, I drink, Skr. *pibāmi; étar*, invenitur, Goth. *fintha; tess*, heat for *tepest-us*, Skr. *tapas; nia*, gen. *niad* nephew, Latin *nepos; suan*, sleep, Skr. *svapna*. Original *pt* is expressed by *cht* as: *secht* seven, Latin *septem; necht* niece, Latin *neptis; socht* silence, Middle High Ger. *swift* silent, Grk. σιωπη (?). Schuchardt remarks that in words borrowed from the Latin through the Cymric, *p* is represented by *c*, *corcur* purpura, *casc* Pascha.

37. The guttural nasal is only found before *g*: *com-boing* confringit, Skr. *bhanga*, root *bhañj*, *inga* nail, Latin *unguis*.

38. The dental *n* answers to the Indo-Germanic *n*: *nocht* naked, Goth. *naquaths; cechtar náthar*, uterque nostrum; *ainm* name, Gr. ὄνομα; *anál* breath, Gr. ἄνεμος.

39. In suffix-syllables an *nn* or *nd* is often found where a single *n* might have been expected; *anmand*, nom. pl. of *ainm* nomen; *gobann*, gen. sg. of *goba* smith; *Erenn*, gen. sg. of *Eriu* Ireland; also *salann*, salt; *torann*, thunder; *croicend*, hide, and many others. In the Modern Irish *íarann* iron for the Old Irish *íarn*, *nn* has been developed after an epenthetic vowel. In the borrowed words, *cucenn*, *cucann* kitchen = Latin *coquina, i persaind* = Latin *in persona*, *nn*, has been developed after accented vowels which were long in Latin. This intensifying of the nasal may be connected with the accentuation (whether the tone be full or secondary), still it must be ancient, for it appears in the Old Gaulish name *Gobannitio* which surely belongs to the Irish *goba*, gen. *gobann*. Note the difference between *cú* hound, gen. *con*, and *brú* womb, gen. *brond*.

40. *m* answers to the Indo-Germanic *m*: *menme*, mind, Skr. *manman; melim*, I grind up, Latin *molo; fo-imim, foemaim*, I receive; *ar-fo-imim*, suscipio, Latin *emo, sumo*.

Consonants.

41. For *mr, ml* in initial sound (*m*)*br*, (*m*)*bl* are used: Old Irish *mrecht* later *brecht* pied, Lith. *márgas* pied; *bligim*, I milk, Old High German *melchan; ón mlith* atritione Ml. 23ᵃ 20, later *do bleith, blith*, inf. of *melim*, Latin *molo;* cf. *arindi mblegar* quia mulgetur.

42. The nasals disappear before the tenues and *s*, usually with lengthening of the preceding vowel (§ 74): *dét* tooth, Cymr. *dant*, Skr. *danta;* *bréc, brécc* lie, Skr. *bhraṃça* to fall, to deviate, to lose the way; *lécim* I leave, Latin *linquo;* *mí* month, g. *mís*, Latin *mensis*. In the borrowed word *ifern* = Latin *infernum* the nasal disappears before *f*. The lengthening is absent in unaccented syllables; *berit* ferunt, for prehist. *berant-i;* *cara* friend, gen. *carat;* *brága* neck, gen. *brágat* (suff. *ant*); *air-itiu* receptio (*air-ema* suscipiat) for *em-tiu*, Lat. emtio cf. § 25; *óac* youth, Cymr. *ieuanc*, Lat. *juvencus;* *do-anac, tánac* veni, Skr. *ānaṃça*. It seems as if the lengthening of the *a o* or *u* was never practised where a nasal had disappeared: *muc, mucc* pig, Cymr. *moch*, for *munc-ā*, Greek μυκτήρ, snout, ἀπο-μύσσω I snort, Skr. root *muc, muñcati* to set free; *oc* at, *ocus*, Cymr. *agos* vicinus, for *anc- onc-*, Goth. *nehva* near, *nehvundja* the next, Old High German *nāh, nāho;* *crocenn* hide, for *crunc-* (Skr. *kruñcati* to bend?), Old Norse *hryggr* back (St. *hrugja*), Old High German *hrucki*.

43. *r* and *l* answer to the *r* and *l* of European languages: *srúaim* stream, Grk. ῥεῦμα; *rigim* I reach, Grk. ὀρέγω; *ad-condarc* conspexi, Skr. *dadarça*, Grk. δέδορκα; *daur* oak, Grk. δόρυ, Goth. *triu* tree; *lenim* adhaereo, Skr. *linámi*, Latin *lino;* *lige* bed, Grk. λέχος, Goth. *ligan;* *lúath* swift, *lúam* celox, Grk. πλεῦμα; *clú* fame, Grk. κλέος; *at-luchur budi* I thank, perhaps the Latin *loquor;* *gelim* consumo, Skr. *gilati*.

44. *f* in initial sound takes the place of the Indo-Germanic *v*, an unaccented spirant for an accented: *fiche*, gen. *fichet* twenty, Latin *viginti; fini* cognati, Old H. G. *wini* friend; *frass* shower, Skr. *varsha; froech, fraech* heather, Grk. ἐρείκη;

12   I. *Phonology.*

flaith lordship, Cymr. *gwlad* (stem *vlati, valti,* whilst the Goth. *valda,* Ksl. *vladą* points to a radical form *valdh*).

45. For the Indo-Germanic *v* there also appears *b* in initial sound before *r* and *l*: *bran* raven, Ksl. *vranŭ*, Lith. *varnas; leblaing* he leaped, perfect of *lingim*. In the perfect only a trace of the original initial *v* is perceptible, Skr. *valg.* *f* and *b* (later *bh*) change in the initial sound of the possessive pronouns *far n-, bar n-* your (cf. Goth. *iz-vara*), and the enclitic affixed *-b* you, appears in *dúib* you, *lib* with you, cf. Skr. *vas.* As to the change of *f* and *s* in initial sound, see § 56.

46. The following appear to be isolated cases of an original *v* dropped in initial sound: *lingim* I leap (§ 45); *oland* wool, Cymr. *gulan*, Goth. *vulla*, Skr. *ūrṇa* (perhaps the accent was on the second syllable). The (proclitic) preposition *fri* contra, loses its *f* in Middle Irish.

47. In median sound an original *v* after single accented consonants is expressed by *b* (later *bh*): *tarb* bull, Old Gaulish *tarvos; marb* dead, Old High German *marawêr* mellow; *berbaim* I boil, Latin *ferveo; delb* form, Cymr. *delw; fedb* widow, Latin *vidua*. It has disappeared in *ech* horse, Skr. *açva;* also, perhaps, in *dess* dexter, Cymr. *deheu,* Goth. *taihsva; árd* high, Latin *arduus.*

48. *b* (later *bh*) also appears for *f* in composition after the preposition *co(n)* which loses its nasal: *fossad* firm (Skr. root vas), *cobsud* stabilis; *fine* cognatus, *coibnes* affinitas; *cobeden* conjugatio; *cobdelach* cognatus (for con-fed-, -fad-), Goth. *ga-vidan* to tie up, *ga-vadjon* to betroth; *fiss* knowledge, *cubus* conscientia.

49. Between vowels the Indo-Germanic *v* has either been dropped as in: *día*, gen. *dé* God, Skr. *deva; dead* finis, Cymr. *diwedd; tana* tenuis, Cymr. *teneu*, Grk. ταναός, Skr. *tanu; mogai* nom. pl. of *mug* servus, for a prehistoric *mogav-es:* or

vocalized: *núe* new, Gothic *niujis*, Skr. *navya;* clú fame, Skr. *çravas*, Grk. κλέος; *cló, clú* nail, Latin *clavus;* bíu, béo living, βίος, Skr. *jīva*, cf. *ho Duid* of David, Ml. 14ᵇ8.

50. *s* in initial sound answers to the Indo-Germanic *s*: *samail* likeness, Latin *similis;* *sen* old, Latin *senex;* *scáth* shadow, Goth. *skadus;* *snám* swim, Skr. root *snā;* *sruth* stream, Skr. root *sru;* *fo-sligim* delino, Skr. root *sarj*, *sṛijati* to pour out (?).

51. Before *t* in initial sound *s* regularly disappears: *tiagaim* I go, Grk. στείχω; *tech* house, Grk. στέγος; *táu* I am, Lith. *stóju;* *tibim* I laugh, Grk. τάφος, Lith. *stebėti-s* to be surprised.

52. Single *s* between vowels disappears: *tó* dumb, Skr. root *tush, tushnim;* *doróigu* elegit, for *do-ro-gegu*, Goth. *kiusa;* *ro dam cloathar* qui me audiat, Old High German *hlosên;* *ál* proles, *alacht* gravid, Old H. G. *fasel* proles (Stokes); *beri* thou bearest for *beres-i*, Skr. *bharasi;* *tige*, gen. sg. of *tech* house, for prehistoric *steges-as*, Grk. στέγεος.

53. *s* between consonants has disappeared; *echtar* without, Latin *extra;* *tart* thirst, Skr. root *tarsh*.

54. *s* or *ss* in median or in terminal sound has arisen by assimilation from *ks*: as *dess* to the right, Latin *dexter;* from *gs*: as *-tías* I shall go, fut. of *tiagaim*, Grk. στείξω; from *ts* as *contotsat* 3 pl. fut. of *tuitim* I fall (that is *to-thitim, -titim* for *tetim* that is *do-étim* adeo, from *ét-* for *pent*, Goth. *fintha*, Skr. root *pat*); from *ds*: as *fessur* sciam, root *vid*; from *st*: as *acsin* to see for *ad-castio*, root *cas* (cf. Skr. *caksh* for *cakas*); *brissim* I break, Old H. G. *brëstan;* *less-* in *less-ainm* nickname, *less-mac* stepson, Old H. G. *lastar* abuse, scorn, Grk. λάσθη (?); *ocus* near, for prehist. *ancast-us;* from *dt*: as *fiss* knowledge, for prehist. *vidt-us;* from *tt* as *ind-risse*, invasus for *rit-te* § 354ᵇ.

55. Before *sc* in initial sound the consonant of the terminal sound of the root is lost: *mesc* ebrius, Skr. *mada* drunkenness; *lesc* piger, Goth. *lats* l. zy(?); *usce* water, Skr. *udaka;*

nasc band, ring; *nascim* I bind, Skr. root *nah*, Latin *necto;* *com-mescatar* miscentur, Old H. G. *miskan*, Skr. *miçra*, Grk. μίγνυμι (original root *miç*); *miscais* hate, Skr. root *mith*, to reproach, μισέω.

56. *s* and *f* change in initial sound, where *sv* originally existed: *siur* and *fiur* sister, Skr. *svasar;* *sollus* and *follus* clear, Skr. root *svar;* *súan* sleep, and *feotar* (for *fefotar* perf.) they slept, Skr. root *svap;* *do-sefainn, -sephainn*, pl. *do-sefnatar*, perf. of *do-sennim* I drive, hunt, Irish root *svand* (Skr. *sūd?*). In borrowed words in the initial sound a Latin *f* is represented by *s*: Irish *srían* = Latin *frenum;* Irish *senister* = Latin *fenestra*. Schuchardt remarks that the words in which this change is found have in many cases come into use in Irish through the Cymric and not directly from the Latin.

57. The Indo-Germanic *j* has disappeared in initial sound: *oac, óc* youth, Cymr. *ieuanc* Latin *juvencus;* *aig* ice, Cymr. *ia*, Old Norse *jökull* glacier. The *j* is in rare cases vocalized: *íc* salus, *ícaim* I heal, Cymr. *iach* healthy; in the same way *Ísu* Jesus.

58. In median sound *j* has disappeared: *fátho* gen. of *fáith* seer, for prehistoric *vātaj-as* (*os?*): *táu* I am, for prehistoric *stáju*, Lith. *stóju;* no *charu* I love, for prehistoric *cara-u, caraj-ō*; *clé*, Cymr. *cledd*, to the left, appears to stand for *clija*, Goth. *hlei-duma* the left hand.

Aspiration.

59. *c* and *t* become *ch* and *th* by aspiration, if they stand between vowels or originally did so: *lóche* lightning, Goth. *lauhmuni;* *loch* lake, Latin *lacus;* *fiach* debt, *féchem* debitor, Goth. *veihs* holy; *bráthir* brother, Latin *frater;* *cath* battle, Old H. G. *hadu*. Thus also *ct* becomes *cht*: *oct* and *ocht* eight; *rect* and *recht* right.

60. *d* (later *dh*) is made use of for *th* after an unaccented vowel, especially in terminal sound and in suffixes: *berid* he

bore, Skr. *bharati;* *lécud* inf. of *lécim* I leave, suffix *-tu;* *beothu* life, gen. *bethad,* suffix *-tāt,* Grk. βιότητ-ος. In median sound the method of writing varies, *d* is the rule before slender vowels: *ni agathar* non timet; *firfidir* verum fiet. Sometimes *d* is also used in radical terminal sound under the influence of slender vowels: *maided* clades, Skr. root *math.*

61. *d* for *t* is also found in the initial sound of single little words which are used proclitically: *do* thy, *do bráthir* thy brother, but after elision of the *o*: *th' athair* thy father; *dar* over, Latin trans, but by suffixing the enclitic pronoun to the now accented preposition, *tairis* over him, *tairsiu* over them.

62. *g* is only used for *ch* after slender, unaccented vowels: *cathir* town, gen. *cathrach,* dat. *cathrig;* *uallach* arrogans, *ualligim* sum arrogans. In the same way; *sudigim* I sit, from *sude* seat (the intermediate *sudech* does not occur).

63. In the terminal sound of words of one syllable (ending the radical syllable) *ch* is so much liked, that in this case it even answers to an original *g* (Indo-Germanic *g* or *gh*): Old Irish *teg* and *tech,* later only *tech* house (gen. *tige*), Grk. τέγος; *scáig* and *scáich* praeteriit, Old Saxon *skôk;* *tor-mach* auctio, Skr. root *mah;* *immach* out, from *mag* plain.

64. If *th* comes to stand directly after *l n* or *s*, after suppression of the preceding vowel, then the aspiration does not take place: *rélad* manifestatio (suffix *-tu*), gen. *rélto;* *cumsanad* quies, gen. *cumsanto;* *césad* passio, gen. *césto.* Sometimes *t* takes the place of two dentals which have come together after suppression of a vowel: *adfét* for *adfeded;* *fóitir* mittitur, for *fóidithir.* In the same way *cóica* fifty stands for *cóicecha.*

65. The unaspirated tenuis after a vowel is found in median sound, if a nasal (§ 42) or a liquid (§ 79) originally went before it, besides certain cases of coalescence in the composition of words (§ 73). In a few cases a prehistoric *qu* = Brit. *p* appears to be represented by *c* or *cc*, *e.g.* in *mac, macc,* gen.

maqi, Old Cymr. *map*. The etymology of many other words which might here be considered is not fully determined.

66. After consonants the tenuis in Old Irish is firm in the groups *cht, rt, lt, rc, lc, sc*: *recht* right; *gort* garden, Latin *hortus;* *ro alt* educatus est; *marc* horse, Old H. G. *marah;* *serc* love; *olc* malus; *mesc* ebrius. The firmness is often expressed by doubling the letter, *olcc, mescc,* and so on.

67. In the same way the media is firm after *r* and *l*: *árd* high, Latin *arduus;* *garg* rough; *serg* illness, Old Sax. *swerkan* become dark, sad. The media in this situation is also often written double *árdd, gargg,* or expressed by the tenuis *ferg, ferc* wroth, Greek ὀργή, Skr. *ūrj* strength; *orcun* caedere, *frith-orgun* offendere, Old Gaulish *Orgeto-rix*, Skr. r̥ghāyati to rage (?); *cerd* and *cert* trade, artist, Latin *cerdo*, Grk. κέρδος; *com-arpi* coheredes, Goth. *arbja*.

68. Aspiration early came into use in pronunciation with *b, d, g,* and *m,* between vowels (*bh, dh, gh, mh*), but first finds written expression in later manuscripts. The first trace is to be found in words borrowed from the Latin where *b* between vowels is rendered by *m* (*bh* pronounced as *mh*, § 3); *am-prom*, Latin *improbus;* *mebuir*, Latin *memoria*. The next is that in Middle Irish *b* is written for *m* between vowels; *mebaid* he broke, pl. 3 *mebdatar*, for Old Irish *memaid, memdatar*. The last is that *mh* is written for *bh*: *claidheamh*, sword, for Old Irish *claideb*.

Assimilation.

69. As to the change of *ks, gs, ts, ds, st, tt, dt* into *ss, s,* see § 54. *sm* changes to *mm*, later *m* (never *mh*): *druimm, druim* back, for prehistoric *drosm-e*, Latin *dorsum*. *sl* changes to *ll*: *coll* corylus, Old H. G. *hasala;* *giall* hostage, Old H. G. *gîsal*, Cornish *guistel*. *rs* changes to *rr*: *tarrach* timid, Skr. *tras*.

Assimilation. 17

70. *nd* changes to *nn* and *mb* to *mm*, *m*: *ad-greinn* persequitur, Old Slavonian *grędą*; *mennat* dwelling, Skr. *mandira* dwelling; *imb*, *imm*, *im* about, Grk. ἀμφί; *imbliu*, gen. *imlenn* navel, Grk. ὀμφαλός; in Modern Irish *m* is written for *mm*, whilst an original single *m* has become *mh*. As to the assimilation of *ngm* and *ndm* to *mm*, *m* see § 76.

71. *ln* changes to *ll*: Old Irish *com-alnaim* impleo, later *com-allaim*, with *com-all* praegnans, Goth. *fulls*, Skr. root *par*, *pṛināmi*, *pūrṇa*; *collo* for *colno*, gen. of *colinn* flesh; *ld* changes to *ll*: *meldach* gratus, later *mellach*; *accaldam* discourse, later *accallam*; *ildatu* quantity, later *illatu*; *mall* slow, Grk. βραδύς; *caill*, *coill* wood, Old S. *holt*. The gradual preponderance of the *l* is indicated by the written forms *melltach*, *illdathach* many-coloured (*il-dathach*), and the inclination to pronounce the *l* with especial force before a following dental is also shown in the orthography *ni cheilltis* they concealed. Even *lnd* is thus assimilated: *álind* pretty, compar. Old Irish *áildiu*, later *áilliu*, *áilli*, *áille*. A solitary case is *lb* to *ll*: *úall* superbia, gen. *úailbe*, *úaille*.

72. *rnd* is assimilated to *rr*: *cruind* round (for *curind*), compar. *cuirre*, *cuirrither* (for *curind-iu*, *-ither*). It deserves note that sometimes (in Lebor na huidhri) *rd* is written for *rn* in words in which an assimilation has not taken place, e. g. *iferd* for *ifern* = Latin *infernum*; *card* for *carn*. In such cases *d* is a contraction for *nd* = *nn*, since *ifernd* occurs.

73. The final *t* (*th*) or *d* of prepositions is in composition assimilated to the following consonantal initial sound: *frithgart* becomes *frecart* respondit; *adbeir* dicit (prep. *aith-*), past *epert* dixit; *ad-gládur* appello, inf. *accallam*; *aith-od-bart* becomes *adopart* obtulit; *ad-daimet* and *ataimet* profitentur; *ad-ċiu* becomes *acciu* (besides *adchiu*, *atchiu*).

74. The vowels *á*, *é*, *í*, *úa*, *ó* are due to disappearance of a consonant with compensatory lengthening. Thus every

I. G. 2

explosive sound is lost before a following liquid, guttural and dental before a following nasal. As to the disappearance of the nasal before *c*, *t*, *s* see § 42.

ám battalion, Latin *agmen*, *examen*; *ár* clades, Cymr. *aer* (points to *agr-*); *mál* prince, cf. Old Cymric proper names as *Seno-magli* (gen. in an inscription); *dál* assembly, Old Cymr. *datl* forum; *sál* heel, Cymr. *sawdl*; *anál* breath, Cymr. *anadl*;

fén wagon, Old Norse *vagn*; *dér* tear, Grk. δάκρυ; *én* bird, Old Cymr. *etn*, Latin *penna*; *cenél* kind, Old Cymr. *cenetl*;

mí month, gen. *mís*, Latin *mensis*; *cís* vectigal = Latin *census*, rent;

úan lamb, Latin *agnus*; *búain* harvest, inf. of *bongaim* I harvest (break), Skr. *bhañga*; *cúala* audivi, Skr. *çuçrāva*;

srón nose (points to *srogn*); *doróni* fecit, *dorónad* factum est for *do-ro-gni*, *do-ro-gniad*.

The following show an abnormal transformation: *con-goite* part. compunctus; *ro gaet* past pass. was killed, of *gonaim* vulnero.

75. To this place belong the perfect and future forms which are characterized by an *é*: *génar* natus sum for *gegn-*, Grk. γέγνημαι; *do-bér* dabo for *bebr-*. In these tenses other combinations of consonants are treated in the same way: *ménar* putavi for *memn-*, Skr. *mene*; *in-géb* comprehendam for *gegb-*.

76. Assimilation of the consonant before *m* and at the same time lengthening of the preceding vowel are introduced in the formation of the neuter nomina actionis in *man* from radical syllables in *ng*, *nd*: *léimm* to leap, leap, to *lingim* I leap, for *lengm-e* (*-en*?); *céimm* to walk, step, from *cingim* I stride, for *cengm-e*; *gréimm* progressus to *in-grennim* persequor, for *grendm-e*. In the same way is formed *béimm*, *béim* to beat, blow, from *benim* I beat.

77. In composition, where the accent advances to the first syllable of the word the length of the vowel is given up: *tochimm*, *tochaim* to march, from *céimm*; *in-greimm*, *in-grimm* to pursue, from *gréimm*; in the same way *fo-glaim* to learn

from *fo-gliunn* disco; *tó-thim* (later but less correct *tuitim*) to fall, to *tuitim* I fall (§ 54), -*thim* for *do-éimm*, *éimm* for *entm-e*, root *pat*, nasalized *pent*.

78. Certain groups of consonants are separated by introduction of a vowel if they happened to be at the end of a word after the disappearance of the last syllable. This is particularly the case with the *mn* derived from *bn*: *omun* fear, *ess-amin* fearless, cf. Old Gaulish *Exobnus*; *domun* world, cf. Old Gaulish *Dubno-rix*; *tamun* stem, Old S. *stamn*, Old H. G. *stam*, and with the *tr* of the suffix trā: *críathar* sieve, Old H. G. *rîterâ*, Latin *cribrum*; *arathar* plough, Grk. ἄροτρον; *bríathar* word, Grk. Fράτρα (?).

The Old Irish *iarn* iron becomes later *iarann*. Perhaps *olan, oland* wool (§ 46) may be explained in the same way, cf. Skr. *ūrṇa*, Goth. *vulla*. The inclination to split up combinations of consonants is strongly developed in Modern Irish. O'Donovan (Irish Gr. pp. 57 and 58) gives the pronunciation of: *dlúth* as *dŏluth*, *bolg* as *bŏllŏg*, *borb* as *borŏb*, *garg* as *garăg*, *corn* as *corrŏn*. Examples of similar written forms are to be found in the Book of Lecan (see Windisch, Irish Texts, p. 84). Nevertheless this pronunciation cannot be old at least as regards *lg, rg, rb*, cf. § 67.

METATHESIS.

79. Metathesis sometimes occurs with and sometimes without lengthening of the vowel. (1) With lengthening of the vowel: *lám* hand, Latin *palma*; *lán* full (for *paln* = *all* in *com-all* praegnans), Gothic *fulls*, Sanskrit *pūrṇa*; *bráge* neck, Latin *gurges*; *cnáim* bone, Greek κνήμη, Old High German *hamma* hind leg; *ad-gládur* appello, infinitive *accaldam*. (2) Without lengthening of the vowel: *bligim* I milk, Old High German *melchan*; *dligim* I owe, Gothic *dulgs*; *cruim* worm, genitive *croma*, Lithuanian *kirmélĕ*; *srub* snout, Latin *sorbeo*; *cride* heart, Greek καρδία, Lithuanian *szirdìs*; *fliuch* wet, beside *folcaim* humecto; *fr, fl.* frequently arise thus in initial sound:

frith versus, root *vart*; *frass* shower, Sanskrit *varsha*; *flaith* sway, originally *valt-is*. When the combinations *rc*, *lc* are broken up by metathesis *c* remains unaspirated: *du-thracair* voluit connected with *du-fu-tharcair*, Skr. root *tark*, *tarkayati* to imagine, to remember to do something, *tuaslucud* resolutio beside *tuasulcud* (*do-fo-od-salciud*).

80. Besides the above cases of metathesis which are in part common to all Celtic languages there are others which are first perceived in Later and Modern Irish. Old Irish *baitsim* I baptize (from *baithis* baptism), Later Irish *baistim, baisdim;* Old Irish *éitsim* I hear, Later Irish *éistim, éisdim;* Old Irish *do acsin* to see, Later Irish *do aiscin;* Old Irish *bélre* speech, Modern Irish *béurla*.

CONTRACTION.

81. Similar vowels or vowels assimilated to one another which, owing to the disappearance of a consonant, have become directly contiguous might be contracted to one long vowel if one of them was accented (especially the first); *dead* finis, Cymr. *diwedd*, whence *dédenach* finalis; *tee* hot for *tepe* (Latin *tepens*) becomes *té*, nom. pl. *téit*; *lathe* day already in Old Irish *laa, lá*; *ad-chíu* I see, for *-cisiu*, Skr. root *caksh* (fr. *cakas*); *biid* gen. of *biad* victus becomes *bíd*; *broo, bró* millstone, gen. *broon, brón*, Skr. *grāvan*.

82. Dissimilar vowels, which were not assimilated to one another, remain side by side and often count in verses as two syllables, *e.g. biad* victus for *bivat-am*, Grk. βίοτος. In like manner, perhaps after loss of a consonant, the following are dissyllabic; *iach* (Hy. 5. 72) *immedon iach* in a salmon's belly; *niad* (Hy. 5. 71), gen. of *nia* hero, warrior.

83. If neither of the two vowels was accented, one of them, most likely the first, was simply suppressed; Old Irish *carid* amat (a form like the Sanskrit *sukhayati* he rejoices) goes back through *car'-ati* to *cara-ati*, *caraj-ati* as *for-chongrimm* praecipio is contracted from *for-chon-garimm*. In the

same way *no chara* amat (of the conjoined flexion) does not go back to a contracted form *carāt*, but stands for *cara-at*, with loss of the last syllable according to the rule of termination.

84. In the same way contraction is not to be assumed where an original *ia* is represented by *e*: *cride* heart stands for prehist. *cridi-am*, *e* is the mutation of *i* due to a following *a* (as in *fer* for prehist. *vir-as*) and the syllable *am* has disappeared according to the rule of termination. In the same way the *e* in *no guidem* we pray may be explained for a prehist. *godiam-as*.

85. It is a form of absorption when *e* and *a* disappear after *ó* or *ú*: *óac* (dissyllabic Serclige Concul 37. 14, Old Cymr. *ieuanc*, Latin *juvencus*) youth, becomes *óc*; *aue* grandson becomes *ó*, *ú*, through *óa*, *úa*; *núe* new (Skr. *navya*) becomes *nú*.

Terminal Sound.

86. Comparison with the allied languages teaches that numerous Irish word-forms have lost a syllable at the end, and Irish itself affords ground, in many cases, for the determination of how these syllables were sounded before they were lost. The prehistoric word-forms thus inferred are by no means Indo-Germanic primary forms, but stand in the process of individualizing language, at the same stage as the corresponding Latin and Greek forms. The traces of the lost syllable appear in Irish in two directions, viz. in the preceding syllable of the same word and in the initial sound of the following word.

87. The vowel of the last syllable was introduced in the preceding syllable and has affected the vowel of that syllable as shown § 16 *et seq*. The alteration of the short *a* of the last syllable to *e* or *i* can be clearly perceived but not so the alteration of the *a* to *o*. The short *o*, before the syllable was lost, was either not sharply distinguished from a short *a*; or it has only produced effect as a short *a* upon the vowel of the preceding syllable. Traces of the alteration perhaps are to be

found in the most ancient genitive-forms of stems in *i*, *u*, and *n*: *fáith* vates, gen. *fátho* for *vātaj-os*; *suth* fetus, gen. *sotho* for *sutav-os*; *brithem* judge, gen. *brithemon* for *briteman-os*. The nominative *Corpimaquas* (whence the *Corbmac*, *Cormac* of the manuscripts) from an Old Irish Ogham inscription, may be put forward against assuming the alteration. The numerous Old Gaulish nominatives in *os* (*e.g.* *tarvos*, Old Irish *tarb* bull) correspond only for the area of the Old Gaulish language.

88. The following table, without claiming to be complete, demonstrates how the vowels of the last syllable are treated in Irish:

Indo-Germanic.	Prehistoric Irish.	
a	e, i	Voc. Sg. *a maic* O son for *maqu-e*, Greek φίλε, Latin *amic-e*: Nom. Du. *dá druid* two soothsayers for *druid-e*, Grk. Αἴαντ-ε: 2 Sg. Imperat. *beir* for *ber-e*, Grk. φέρε, Latin *ag-e*: 2 Pl. Imperat. *berid* for *beret-e*, Grk. φέρετ-ε, Latin *agit-e*: 3 Sg. Perf. *cechuin* cecinit for *cecan-e*, Grk. γέγον-ε: *cóic* five for *quenqu-e*, Latin *quinqu-e*, Greek πέντ-ε.
as	as, os	Nom. Sg. *fer* man for *vir-as*, Greek λύκ-ος, Latin *lup-us*: Gen. Sg. *máthar* for *mātur-as*, Grk. μητρ-ός, Old Latin *Vener-us*: *fátho* (later *fátha*) poetae for *vātaj-os*, Grk. πόλε-ως: Nom. Sg. *teg*, *tech* house (Modern Irish *teach*) for *teg-as*, Grk. τέγ-ος, Latin *gen-us*: *do-beram* damus for *beram-as*, Latin *agi-mus*: 2 Sg. Perf. *cechan* cecinisti for *cecan-as*, Grk. γέγον-ας.
as	es, is	Nom. Pl. *carit* amici for *car-ant-es*, Grk. φέροντ-ες: *teoir* Fem. three for *tesor-es*, Skr. *tisr-as*: 2 Sg. Pres. *do-beir* thou givest for *ber-is*, Grk. ἔφερ-ες, Latin *agis*, cf. *tige* houses for *teg-es-a*, Grk. τέγ-ε-α, Latin *gen-er-a*.
am	an, on	Nom. and Acc. Sg. N. *nemed* n- holy place, for *nemet-an*, Old Gaulish νεμη-τον, Grk. μέτρ-ον, Latin *jug-um*: Acc. Sg. *fer* n- for *vir-an*, Grk. λύκ-ον, Latin *vir-um*.
	en, in	Acc. Sg. *menmain* n- mentem for *mene-man-en*: *bráthir* n- for *bráter-en*, Latin *fratr-em* (Grk. πατέρ-α).

Terminal Sound. 23

Indo-Germanic.	Prehistoric Irish.	
an (?)	en, in	nói n- nine for nov-en, Latin nov-e-m (Grk. ἐννέα): deich n- ten for dec-en, Latin dec-em (Grk. δέκα): Nom. and Acc. Sg. N. ainm name for anm-en, Latin nom-en (or for anm-e, Skr. nām-a, cf. § 100).
ar	er, ir	eter, etir between, Latin inter, Skr. antar: Voc. Sg. a bráthir O brother, Grk. ὦ πάτερ.
at	et, it	3 Sg. Pres. do-beir dat for ber-it, Grk. ἔφερ-ε, Latin ag-it.
ā	a	Nom. Sg. F. túath people, Latin mens-a, Grk. χώρ-α, Goth. thiud-a: Nom. Du. M. and N. dá fer two men for dvā vir-a, Grk. δύο ἵππ-ω, Latin du-ō: Nom. Pl. N. grán for grān-a, Latin gran-a, Grk. μέτρ-α: 1 Sg. Conj. ér-bar dicam for (ass-ru-) ber-a, Ved. stav-ā I will praise: Nom. Sg. flaithem prince for valtim-a, Skr. brahm-ā.
	o, u	1 Sg. Pres. as-biur dico for ber-o, ber-o, Lat. fer-o, Gr. φέρ-ω: no rádiu loquor for rādio, Latin fugio: Nom. Sg. airmitiu reverentia for mentio, Lat. mentio.
ās	ās	Nom. Pl. F. túatha for tōtās, Goth. thiudos: 2 Sg. Conj. Pres. as-bere, -beræ, -bera dicas for berās, Latin feras, Skr. bharās.
ām	an	Gen. Pl. of all declensions fer n- for viran, Grk. θε-ῶν, Latin de-um, Goth. fisk-e: túath n- for tōt-an, Goth. thiudo: bráthar n- for brātar-an, Lat. fratr-um, Grk. πατέρ-ων, Goth. brothr-e: fáithae, fáithe prophetarum for vātej-am, Grk. πόλε-ων (from Irish alone the length of the a cannot be inferred; beside bráthar also bráthre).
āt	āt	3 Sg. Conj. Pres. as-bera dicat, for berāt, Latin ferat, Ved. bharāt; cf. niæ, nia filius sororis, Gen. niad for nep-at-as, Latin nepotis.
tād		2 Sg. Imperat. cluinte hear, Ved. vahatād.
ār	ēr, īr	máthir, Latin mater, Grk. μάτηρ: athir Lat. pater, Grk. πατήρ: bráthir, Lat. frater, Grk. φρατήρ.
ār	ôr	siur sister, Lat. soror.
ant	ant	3 Pl. Pres. as-berat dicunt for berant, Grk. ἔφερον, Latin ferunt.
ans	ons, ōs	Acc. Pl. firu, Lat. viros, Cret. τovs, Herakl. τως, Attic τούς.
ans	ass	Nom. Sg. menme mind, Gen. menman; cf. Grk. μέλας.

24   I. Phonology.

Indo-Germanic.	Prehistoric Irish.	
tāts	tōs	Nom. Sg. *beothu* life, Gen. *bethad* (for *bivat-at-as*), Grk. βιότης, Latin *aetas*.
āts		Nom. Sg. *niæ*, *nia* filius sororis, Gen. *niad* (for *nepāt-as*), Latin *nepōs*. The Irish *niæ* might also contain the suffix *-at* (with short vowel).
ats	ass?	Nom. Sg. *tenge*, *tenga* tongue, Gen. *tengad* (for *tengat-as*); cf. Old Gaulish *Attrebas*.
ats	ess?	Nom. Sg. *fili*, *file* poet, Gen. *filed* (for *velet-as*).
ants	ass?	Nom. Sg. *tricha* thirty, Gen. *trichat* (for *tri-cant-as*); cf. Grk. τριάκ-οντ-α: *care*, *cara* friend, Gen. *carat* (for *caraj-ant-as*); cf. Grk. ἐλέφας, ἱμάς, τύψας.
ants	ess?	Nom. Sg. *fiche* twenty, Gen. *fichet* (for *vicent-as*); cf. Latin *vig-int-i*: *lóche* lightning, Gen. *lóchet* (for *lōcent-as*), Latin *torrens*, *agens*.
i	i	Nom. Sg. N. *muir* sea for *mor-i*, Latin *mar-e*: 3 Sg. Pres. Act. *berid* for *beret-i*, Grk. φέρει, Skr. *bharat-i*: 3 Pl. *berit* for *berant-i*, Doric φέροντ-ι, Skr. *bharant-i*.
is	is	Nom. Sg. *fáith* vates for *vāt-is*, Grk. πόσ-ις, Latin *ign-is*.
im	in	Acc. Sg. *faith n-* for *vāt-in*, Grk. πόσ-ιν.
ins	īs	Acc. Pl. *fáthi* for *vātis*, Skr. *kavīn*, Goth. *balgins*.
ī	ī	Nom. and Acc. Dual *di sūil* two eyes for *sūl-i*, Skr. *kav-ī*.
u	u	Nom. Sg. *rect* right for *rect-u*, Latin *corn-u*: 3 Sg. Imperat. *berad* for *berat-u*, Skr. *bharat-u*: 3 Pl. Imperat. *berat* for *berant-u*, Skr. *bharant-u*.
us	us	Nom. Sg. *bith* world for *bit-us*: *mug* servus for *mog-us*: *fiss* knowledge for *viss-us*, Goth. *magus*, Latin *fructus*.
um	un	Acc. Sg. *bith n-* for *bit-un*, Latin *fructum*, Goth. *magu*.
uns	ūs	Acc. Pl. *mogu*, Goth. *maguns*, Lat. *fructus*.
ū	u	Nom. and Acc. Du. *dá mug* for *mog-u*, Skr. *bāhū*, two arms.
ai	i	Nom. Pl. M. *eich* for *equ-i*, Latin *equ-i*, Grk. ἵππ-οι: Nom. Du. Fem. *di choiss* two feet for *coss-i*, Skr. *kanye* two maids: Dat. Sg. *don menmain* menti for *meneman-i*, Skr. *manman-e*, Latin *patr-i*.
āi	o, u	Dat. Sg. M. and N. *don fiur* to the man for *vir-u*: *dond eoch* to the horse for *equ-o*, Latin *vir-o*, Grk. ἵππῳ.
āi	i	Dat. Sg. F. *don túaith* to the people, for *tōt-i*, Grk. χώρᾳ, δίκῃ?

Aspiration.

89. The effect of the original terminal sound is only discoverable in the initial sound of the following word, when both words according to the construction are very nearly connected with one another: as article and substantive, substantive and adjective, numeral and substantive, preposition and article or substantive, verbal particle and verb, negative and verb, relative pronoun and verb, conjunction and verb, infixed pronoun and verb. These combinations are treated as if they were one word. The terminal sound of the first part and the initial sound of the second part are treated almost as if they were standing in the median sound. An attributive modification with a preposition may closely belong to the preceding noun: *fúan cáin corcra n-imbi*, a beautiful purple cloak about him, FB. 45: *ose cen udnucht n-imbi*, SP. III. 6: *dobera muin n-immi*, Ir. T. p. 144, 31.

90. Three things may occur as to the initial sound of the following word: (1) it exhibits aspiration: (2) it exhibits a nasal: (3) it exhibits no change of the kind.

Aspiration.

91. Aspiration has taken place after an original vowel terminal sound of the preceding word. Aspiration changes *c* and *t* to *ch* and *th*; *s* and *f* to *ṡ* and *ḟ* (§ 4) and in Middle and Modern Irish also *b, d, g, m* to *bh, dh, gh, mh*. The remaining sounds are not affected by aspiration.

92. The following forms and words are followed by aspiration (cf. Z.² p. 180, Stokes, Fís Adamnáin, p. 38): (1) The article in the Gen. and Dat. Sg. M. and N. (τοῦ, τῷ), the Nom. Pl. M. (τοί), the Nom. and Dat. Sg. F. (ἡ, τῇ), see § 171. (2) The nominal *a*-stems in the same cases, if an adjective or a genitive follows after them: Gen. Sg. M. *oc fennad lóig fothlai: fiad a chlaidib thana deirg: in trir churad:* Dat. Sg. M. N. *co n-galur fúail: co n-ilur thor: a triur churad: do airiuc thuile: ón mud*

chetna: Nom. Pl. M. *naim thuascirt in domain: a thárraluig slighith:* Nom. Sg. F. *fled chaurad: rigon...chaemcasto: tegdas chumtachta:* Dat. F. *di chlaind chéit ríg: alleind chorcra: co m-binne cheóil.* Also in Voc. Sg. *a ingen fial:* Nom. Du. *dá grúad chorcra* Lg. 18, 13. (3) In general all stems in the Dat. Sg. *co mid chollan chain: iar cuairt chaille: do gin chlaidib: ón chomdid chumachtach: ó Choin cherda Conchobair: na leth chli: do denam thole Dé: sin t-síd thréll: im lín chein.* Also in the case originally distinguished from the dative (instrumental?) which is used to note time: *ind adaig thússech,* in the first night. (4) The Nom. Sg. *cú; Cúchulaind,* literally, the hound of Culann. (5) The vocative particle *a.* (6) The possessive pronouns *mo* my, *do* thy, and the masculine, *a* his, of the third person. (7) The Nom. Acc. Du. M. *dá* and F. *di* two: the Nom. Acc. N. *tri* three (*trí chét*), *cethir* four. (8) The prepositions *di, do, fo, ó, tré, air* (*ar*), *cen, fiad, imm, ol, ós:* also *eter* (though as to Old Irish the reverse is noted, Z.² 656). (9) The negations *ni* (*mani*), *na, nach, nad.* In Old Irish, according to Zeuss² 179, aspiration is often absent after *ni.* Probably in this case the two words are not to be pronounced quickly one after the other but separately with emphasis, *e.g.* if, as in *ni clóin* non injustus, the copula is absent between the negation and the predicate. (10) The verbal particles *no, ro, do.* (11) The enclitic infixed pronouns *-m* me, *-t* te; of the pronouns of the 3rd person according to Z.² 181: "*d, n* (eum, id), *a* (id, eos)," which is supported in the Irish texts by *nod chluined* Lg. 8 (referring to *andord* M. or N.), *conda thanic adiit eos* Hy. 2. 39. (12) The 3rd Sg. rel. *as, bas,* the 3rd Sg. Second Present *bad,* the 3rd Sg. Perf. *bu, bo, ba;* according to Z.² 181 also other forms of the verb substantive: *as chóir,* and so on; *bas ferr* Sc. M. 2; *ro bad chomairche,* SC. 10; *diammad chara* SC. 10. 7; *co m-bo chomsolus* FB. 2 and so on. After *bad* and *bu* aspiration is still usual in Modern Irish (O'Donovan, Gr. p. 386). (13) Isolated forms of other verbs: *fuachimm chein* SP. II. 10: *hi tucu cheist* SP. II. 12; *nad déni thoil* SP. IV. 2; *tairces churathmír* FB. 73. (14) Certain pro-

Aspiration. 27

nouns: *os me chene* SP. II. 12; *coich thussa* SC. 12; *cia thoetsat* Sc. M. 3. 16; *is sí thorrach* Lg. 1; further *ciaso thú* TE. 13, LU.; *masa thú* SC. 33. 30. (15) The conjunctions *ce cia* though, *ó* since; *mar* as; *feib* how: *ciá thíastaís* FB. 61; *o thanic* 81; *mar charas* SC. 44. 10; *feib thallad* FB. 82. According to Zeuss[2] 182 also *má* if, *air* then. Moreover the conjunctions *ocus, is* and, *nó* or: *lígrad óir...ocus charrmocail* FB. 2; *do brothrachaib...ocus cholcthib* 4; *ocus chineul* TE. 2 Eg.; *eter aite is chomalta* SC. 29. 3; *itir suide no šessam* Hy. 1. 3; *cuslennaig nó chornairi* Lg. 17, 22.

93. Aspiration has come to be used as a grammatical instrument in cases where it has no etymological ground. To this some of the above-indicated cases may belong which may be indicated as follows: (1) Aspiration appears as a mark of the feminine, after the Nom. Sg. of *i* stems also, although this originally terminated in *is*: *súil cháirech; turbaid chotulta; gáir chommaidmi; gáir chuitbiuda.* In the same way of other stems: *nau tholl; ail chloche.* (2) As sign of the masculine also after a genitive which originally terminated in *as*; *glond catha chomramaig; in chon chetna; bethath che;* perhaps also *ind ríg thuas* SP. IV. 2. (3) In the initial sound of verbal forms before which the relative pronoun is absent: *in cúach thucais* FB. 74; *ni fri biasta chathaigmit-ni* 57, 73; *bá tú theis* 17; *is mé thuc* 73; *co fult budi thic immach* SC. 33. 26; *is messi thall* TE. 13, Eg. Aspiration here expresses a dependence or close conjunction; and it has the same significance when the object appears aspirated after verbal forms of various kind (cf. also *co n-den-sai chorai* Ir. T. p. 130, 29), or the predicate after any form of the verb substantive. In Modern Irish the Acc. *thú* thee is distinguished by its permanent aspiration from the Nom. *tú*.

94. Later aspiration is sometimes made use of after word forms which were distinguished within the historic period by a vowel termination, although they have lost a consonant at the end: *rí chóigith* TE. 1 Eg.: *re se thráth* Sc. M. 21. 36.

95. In some words a certain fleetness in the articulation

appears to have led to a permanent aspiration of the initial sound: *chucai, chucu* (ad eum, ad eos), *chena, thra*, as for *ind ríg thúas* of the king above, SP. IV. 2 (cf. § 61).

96. Aspiration is regularly employed in the second member of a compound. Most of the stems which stand in the first part of a compound terminated originally in a vowel, and these have given the rule for every compound: *dobar chú* otter (literally water-hound), *roth-chless* play of wheel; *briathar-chath* word-battle; *óen-fecht* once; *ard-chend* high-headed; *óenchossid* one-legged: thence also *ríg-thech* king's house (stem *ríg-* with "composition" vowel); often after *so-*, Skr. *su-*, e.g. *so-chumact* potens, but also after *do-*, although this originally (Skr. *dus-* Grk. δυσ-) terminated in a consonant, e.g. *do-chumact* impotens; after *mí-, miss-,* e.g. *mi-thoimtiu* bad intention, cf. Goth. *missa-deds* misdeed.

Eclipsis.

97. A nasal appears before the initial sound of the following word, if the preceding word originally had a nasal as its terminal sound. This nasal is drawn to the following word, and its form is directed by the nature of the subsequent initial sound. It appears as *n* before *d, g* and vowels; as *m* before *b*; before *c, t, f, s* it disappears (§ 42); it becomes assimilated to a subsequent *n, m, r, l*, though, even in Old Irish, these sounds are not always written double (gen. pl. *narrúun*, commonly *na rún* of the secrets). Perhaps the disappearance of the nasals before *c, t, f, s* is, at least in part, founded on assimilation.

98. Modern Irish grammarians call this change of initial sound ECLIPSIS. The preceding sound eclipses the original initial sound in the pronunciation: *na mbárd* of the bards is pronounced *na márd*, &c.; *c, t,* and *f* are also affected by this *eclipsis* in later Irish writing, receiving before themselves *g, d,* and *bh: na gceart* of the rights is pronounced *na geart*. This change has nothing to do directly with the original nasal, but it

is the same which in ordinary internal sound has affected the unaspirated *c* and *f* in Old Irish (*éc* death, Modern Irish *éug*, and in the same way Old Irish *na cert*, Modern Irish *na gceart*).

99. The following forms have a nasal after them:

(1) The article in the nom. sg. neuter, acc. sg. and gen. pl. of all three genders.

(2) All *a*-stems in the same cases, nom. sg. neuter: *dliged n-doraid*, *lestar n-arggit*, acc. sg. masc. *ar fer n-aile*, fem. gen. pl. *co mathib fer n-Ulad*.

(3) Generally all masculines and feminines in the acc. sg. and all three genders in the gen. pl. *ríg n-amra*.

(4) The nom. dual neuter and the dative dual of all three genders of *dá* (*dá n-*, *dib n-* two).

(5) The plural possessive pronouns *ar* our, *far* your, *a* their (French *leur*).

(6) The prepositions *co* with; *i* in, *íar* after, *ré* before.

(7) The numerals *secht*, *ocht*, *nói*, *deich* (*ocht* probably after analogy of the three others).

(8) The infixed pronouns *a*, *da* eam, *s* eam, eos. After suppression of the *a* there remains of the first two only *-n-* and *-dn-*; *rom-bertaigestar*, *rod m-bertaigedar*, Sc. M. 15.

(9) The relative pronoun *a*.

100. Here also transfers have taken place: after analogy of neuters in *a*, neuters in *i* and *as* have also received such an *n*: *muir n-Icht*, *mind n-óir*, *inmain n-ainm...Aeda*, dear the name of Aed; *hi tech n-óil*.

In neuters in *man* the nasal may belong to the stem: *léim n-úathmar ainm n-Aeda*.

101. On the other hand, as the neuter as a separate gender gradually dies away, so also sometimes the *n* before neuter *a*-stems is wanting.

102. In all remaining cases, where in the grammatical formulæ mentioned in § 89 neither aspiration nor the nasal is

observable, the first word-form originally had as terminal sound any consonant except *m* or *n*.

103. Cases occur in which the last syllable of words of more than one syllable has remained as such, even when not in their original condition. The last syllable is preserved :

(1) when it ends in *r:* *bráthir*, Latin *frater;* *eter*, Latin *inter;*

(2) when it terminates in a double consonant: *do-berat* they give, for *berant*, Greek ἔφερον; *firu*, Latin *viros*, Goth. *vairans;* *lóche* lightning, a nominative form like the Latin *lucens;*

(3) when it contained a long vowel with final *s*, *t*, or *d:* *tuatha* the peoples, nom. pl., as Goth. *thiudos*, Skr. *kanyās* the maidens: *do-bera* he may give, 3 sg. conj. pres. as Latin *ferat*, Skr. *bharāt*.

104[a]. Of final consonants except the nasal (in the cases mentioned § 97) only *r* and the *t* of the group *nt* are preserved. *gs*, *ks*, *ts*, *nts*, *ns* were assimilated to *ss*, *s*, and have disappeared: *rí* king, Latin *rex;* *mí* month, Latin *mensis;* *lóche*, lightning (gen. *lóchet*); cf. Latin *lucens*.

104[b]. Rarely an original *s* in terminal sound is assimilated to a following *m*, *n*, *r* or *l*: e.g. the *s* of the form *inna*, *na* of the article; gen. sg. fem. *nammucci* of the pig; gen. sg. fem. *nallongsi* of the banishment; cf. *allatin* e Latino, prep. *ass a*, Latin *ex*.

105. In the third sg. of the *s*-future of the conjoined flexion a similar *ss*, *s* has disappeared, although it did not originally stand in the final sound: *téi* stands for a pre-historic *tēss-it*, cf. Grk. στείξει.

106. In the gen. sg. of masculine and neuter stems in *a* and in the dat. sg. of neuters in *as* more than one syllable has been lost: *eich* equi appears to answer to the Skr. *açvasya:* *tig*,

dative of *teg* house, must have had a termination after the stem-form *teges-*.

PROSTHESIS.

107. *h* is often placed as in mediæval Latin before an initial vowel. This is without fixed rule in Old Irish, but gradually becomes invariable in particular cases:

(1) after the forms *inna* and *na* of the article (gen. sg. fem., nom. pl.), e.g. *na hingine* of the girl; *na heich* the steeds;

(2) after the possessive *a* fem. gen., e.g. *a ech* his steed, *a hech* her steed;

(3) after the prepositions *co, fri, la, a (ass)*, e.g. *co hEmain, fri hór, la háes, a hEmain*;

(4) after *ba* fuit, e.g. *bá halaind, ba hé*, but also in any other situation often *hé*, he;

(5) in general before certain words without regard to the preceding word, e.g. before the preposition *in-* when its nasal has disappeared: *hí Temraig* in Tara; *hitá* ubi est; very often *hEriu, hErend*.

108. In Middle and Later Irish an *f* is placed before certain words: *focus, comfocus* near, Old Irish *ocus; fúacht* cold, Old Irish *úacht; for* inquit, Old Irish *or, ol; fur-áil* enjoin, Old Irish *ur-, er-áil; ros-fuc* tulit eos, Old Irish *ro uc, ruc; dos fanic* came to them, Old Irish *do anic, tánic; con facca* vidit, Old Irish *con acca; dona fib* eis qui, Old Irish *donaib hí*.

APHÆRESIS.

108[b]. Sometimes, especially in Later Irish, the initial vowel in small proclitic words is suppressed: *con tein* for *ocon tein* by the fire; *má tudchatar* for *imma tudchatar* wherefore they are come; *sin maig* for *isin maig* on the plain; *na lámaib* for *inna lámaib* in their hands. Thus also in the article *na* has arisen from *inna*.

108ᶜ. Thus also the *s* of the initial sound of the proclitic article and relative pronoun has disappeared and has only survived in union with prepositions which had a consonantal terminal sound (cf. § 169 and § 207). Thus also the conjunction and preposition *amal, amail* may be put with *samail* likeness, Latin *simile*.

II.

DECLENSION.

109. Declension varies according to the original terminal sound of the stem. The following may be distinguished:

I. Stems in *a*, with the subdivision of stems in *ia*, Masculine, Feminine and Neuter;

II. Stems in *i*, Masculine, Feminine and Neuter;

III. Stems in *u*, Masculine and Neuter;

IV. Stems with consonantal terminal sound, namely (*a*) stems in *d*, *th* (originally *t*) and *t* (originally *nt*), (*b*) stems in a guttural, (*c*) stems in *r* (the terms of kinship), (*d*) stems in *n*, Masculine and Feminine, (*e*) Neuters in *man*, (*f*) Neuters in *as* and other stems in *s*.

I.

(*a*) Stems in *a*.

110. Paradigms: *fer* Masc. man, *túath* Fem. people, *dliged* Neut. law.

Singular.

N. *in fer*	*in túath* (§ 64)	*a n-dliged n-*
G. *ind fir*	*inna túaithe*	*in dligid*
D. *dond fiur*	*don túaith*	*don dligud*
A. *in fer n-*	*in túaith n-*	*a n-dliged n-*
V. *a fir*	*a thúath*	*a dliged n-*.

II. Declension.

Plural.

N. *ind fir*	*inna túatha*	*inna dliged, dligeda*
G. *inna fer n-*	*inna túath n-*	*inna n-dliged n-*
D. *donaib feraib*	*donaib túathaib*	*donaib dligedaib*
A. *inna firu*	*inna túatha*	*inna dliged, dligeda*
V. *a firu*	*a thúatha*	*a dligeda.*

Dual.

N. A. *in dá fer*	*in dí thúaith*	*in dá n-dliged*
G. *in dá fer*	*in dá túath*	*in dá dliged*
D. *in dib feraib*	*in dib túathaib*	*in dib n-dligedaib.*

111. In the same way are declined the Masculine nouns: *ball* limb, *bél* lip, *cenn* head, *fiach* debt, *íasc* fish, *folt* hair, *macc* son, *láech* hero, *día* God; and the Feminine nouns: *áram* number, *rann* part, *cland* progenies, *lám* hand, *breth* judgment, *serc* love, *ferc* wrath, *delb* form, *ingen* girl, *bairgen* bread, *tol* will, *coss* foot, *crích* end, *grían* sun, *cíall* sense, *úall* superbia, *bríathar* word; and the Neuter nouns: *bás* death, *grád* gradus, *rath* grace, *scél* story, *accobor* will, *sáithar* trouble, *galar* sickness, *cenél* kind, *foraithmet* memoria, *etach* dress, *biad* food, *bunad* origo, *torad* fruit, *úathad* singularitas; the adjectives *mall* slow, *marb* dead, *slán* whole, *mór* great, *bec* little, *trén* brave, *olc* evil, *lond* bold, *cóem* soft, *nóeb* holy, *sóer* free, *lúath* swift, *fercach* wrathful, *iressach* faithful, *buidech* thankful, *toirsech* mournful, *beo* alive.

111[b]. The *u* peculiar to the Dat. Sg. M. and N. (or *o*, e.g. *eoch* Dat. of *ech*) is gradually given up again (*fir, cinn* for the more ancient *fiur, ciunn*); in syllables with *á, í, ia, ó, úa, ói, óe*, as in some other words such as *mac, rath* and in adjectives in *-ach* it has never been observed at all. (Cf. § 22.)

112. The following are noteworthy: *fiach*, Gen. *féich*, but *biad*, Gen. *biid, bíd*, Dat. *biud* (§ 11); *grían*, Dat. *gréin*; *bríathar*, Dat. *bréthir*; N. *día*, G. *dée, dé*, D. *día*, A. *día n-*, V. *a dé*, Pl. N. *dée, dé*, G. *día n-*, D. *déib*, A. *déo*.

Stems in ia.

113. *Ben* woman is irregular and is declined thus:
N. *ben,* G. *mná,* D. *mnái,* A. *mnái n-,* V. *a ben,* Pl. N. *mná,* G. *ban n-,* D. *mnáib,* A. *mná,* Dual N. A. *di mnái,* G. *dá mná,* D. *díb mnáib.*

114. In Middle Irish the feminine form in *-a* of the Nominative Plural is introduced also into the masculine of adjectives: *marba* besides *mairb*. Cf. § 180.

(b) Stems in *ia*.

115. Paradigms: *céle* M. fellow, *aidche* F. night, *cride* N. heart.

Singular.

N. *in céle*	*ind aidche*	*a cride n-*
G. *in chéli*	*inna aidche, haidche*	*in chridi*
D. *don chéliu*	*dond aidchi*	*don chridiu*
A. *in céle n-*	*in n-aidchi n-*	*a cride n-*
V. *a chéli*	*a aidche*	*a chride n-.*

Plural.

N. *in chéli*	*inna aidchi, haidchi*	*inna cride*
G. *inna céle n-*	*inna n-aidche n-*	*inna cride n-*
D. *donaib célib*	*donaib aidchib*	*donaib cridib*
A. *inna céliu*	*inna aidchi, haidchi*	*inna cride*
V. *a chéliu*	*a aidchi*	*a chride.*

Dual.

N. A. *dá chéle*	*dí aidchi*	*dá cride*
G. *dá céle*	*dá aidche*	*dá cride*
D. *dib célib*	*dib n-aidchib*	*dib cridib.*

116. In the same way are declined the Masculine nouns: *dalte* pupil, *rectire* præpositus, *tigerne* lord, *uisce* water; and the Feminine nouns *córe* peace, *gorte* hunger, *insce* speech, *sétche* wife, *sochude* crowd, *cense* mildness, *fáilte* joy, *soillse* light; and the Neuter nouns *bélre* speech, *comarde* sign, *cumachte* power, *esseirge* resurrection, *tairngire* promise; and the adjectives *asse* easy, *anse* difficult, *doe* slow, *núe* new, *uile* all, *colnide* carnal, *nemde* heavenly, *cétne* same.

117. In many of these words already in the older language *e* has been expanded to *a*, especially after a broad vowel: *dalta* (Gen. *daltai*), *córa, gorta, comarda, cumachta, assa, ansa, nemda, cétna, tigerna, bélra*. The writing *cumachtæ, censæ* indicates an intermediate stage.

118. In the Dative Sg. Masc. and Neuter the *i* is suppressed after a broad vowel: *daltu, gortu,* and later *a* appears in place of *u: dalta*. In words with a slender vowel after the disappearance of the *u* an *i* remains: *céli*.

119. In later manuscripts terminal *i* and *e* are not sharply distinguished.

120. *Duine* M. man, Gen. *duini* has in the Plural *dóini*, Gen. *dóine*, and so on. *lathe* N. day, is also contracted to *laa, lá*, Gen. *lái* (besides *lathi*), Dat. *lau, ló, lá*, Acc. *lá n-*, and so on.

II.

Stems in *i*.

121. Paradigms: *fáith* M. poet, *súil* F. eye, *muir* N. sea.

Singular.

N. *in fáith*	*in t-súil*	*ammuir, a muir n-*
G. *ind fátho, fátha*	*inna súlo, súla*	*in mora*
D. *dond fáith*	*don t-súil*	*don muir*
A. *in fáith n-*	*in súil n-*	*ammuir n-*
V. *a fáith*	*a súil*	*a muir.*

Plural.

N. *ind fáthi*	*inna súli*	*inna mora*
G. *inna fáthe n-*	*inna súle n-*	*inna more n-*
D. *donaib fáthib*	*donaib súlib*	*donaib muirib*
A. *inna fáthi*	*inna súli*	*inna mora*
V. *a fáthi*	*a súli*	*a mora*

Dual.

N. A. *dá fáith*   *dí súil*   *dá muir*
G. *dá fátho, fátha*   *dá súla*   *dá mora*
D. *dib fáthib*   *dib súlib*   *dib muirib*

122. In the same way are declined the Masculine nouns: *cnáim* bone, *cimbid* prisoner, *tuistid* parens, *dorsid* and *dorsióir* door-keeper; and the Feminine nouns: *biáil* (Gen. *béla*) hatchet, *colinn* flesh (Gen. *colno*), *cruim* worm, *dúil* element, *flaith* lordship, *fuil* blood, *fochith*, *fochaid* suffering, *iarfaigid* (Gen. *iarfaigtho*) asking; and the Neuter nouns: *búaid* victory, *guin* wound, *mind* crown, *rind* star, *tír* land; and the adjectives: *cóir* uniform, just, *léir* industrious, *erdirc* famous, *maith* good, *sain* different, *cosmil* like, *mithig* fitting, *álind* lovely (Nom. Pl. *áildi, ailli*), *allaid* wild.

123. Neuter nouns with a slender vowel have *e* in place of *a*: *tír* country (Gen. *tíre*); *rind* has in the Nom. Pl. *rind* and *renna*, the latter (also *mora?*) perhaps in transition to Declension Ia.

124. Some Feminine nouns fluctuate between this and the first declension, especially the infinitive *gabál* and *gabáil* take, *tabairt* and *tabart* give, *tomailt* and *tomalt* consume.

125. In the same way adjectives in many instances fluctuate between the *i-* and the *a-* declension; the genitive singular masculine and neuter is formed always according to the first declension: *maith* good, Gen. *maith*.

III.

Stems in *u*.

126. Paradigms: *gním* M. deed, doing, *recht* N. right.

Singular.

N. *in gním*   *arrecht (n-)*
G. *in gnímo, gníma*   *in rechto, rechta*
D. *don gním*   *dond recht*
A. *in n-gním n-*   *arrecht (n-)*

II. Declension.

Plural.

N. *in gnímai, gníma*   *inna rechte, rechta*
G. *inna n-gníme n-*   *inna rechte n-*
D. *donaib gnímaib*   *donaib rechtaib*
A. *inna gnímu*   *inna rechte, rechta*

Dual.

N. A. *dá gním*   *dá recht*
G. *dá gnímo, gníma*   *dá rechto, rechta*
D. *dib n-gnímaib*   *dib rechtaib.*

127. In the same way are declined the Masculine nouns: *bith* world, *bráth* judgment, *cruth* figure, *guth* voice, *fid* tree, *mug* slave, *áis, óis* aetas, *senchas* antiquity, *fiuss, fiss* knowledge, *cotlud* sleep, and all other infinitives in *-ud* and *-ad*.

128. The Neuter nouns are not sharply distinguished from the Masculine. The following may, with more or less certainty, be classed as neuter: *ith* corn (Gen. *etho*), *lin* number, *lind* drink, *loch* lake, *med* mead, *sruth* stream, *suth* fetus, *tes* heat, *dorus* door.

129. The infinitives in *-ud* of verbs of the III. Conjugation show especially the after effect of the original *u* in the Nom. Sg.: *loscud* to burn, *foillsigud* to show. In the later language this *-ud* is changed in many verbs to *ad*: *loscadh*. More frequently Old Irish had a *u* in the Dative Sg. *isin biuth* in the world, *dind riuth* de cursu (Nom. *bith, rith*), but it was gradually given up even here.

130. After a slender vowel *-e* shows itself for *-o, -a* in the Gen. Sg.: *suidigud* positio, Gen. *suidigthe*.

131. A great variation of the ending is observed in the Nom. Pl.: besides *gnímai* and *gníma* there are found *gními, gnímæ* and *gníme*.

132. Adjectives in the plural pass into the *i* declension: *follus* clear, Nom. Pl. *foilsi;* *il* much, Acc. Pl. *ili.*

(a) Dental Stems.

133. Many words follow later the *a*-declension: *dorus*, later *doras* door, Gen. *dorais*.

IV.

(a) Dental stems.

134. Paradigms: *fili* M. poet, *ara* M. charioteer, *cara* M. friend, *beothu* M. life.

Singular.

N. *in fili*	*in t-ara*	*in cara*	*in beothu*
G. *ind filed*	*ind arad*	*in charat*	*in bethad*
D. *dond filid*	*dond arid*	*don charit*	*don bethid*
A. *in filid n-*	*in n-arid n-*	*in carit n-*	*in m-bethid n-*
V. *a fili*	*a ara*	*a chara*	*a beothu*

Plural.

N. *ind filid*	*ind arid*	*in charit*
G. *inna filed n-*	*inna n-arad n-*	*inna carat n-*
D. *donaib filedaib*	*donaib aradaib*	*donaib cairtib*
A. *inna fileda*	*inna arada*	*inna cairtea*
V. *a fileda*	*a arada*	*a chairtea*

Dual.

N. A. *dá filid*	*dá arid*	*dá charit*
G. *dá filed*	*dá arad*	*dá carat*
D. *dib filedaib*	*dib n-aradaib*	*dib cairtib*

135. Like *fili* are declined: *óigi* guest, *slige* way, *tene* fire, *léine* shirt, *cóimdiu, coimdi* (Gen. *cóimded*) Lord, *eirr* curruum princeps, *traig* foot, *míl* miles, *drui* Druid (but Gen. Sg. and Pl. and Du. *druad*).

136. Like *ara* are declined: *nia* hero, *nia niæ* nepos, *asca* rival, enemy, *tenge, tenga* tongue, *Ulaid* Ultonii, *sab* princeps, fortis, *cin* guilt.

II. Declension.

137. Like *care*, *cara*, are declined: *námæ*, *náma* enemy, *tipra* spring, *tricha* thirty, *dínu* lamb, *fiadu*, *fiada*, Lord, God, *Núadu* Nom. pr., *bráge* neck, *lóche* (Gen. *lóchet*) lightning, *fiche* (Gen. *fichet*) twenty, *tee*, *té*, hot.

138. Like *beothu* are declined numerous abstract nouns in *-tu* and *-datu*, the latter being derived from adjectives in *-de*: *óentu*, unitas, *aurlatu* obedience, *cródatu* hardness, *esbatu* inutilitas, *óendatu* unity, *mórdatu* greatness.

139. The stem of the paradigms *fili*, *ara*, *beothu* had an original terminal sound in *t*; hence *th* is still found instead of *d*, and unaspirated *t* in the immediate contact of the dental with *l* or *n*: *niath* nepotis, *bethath* vitae, *tengthaib* linguis, *sligthi* viae, *tenti* ignes, *Ultaib*.

140. The stem of the example *cara* had an original terminal sound in *-nt*. The *t* of *cara* becomes *d* in Middle Irish by direct contact with *r*: *cairdib*.

141. For *-id*, *-it* in the Dative and Acc. of all numbers of the paradigms *ara*, *cara*, *beothu* *-aid*, *-ait* came to be written in Middle Irish. Simple *i* remains after a slender vowel: *fiche* twenty, Acc. *fichit*.

142. Even in Old Irish in the Dat. Sg. of the paradigm *beothu*, a form resembling the Nominative is found: *i m-bethu* in life; so also *it chin* besides *it chinaid* through thy guilt. Also instead of the Nom. Dual the form of the Nominative Singular is used.

143. In Middle Irish such forms occur in the Nom. Pl. as *tenti*, *sligthi*, *traigthi*; in the Accusative Plural forms in *-u*, *-o*, replace the older forms in *-a*: *Ulto*, *Ultu*, *filedu*.

(b) Guttural stems.

144. Paradigm: *cathir* F. town.

Singular.	Plural.	Dual.
N. *in chathir*	*inna cathraig*	*dí chathraig, chathir*
G. *inna cathrach*	*inna cathrach n-*	*dá cathrach*

(c) *Terms of kinship in r.*

D. *don chathraig, chathir*	*donaib cathrachaib*	*dib cathrachaib*
A. *in cathraig n-*	*inna cathracha*	*dí chathraig*
V. *a chathir*	*a chathracha*	

145. In the same way are declined: *nathir* water-snake, *lassair* flame, *láir* (Gen. *lárach*) mare, *dair* oak, *Temair* Tara, *ail* (Gen. *ailech*) rock, *Lugaid* (Gen. *Luigdech* and *Lugdach*); and with a terminal vowel: *coera* sheep, *mala* eyebrow, Acc. Plur. *mail-gea, eola* knowing, *rure* king (Gen. *rurech*), *aire* nobleman (Gen. *airech*).

146. The Nom. *daur* oak belongs to an old *u* stem, as also the Gen. *daro, dara*. Some other words of this kind form single cases without the guttural. Dat. Sg. *cathir, Temair,* Acc. *ail,* Dat. Pl. *cáirib.*

147. *Lia, lie* M. stone, Latin *cos*, is an isolated stem in *cc, c*, and is thus declined: N. *lia, lie*, G. *liacc*, D. *liic* and *lia*, A. *liic n-*, Pl. N. *lieic*, G. *liacc n-*. Another word is *lecc* F. stone, flagstone, N. *lecc*, G. *licce*, D. *leicc*, A. *leicc n-*, Pl. N. A. *lecca*, G. *lecc n-*, D. *leccaib*.

148. *Rí* M. king is an isolated stem in *g*, and is thus declined, N. *rí*, G. *ríg*, D. *ríg*, A. *ríg n-*, V. *a rí*, Pl. N. *ríg*, G. *ríg n-*, D. *rígaib*, A. *ríga*, Middle Irish *rígu*, Dual N. A. *dá ríg*, G. *dá ríg*, D. *dib rígaib*. A similar stem is *brí* hill, Gen. *breg*.

(c) Terms of kinship in *r*.

149. Paradigm: *bráthir* M. brother.

	Singular.	*Plural.*	*Dual.*
N.	*in bráthir*	*in bráthir*	*dá bráthir*
G.	*in bráthar*	*inna m-bráthre n-*	*dá bráthar*
D.	*don bráthir*	*donaib bráithrib*	*dib m-bráithrib*
A.	*in m-bráthir n-*	*inna bráithrea*	*dá bráthir.*
V.	*a bráthir*	*a bráithrea*	

150. *Bráthar* is found in the Gen. Pl. as well as *bráthre*.

II. Declension.

Later *bráithre* is also met with in the Nom. Pl. In the same way are declined: *máthir* mother, *athir* father, in Middle Irish *bráthair, máthair, athair*. Also *siur* sister, Gen. *sethar, fethar*, § 56, Dat. *siair, fiair*.

151. In the later language these words have come to be inflected like *cathir*: *úasal-athraig* patriarchæ, Modern Irish Nom. and Acc. Pl. *bráithreacha*.

(d) Masculine and Feminine stems in *n* and *nn* (*nd*).

152. Paradigms: *brithem* M. judge, *inga* F. nail, *toimtiu* F. meaning, *goba* M. smith.

Singular.

N. *in brithem*	*ind inga*	*in toimtiu*	*in goba*
G. *in brithemon, -an*	*inna ingan*	*inna toimten*	*in gobann*
D. *don brithemain*	*dond ingain*	*don toimtin*	*don gobainn*
A. *in m-brithemain n-*	*in n-ingain n-*	*in toimtin n-*	*in n-gobainn n-*
V. *a brithem*	*a inga*		*a goba*

Plural.

N. *in brithemain*	*inna ingain*	*inna toimtin*	*in gobainn*
G. *inna m-britheman n-*	*inna n-ingan n-*	*inna toimten n-*	*inna n-gobann n-*
D. *donaib brithemnaib*	*donaib ingnaib*	*donaib toimtinib*	*donaib gobannaib*
A. *inna brithemna*	*inna ingna, -e*	*inna toimtena*	*inna gobanna*
V. *a brithemna*	*a ingna*		

Dual.

N. A. *dá brithemain*			*dá gobainn*
G. *dá britheman*			*dá gobann*
D. *dib m-brithemnaib*			*dib n-gobannaib*

(e) Neuter Nouns in man (nn).

153. Like *brithem* are declined other Nomina actoris, e.g. *dúlem* creator (from *dúil* element), *flaithem* ruler (from *flaith* lordship), also *ollam* princeps poetarum (Gen. *ollaman*), *talam* F. earth (Gen. *talman*), and with a terminal vowel *menme* M. sense (Gen. *menman*).

154. *Anim* F. soul has G. *anme*, D. *anmin*, *anmain*; A. *anmin*, *anmain n-*, Pl. N. *anmin*, and so on, but in Middle Irish comes to be inflected in the Plural like the Neuter noun *ainm* name, Pl. N. A. *anmand*, G. *anmand n-*, D. *anmannib*.

155. Like *inga* are declined *ára*, *áru* kidney, *aursa* doorpost, *gulba* bill, *leco* cheek, *lurga* shinbone, *lúta* little finger, *ulcha* beard, *Alba* North Britain, *Muma* Munster, *patu* hare, and without a vowel in the Nominative, *triath* sea, Gen. *trethan*.

156. In the Nom. Pl. such forms as *ingni* are found later (cf. § 143).

157. *broo*, *bró* millstone, G. *broon*, *brón*, D. *broin*, Ac. *broin n-*; *cú* M. hound, G. *con*, D. *coin*, Ac. *coin n-*, V. *a chú*; Pl. N. *coin*, G. *con n-*, D. *conaib*, Ac. *cona*.

158. Feminine abstract nouns in -*tiu*, -*tu* are declined like *toimtiu*; *foisitiu* confessio, *ditiu* protection, *tichtu* advent, *aicsiu* vision; also *nóidiu* child, Acc. Pl. (in Middle Irish) *nóidenu* (cf. § 143).

159. Like *goba* are declined *gúala* shoulder, *bara* anger, *cuisle* vein, Gen. *cuislenn*, *uile* elbow, *Ériu* F. Ireland (G. *Érenn*, D. *Érinn*), *brú* F. womb (G. *bronn*, *brond*, Dat. *broind*).

(e) Neuter nouns in *man* (*nn*).

160. Paradigm: *ainm* name.

Singular.	Plural.	Dual.
N. A. *a n-ainm n-*	*inna anmann*	*dá n-ainm*
G. *ind anma, anme*	*inna n-anmann n-*	
D. *dond anmaimm, ainm*	*donaib anmannaib*	*dib n-anmannaib*.

II. Declension.

161. In the same way are declined *coirm* beer, *gairm* shout, *druimm* back (Gen. *drommo*), *maidm* eruption, *teidm* pestis, *senim* sonitus, *tochimm* striding, *ingrimm* pursuing, *tóthim*, later *tuitim* fall.

162. The following have *-enn* in place of *-ann*: *béim*, *béimm* blow, *céimm* step, *léimm* leap, *réimm* cursus, nominative plural *bémen*, *cémenn*.

163. In Old Irish only one *n* is often written (*bémen*) and in Middle Irish often *nd* for *nn* (*anmand*).

(*f*) Neuter nouns in *as* and other stems in *s*.

164. Paradigm: *teg, tech* N. house.

	Singular.	Plural.	Dual.
N. A.	*a teg, tech* n-	*inna tige*	*dá tech* (?)
G.	*in tige*	*inna tige* n-	*dá tige*
D.	*don tig*	*donaib tigib*	*dib tigib*.

165. In the same way are declined the Neuter nouns: *nem* heaven, *leth* side, *mag* plain, *slíab* mountain, *glend* dale: *dún* castle and *glún* knee vary in the later language, G. *dúne*, D. *dún, glún*, N. Pl. *dúine*, N. Du. *da prim-dún, da glún*.

166. Comparatives in *-iu, u (o)* may be placed here, but they show no differences of case as they are only used in the nominative, Nom. Sg. and Pl. *laigiu, lugu* less, *máo, móu* greater, *lia* more.

167. *mí*, month, G. *mís*, D. *mís*, A. *mís* n-, Pl. N. *mís*, G. *mís* n-, D. *mísaib*, A. *mísa*.

Isolated stems and stems difficult to class.

168. *Bó* cow (stem *bó-, bov-*), G. *bou, bó*, D. *boin*, A. *boin* n-, Pl. N. *bai, ba*, G. *bó* n-, D. *buaib*, A. *bú*; Du. N. *dí ba*, D. *dib m-buaib*, A. *dí ba, dí boin*.

169. *die* day (put under *s* stems in Zeuss, ed. II. p. 270), Acc. *fri dei, de* by day, with two cases used adverbially, *in diu* to-day, and *dia* followed by a genitive, e. g. *dia brátha* at doomsday.

170. *gné* form, *glé* resplendent, and the composite nouns *to-gu, ro-gu* choice, show no distinctions of case.

III.

THE ARTICLE.

171. A rough breathing after the form is to show that it causes aspiration. Paradigms:

Singular.

	M.	F.	N.
N.	*in, in t-*	*in‛, ind‛, in t-*	*a n-*
G.	*in‛, ind‛, in t-*	*inna, na*	as M.
D.	*don‛, dond‛, don t-*	as M.	as M.
A.	*in n-*	as M.	*a n-*

Plural.

	M.	F.	N.
N.	*in‛, ind‛, in t-*	*inna, na*	as F.
G.	as F.	*inna, na n-*	as F.
D.	as F.	*donaib, dona*	as F.
A.	as F.	*inna*	as F.

Dual.

	M.	F.	N.
N.	*in dá*	*in di*	*in dá n-*
G.	*in dá*	*in dá*	*in dá*
D.	*in dib n-*	*in dib n-*	*in dib n-*
A.	*in dá*	*in di*	*in dá n-.*

172. In the nominative singular masculine the *t-* comes before a vowel initial sound, *in t-athir* the father, in all other cases before an initial *s*, in place of which it is pronounced, *in t-serc* the love.

173. The change between *n* and *nd* is only found in those cases which cause aspiration. *nd* is used regularly in Old Irish before those sounds which have never been aspirated, viz. before *l r n* and before vowels, also before *f* which when aspirated disappears altogether, so that a vowel, an *r* or an *l* may be taken for the proper initial sound of the word: N. Sg. F. *in chathir* the town, *ind flaith* the lordship, G. Sg. M. *in choimded* of the Lord, *ind athar* of the father, Dat. *don bráthir* to the brother, *don macc* to the son. *t* immediately preceded by *n* is not aspirated (cf. § 64) Gen. Sg. *in tige* of the house. In Modern Irish only forms with *n* occur (*an* and *na*).

174. The article had originally an *s*. This *s* has been retained in the Dat. and Acc. in union with prepositions of consonantal terminal sound. *iarsin* from *iar n-* after, *ressin* from *re n-* before, *cossin, cosnaib* from *co n-* with (c. Dat.), *issin, isnaib, isna, isin dib* (Dat. Du.) from *i n-* in (cum Dat. et Acc.), *lassin n-* (M. F.), *lassa n-* (N.), *lasna* Pl., *lasin di* (Acc. Du. F.) from *la(th)* with, *frissin n-* (M. F.), *frissa n-* (N.), *frisna* (Pl.) from *fri(th)* towards, *trissin n-* (M. F.), *trissa n-* (N.), *trisna* (Pl.) from *tri* through, *cossin n-* (M. F.), *cossa n-* (N.) from *co(th)* to, *tarsin n-* (M. F.), *tarsa n-* (N.), *tarsna* (Pl.) from *tar(s)* over (cum Acc.), *assin* (M. F. N.) from *a, ass* out of (cum Dat.), *forsin* (Dat. M. F. N.), *forsin n-* (Acc. M. F.), *forsa n-* (N.), *forsnaib* (Pl. Dat.), *forsna* (Acc.) from *for* upon (c. Dat. et Acc.).

175. Other instances of union with prepositions which originally had vowel endings are: *ón úan* (Dat. Sg.), *ónaib* (Pl.), *fón* (Dat. Sg.), *fón n-* (Acc. M. F.) from *ó* of, *fo* under, and *ocon* besides *oc in* (Dat.), *immon n-* (Sg. Acc. M. F.), *imma n-* (N.) from *oc* by, *imm* about. Also *don* (Dat. Sg.), *donaib* (Pl.), *din* (Dat. Sg.), *dinaib* (Pl.) from *do* to, *di* of, over.

176. The remaining prepositions cause no alteration of

the article: *ar in* (Dat. Sg.), *ar naib* (Dat. Pl.), *ar na* (Acc.), from *ar* for, before.

177. In Middle Irish the peculiar form of the dative plural -(*s*)*naib* is disused and the accusative form -(*s*)*na* is used in its stead; Middle Irish *dona, dina, forsna, óna* for Old Irish *donaib, dinaib, forsnaib, ónaib* and so on.

178. The abbreviated form *na* by degrees wholly takes the place of the fuller form *inna*. The fuller form is never found after prepositions.

179. The neuter gradually loses in the Nom. and Acc. Sg. its peculiar form; *in tech* the house for the older *a tech:* but again in Modern Irish *an* instead of *in,* for all genders in the Nom. and Acc. Sing.

180. In the Nom. Pl. the feminine form *inna, na* finally also supplants the masculine *in: na maic* the sons for Old Irish *in maic* (cf. § 114).

IV.

COMPARISON.

181. The comparative is usually formed by the suffix *-iu, -u* (Modern Irish *-i, -e*).

Positive	Comparative
sen old	*siniu*
álind pretty	*áildiu, áilliu* (§ 71)
árd high	*árdu*
comacus near	*comaicsiu*
—	*laigiu, lugu* minor.

182. The suffix of the superlative is *-em* (*-am*), less often *-imem*.

Positive	Comparative	Superlative
follus apertus	*foillsiu*	*faillsem*
cóem handsome	*cóimiu*	*cóemem*
adbul prodigious	*aidbliu*	*adblam*
úasal noble	*úaisliu*	*úaislimem*.

183. Irregular comparison:

Positive	Comparative	Superlative
il much	*lía*	
óac young	*óa*	*óam*
már, mór great	*máo, máa má, mó*	*máam*
sír long	*sía*	
trén strong	*tressa, tressiu*	*tressam*
ocus near	*nessa, nessu*	*nessam*
olc bad	*messa, messu*	
maith good	*ferr*	(*dech*)
bec little	*laigiu, lugu*	*lugam, lugimem*.

I. G.

IV. Comparison.

184. Instead of the special superlative form the comparative is generally used with the preceding relative *as, bas* (qui est): *intí diib bes tresa orcaid alaile* the strongest of them kills the other; *dá ech bas ferr la Connachtu* the two best horses in Connacht.

185. There is a second disused comparative form in *-ither, -ithir, idir: léir* industrious, comparative *lériu* and *lérithir; lúath* swift, comparative *lúathiu* and *lúathither*.

186. "The," Latin *eo*, with the comparative is expressed by *de* placed after the adjective: *ferr de* the better. Better and better *ferr assa ferr*; worse and worse *messa assa messa*.

187. "Than," Latin quam, after the comparative is expressed by *ol* or *inda*. *Ol* is without exception associated with a relative form of the verb substantive and *inda* is usually so: *olda-as oldás, inda-as indás* quam est; *oldáte indate* quam sunt.

188. As in Latin the ablative is used instead of this form, so in Irish the dative of the compared object is employed: *ni diliu nech limm alailiu* non carior mihi quisquam altero. In feminine stems in *a* this case of the comparative (originally an instrumental?) sounds sometimes like the nominative.

In Middle Irish the accusative is used in the same way: *it lúathidir gáith n-erraig* they are swifter than a spring gale.

V.

ADVERB.

189. Adverbs are formed from adjectives

1. By the dative singular masculine or neuter with the article: *bec* little, adverb *in biucc* paullatim; *laigiu* minor, adverb *ind laigiu* minus.

2. By a peculiar form in *-ith, -id* with the same case of the article: *óinde* singularis, adverb *ind óindid* singulariter.

3. By prefixing the preposition *co*: *dían* swift, adverb *co dían* swiftly.

The third becomes the usual form in Middle Irish.

VI.

PRONOUNS.

Demonstrative.

190. To the Greek οὗτος answers substantivally *side, suide*, less often *ade*, and adjectivally the indeclinable suffix *sin*; *in fer sin* this man, genitive *ind fir sin* and so on (compare the French *cet homme-ci*). *sin* occurs also without substantive: *íar sin* μετὰ τοῦτο; *in sin* (indeclinable) substantival, for all three genders.

191. To the Greek ὅδε answer the demonstratives *se, sa* and *so*, indeclinable and placed after the substantive: *in fer so ὁ ἀνὴρ ὅδε*; substantivally *so* and *in so* (indeclinable) for all three genders.

se, sa and *so* become *si, sea* and *seo* or *siu* after a slender vowel.

192. All these demonstratives also become adverbial, intensifying the meaning when added to the adverb *and*, here: *andsin, andso, andside, andaide*.

193. Some of the particles (particulæ augentes) which serve for the stronger enunciation of the personal pronouns are of the same origin: *-se, -sa* for the 1 Sg., *mésse, mesi* I, *ro-básа* I was; *-su, -so* for the 2 Sg., *tússu* thou, *do ara-so* thy charioteer, *foracbaisiu* thou didst abandon (for *foracbais-siu*); *-som, -sam,-sem* for the 3 Sg. M. and the 3 Pl. of all three genders, *ésseom* he, *rigid-som* he stretches out.

194. To the Greek τοῦτο answer also *ón, són*. *Sodin, sodain* οὗτος is rarely used in other than a neuter sense: *la sodain* thereon.

195. The enclitic *-í* has a more determinative character. When united with the article (M. *intí*, F. *indí*, N. *aní*) it is followed by a proper name, or by a demonstrative or relative clause: *intí Labraid* this (aforesaid) Labrid, *aní sin τοῦτο*, *intí siu ὅδε, intí thall* ille; *intí cretfes* French celui qui croira, Dat. Pl. Old Irish *donaib hí gníte* iis qui faciunt, Middle Irish *dona fíb no chretitis* to those who believed, *cosna fíb filet intib* with those who are therein, or placed after the substantive as: *lasin screich í sin* upon this cry.

196. The Greek ἐκεῖνος is expressed by means of the adverbs *tall, út, sút, ucut, sucut* illic, subst. *intí thall* yon, adj. *in fer tall*, French cet homme-là, *na tri dath ucut* those three colours.

197. To the Latin idem correspond *inonn, inunn* and *cétne, cétna: in fer cétne* idem vir (but *in cétne fer* primus vir).

198. *Side, suide* and *ade* hic (§ 190) with the neuter *se* hoc (e.g. *re siu* antehac) are alone declinable without the article. Their form of declension is that of noun-stems in *ia* (§ 115) but *side* is also in use undeclined for the Nom. Pl. of all three genders.

Personal Pronouns.

199. The personal pronouns are frequently strengthened by an enclitic pronominal particle (particula augens), cf. § 193.

In the 1 and 2 persons pl. the strengthening takes place by reduplication of the pronoun. The strengthened form is within parentheses:

Singular.
mé I (*messe, mesi*)
tú thou (*tussu, tuso*)
é he, *si* she, *ed* it (*é som, sisi, ed ón*)

Plural.
ni, sni we (*snisni, snini, ninni*)
sib you (*sissi*),
é, íat they (*é som, íat som*).

VI. Pronouns.

200. These forms also occur in the accusative. In the later language a distinction is attempted between the Nom. and Acc.

	Singular.		Plural.
Nom.	Acc.	Nom.	Acc.
1 mé	mé	1 sinn	sinn, inn
2 tú	thú	2 sib	sib, ib
3 sé, sí (í)	é, í	3 síat	íat.

201. The pronoun governed by a preposition (pron. suffixum) is blended with the preposition. The pronoun governed by a verb is in Old Irish blended with the preceding verbal particle, conjunction, negative particle, or preposition (pron. infixum). In the second case the particle *do* is often put before the verb in order to suffix the pronoun to it.

202. These enclitic dative and accusative forms sound as follows: in the 1 Sg. -*m*, -*mm* (aspirating), 2 Sg. -*t* (aspirating), in the 1 Pl. -*n*, -*nni*, -*nn* (-*nd*), 2 Pl. -*b*: *dam, damsa* to me, *frimm* towards me, *indium* in me, *mani-m berasu* nisi feras me, *duit, duit-siu* to thee, *immut* about thee, *atotchiat* vident te, for *ad-dot-chiat* (*ad-cíu* I see), *dún* to us, *lin-ni* with us, *ro-nn ain* protegat nos, *dúib, dúib-si* to you, *úaib* from you, *cotob sechaim* coerceo vos (*cosc* hold back; *dob* pushed between *co n-* and *sechaim*). For the 2 Pl. *bar* is also in use (usually a possessive pronoun): *no bor mairfither* ye will be slain, *ro bur fucc* who brought you.

203. The enclitic elements for the dative and accusative of the 3rd person are more difficult to ascertain and can scarcely be differentiated from their union with prepositions. In the plural there is no distinction of genders.

As verbal objects (Acc. or Dat.) the following are discoverable: -*d* (aspirating) for Neuter, Masc., Fem., *rod chluinethar* qui id audiverit; -*n* (asp.) for Masc., Neut., *nin accend* non eum videt; -*a* (asp.) for Plural, Neuter, Fem. (?), *ra chualatar* id audiverunt; *da* (asp.) for Plural, Fem., Neut. (?), *conda thanic* eos adiit; -*a* (*n-*), -*d* (*n-*) for Masc., Neut. (?), *rom-bertaigestar*,

Personal Pronouns.

rod m-bertaigedar he shook himself; *-s (n-), dos (n-)* for Plural, Fem., *dos n-icfed* he would come to them, *-s, dos* for Plur., Masc., Fem., Neut., *ros bia* eis erit.

Sometimes the pronominal element is proleptic whilst the proper object still follows after it, *dos leicim-se...do-som in n-gai cétna* I throw the same spear after him, Sc. M. 10.

204. The following is a table of prepositions united with the personal pronouns. Only the more important variations are given. The forms enclosed in [ ] are from O'Donovan's grammar.

PREPOSITIONS WITH THE DATIVE.

	Sg.	Pl.	Sg.	Pl.	Sg.	Pl.
	ó, úa Latin a.		*oc* apud		*fiad* coram	
1.	*úaim*	*úain*	*acum*	*ocainni*	*fiadam*	
2.	*úait*	*úaib*	*ocut*	*ocaib*		*fiadib*
3. M.	*úad*	*úadib*	*oca*	*ocaib*		*fiadib*
F.	*úadi*		*aci*			
	do ad		*is* infra, *ós, úas* supra		*re (n-), rem* ante	
1.	*dom, dam*	*dún*	*issum*	[*uasainn*]	*rium, remum*	*reunn, remunn*
2.	*dait, duit, deit*	*dúib*	[*uasat*]	[*uasaibh*]	*riut,* [*remut*]	[*romhaibh*]
3. M.	*dáu, dó*	*dóib*	[*uasa*]	*úasaib*	Acc. *remi*	*remib, rempu*
F.	*di*		[*uaisti*]		*rempe*	*rompa*
	di de		*a, ass* ex		*íar (n-), íarm* post	
1.	*diim*	*diin, dind*	[*asam*]	[*asainn*]		
2.	*diit*	*diib*	[*asat*]	[*asaibh*]		
3. M.	*de*	*diib*	*ass*	*essib, estib*	*iarma*	
F.	*di*		*essi, esti*			

PREPOSITIONS WITH THE ACCUSATIVE.

	fri contra		*tar* trans		*imb* circa	
1.	*frim, friumm*	*frinni*	[*thorm*]	*torunn*	*immum*	*immunn*
2.	*frit, friut*	*frib*	*torut*	[*thorraib*]	*immut*	*immib*
3. M.	*friss*	*friu*	*tairis*	*tairsiu*	*imbi*	*impu*
F.	*frie, fria*		*tairse*		*impe*	

VI. Pronouns.

	Sg.	Pl.	Sg.	Pl.	Sg.	Pl.
	tri per		*eter* inter		*cen* sine	
1.	*trium*	*triunni*	*etrom*	*etrunn*		
2.	*triut*	*triib*	[*eadrat*]	*etruib*	*cenut*	*cenuib*
3. M.	*triit*	*treu, trethu*	*etir*	*etarru*	N. *cene*	*cenaib*
F.	*tree, tréthi*					

	la with, through		*sech* praeter		*co* ad	
1.	*lemm, liumm*	*lenn, linn*	[*seacham*]	*sechond*	*cuccum*	*cucunn*
2.	*lat, let*	*lib*	*sechut*	[*seachaibh*]	*cucut*	*cucuib*
3. M.	*leiss*	*leu, lethu*	*secha*	*seccu, seocu*	*cucci*	*cuccu, cucthi*
F.	*lee*		*secce*		*cuicce*	

PREPOSITIONS WITH DATIVE AND ACCUSATIVE.

	ar, air pro		*for* super	
1.	*airium*	*erunn*	*form*	*fornn, forun*
2.	*airiut*	*airib*	*fort*	*foirib*
3. Dat. M.	*airi*	*airib, airthib*	Dat. M. *fora*, F. *fuiri*	*forib*
Acc.		*airriu, airthiu*	Acc. M. *foir*, F. *forrae*	*forru*

	fo sub		*i* (*n*-), *ind* in	
1.	*foum*	[*fúinn*]	*indiumm*	*indiunn*
2.	[*fút*]	[*fáibh*]	*innut*	*indib*
3. Dat. M.	*foa*	*foib, fothib*	Dat. *indid*, Acc. *ind*	*indib*
Acc. M. *foi*, F.	[*fuithi*]	[*fútha*]	Dat. *indi*, Acc. *inte*	*intiu*

205. These same pronominal elements have also become suffixed to verbal forms in the sense of subjects and objects, especially often to the forms of the verb substantive. In Old Irish occur: *at* thou art, *adib* ye are, *baan, ban* simus, *con-dan* ut simus; so also *ro bam* fui, *biam* ero, *ni pam* non ero, *ni dam* non sum, *bát* sis (*ni pat* besides *ni pa* SC. 26), *can dollot* unde venisti (§ 302). And as acc. or dative: *ainsiunn* protegat nos (*ainis* protegat), *taithiunn* (est nobis) (*taith* est), *tuthut* est tibi, *gabsi* cepit eum, *gabsus* cepit eos (*gabis* cepit), *marbthus* occidit eos, *boithus* erat eis.

206. The genitive of pronouns is expressed by prepositions, e.g. *ni sochude diib* non multi ex eis, but there are also

some distinct genitive forms, in first person dual *nathar*, in the third person *ái, ae*, and *de: cechtar nathar* uterque nostrum, *cechtar ái, cechtar ae* and *cechtar de* uterque eorum, *cach ái, cach ae* each of them. Old Irish *ái* suum proprium, Geu. *ind ái* ἑαυτοῦ sui, Pl. *inna n-ái* ἑαυτῶν.

Possessive Pronouns.

207. The possessive pronouns are:

Sg. *mo, mu* (asp.) my *do, du* (asp.) thy *a* M. N. (asp.) his, *a* F. her
Pl. *ar n-* our *far n-, for n-, bor n-* your *a n-* their.

208. The pronouns *mo* and *do* often lose their vowel before an initial vowel, when amalgamated with prepositions they also lose their vowel before an initial consonant. Instead of *do, t* then appears, before vowels *th: m' athir* my father, *th' athair* thy father. With prepositions: *óm, ót, úat* a meo, tuo (*ó*); *dom, dot* meo, tuo (*do*); *dim, dit* de meo, tuo (*di*); *fom, fot* sub meo, tuo (*fo*); *form, fort* super meo, tuo (*for*); *frim, frit* contra meum, tuum (*fri*); *imm, it* in meo, tuo (*i n-*); *ocom, com* (§ 108ᵇ), *icim, iccot* apud meum, tuum; *immom* circa meum.

209. Of other compounds the following deserve notice: *iarna* after his, *iarnar n-* after our; *rena, riana* before his (*re n-*); *fria* towards his, *tria, trea* through his; *inna* in his, *innar n-* in our; *má* for *imma* about his, her; *na* for *inna* in his; *do* becomes *di* (in these possessives) before *a*: *dia* to his, to her, *dia n-* to her, *diar n-* to our.

210. The possessive pronoun with the infinitive marks the pronominal object, less often the subject of the infinitive: *is cóir a thabairt dóib* it is right to give it to them, *tair dum berrad sa* come to shear me, *iarna thichtain ó Róim* when he had come from Rome.

VI. Pronouns.

SELF.

211. The notion of "self" is expressed by several allied composite words, which begin with *fe-, fa- (fo-)* or *ce-, ca-:*

féin 1. 2. 3. Sg. 　　　　*céin* 1 Sg.　*fadéin* 1. 2. 3. Sg.;
fésin 2. Pl. *féisin* 3. Sg. F.　　　　　　　　　　　　　　　　　[M.; 3. Pl.
fessin 3. Sg. M.; 3. Pl.; 2. Sg.; *cesin* 3. Sg.　*fadesin* 3. Sg. M.; 3 Pl.; *cadessin* 3. Sg.
fésine 3. Sg. Pl.　　　　　　　　　　　　*fadesine* 3. Pl.
féisne 2. Pl.; 3 Sg. F.; 3 Pl.　　　　　　*fadéisne* 2. Pl.
　　　　　　　　　　　　　　　　　　　　fanisin 1. Pl.　　　　　*canisin* 1. Pl.

For *fadéin, fodéin* the form *bodein* is also found. The forms *fésin* and *fessin* are perhaps identical.

RELATIVE PRONOUNS.

212. The relative pronoun *a n-* does not change for case, number or gender, and sounds like the nominative and accusative singular neuter of the article. It had originally an initial *s*, which is yet to be traced when it is compounded with prepositions which have a final consonant. *Frissa n-, lasa n-* (§ 174); by composition with *do* is produced *dia n-* (cf. § 209). It stands either at the head of the relative clause or after the particle which may precede the verbal form : *a n-asbiur* quod dico, *tresa m-bí* per quam est, *hua m-bí* e quibus fit, *do-m-bert* quem attulit, *a forcital for-n-dob-canar* doctrina quae vobis praecipitur (*forchun* praecipio).

213. The relative pronoun is often omitted, especially after the relatively employed negative particle *na* and the indefinite *nech* (§ 220), but often its absence is only an apparent one : *it hé do-r-raidchiuir* sunt hi quos redemit (for *do-an-ro-aidchiuir*).

214. The relative pronoun is also used as an explanatory conjunction, e.g. *ron-gníth* that it has happened : less often by itself in the sense of "when," but it is a frequent ingredient of compounded conjunctions, e.g. *ara n-* that (final), *dia -n*

(prep. *di*) if; and in the same way *in tan* during, when, because, *óre, úair* because, *amal* as are followed by the relative pronoun, *in tan m-bímmi* cum sumus, *húare m-bís* quia est, *amal fo-ngníter* sicut voluntur (*fo-gníu* I serve).

Interrogative Pronouns.

215. *Cia, ce, ci* are the interrogative pronouns and are indeclinable being used without distinction of gender for singular and plural, substantivally and adjectivally. Besides these the forms *ca, co* are discoverable in the expressions *cate, cote* quis est, quid est; *cateet* quid sunt; *cani, cini* why not; *can* whence. *Coich* is also used as a synonym of *cia : coich andso* who is this here?

216. In order to distinguish the genders the personal pronoun is added: *ce hé* quis; *cé si, cisi* quae; *ced, cid* (for *ce ed*) quid.

217. The question is always framed so as to have the interrogative pronoun in the nominative case; other cases are expressed by an indefinite or relative pronoun following: *cia dia tibertais rigi* to whom they should give the kingship; *cia ar neoch dorrignis* ad quid hoc fecisti? When the interrogative pronoun is used adjectivally the flexion takes place in the noun only *cia i n-olcaib* in quibus malis.

218. *Ce rét* what thing, *ce airm* what place, *ce indas* what condition, fuse to *crét, cairm, cindas*. These are short interrogative sentences which the special meaning of the question commonly follows in a relative sentence : *cia airm i n-dom facca* what the place in which thou hast seen me = where hast thou seen me?; *cinnas rainnfither* what the manner (in which) it shall be divided = how shall it be divided? *Cindas* associated with a genitive paraphrases the Latin qualis : *cindas in choirp i n-eséirset* quali corpore resurgent?

VI. Pronouns.

219. *Cia, ce* with the conjunctive is used in the sense of the Latin quisquis and quamquam; *ce bé, cipe* quisquis est; *cía no betis fir in chóicid uli immond* even if the men of the whole province were around us.

INDEFINITE PRONOUNS.

220. *Nech* quisquam, aliquis, without distinction of gender is used substantivally and is declined: Nom. *nech*, Gen. *neich*, Dat. *do neuch, neoch*, Acc. *nech*. *Nech* with a relative sentence following it (without a relative pronoun) answers to the Latin *is*, especially to the neuter *id*, and to the *ejus* of *id quod, ejus quod* and so on: *do dénum neich asberat* ad agendum id quod dicunt.

221. *Nach (nách)* ullus, aliqui, Neuter *na n-* is used adjectivally. The following inflected forms are further observable: Dative *do nach*, Accusative, Masculine and Feminine *nach n-*, Genitive Feminine *nacha*.

222. "Something," the Latin aliquid, is usually expressed by the word *ní*, which according to Zeuss is a substantive meaning res: *mór ní* magnum aliquid; *na sothe i. ní dofuisim terræ*, gloss on terræ fetus, i. e. quod generat terra. *Aní* (later *inní*) is very often used in the sense of id quod, with a relative sentence following, a form which may represent both *ní* with the article and the pronominal *aní* (§ 195).

223. *Cách* used substantivally, with the article *in cách* each, without distinction of gender: Genitive *caich*, Dative *do chách*.

224. *Cech, cach* every, used adjectivally: Neuter *cech n-, cach n-*; Genitive, Masculine and Neuter *caich, cech, cach*, Feminine *cecha, cacha*; Dative, Masculine, Feminine and Neuter *cech, cach*; Accusative Masculine, Feminine and Neuter *cech n-, cach n-*; Plural Feminine *cecha, cacha*; Dative *cacha*.

Indefinite Pronouns.

225. The adjectival form *cech, cach* is often associated with *oen : cech oen* every one. When followed by a numeral *cech, cach* is distributive: *cach dá* bini (§ 236).

226. *Nechtar* one of two, *cechtar* either of two.

227. The adjectival pronouns *nach* and *cech, cach* are often followed by *ái, ae* in the sense of the Latin eorum (§ 206): *cach ái, cachœ;* besides *cechtar ái* uterque in the same sense also *cechtar de.*

228. *Aile* and *alaile, araile* alius, *ule, uile* whole, all, are declined like noun-stems in *ia* (§ 115) with the exception of the Neut. Nom. Acc. Sg. *aill, alaill, araill* aliud: *uile* signifies whole, when placed after the substantive; all, when it precedes the substantive. Distinct from *aile* is *ala* (indecl.) *ind ala (indara)* alteruter: *ind ala n-ái* (§ 206); *ind ala...alaile* unus (alter)...alter.

VII.

NUMERALS.

229. Cardinal numbers. The dots accompanying *óen...deac* 11 and so on notify the position of the substantive.

1 *óin, óen*
2 *dá,* F. *di,* N. *dá n-; de-* (Comp.)
3 *trí,* F. *teoir,* N. *trí; tre-* (Comp.)
4 *cethir,* F. *cetheoir,* N. *cethir*
5 *cóic, cúic*
6 *sé*
7 *secht n-*
8 *oct, ocht n-*
9 *nói n-*
10 *deich n-*
11 *óen...déc* or *déac*
12 *dá...déac*
13 *trí...déac*
14 *cethir...déac*
15 *cóic...déac*
16 *sé...déac*
17 *secht n- ...déac*
18 *ocht n- ...déac*
19 *nói n- ...déac*
20 *fiche*
21 *óen...fichet* or *óen...ar fichit*
25 *cóic...fichet* or *cóic...ar fichit*
30 *tricha*

40 *cethorcha* or *dá fichit*
50 *cóica*
60 *sesca* or *trí fichit*
70 *sechtmoga, -o*
80 *ochtmoga* or *cethir fichit*
90 *nocha*
100 *cét* or *cóic fichit* or *dá cóicait*
118 *ocht déac ar chét*
120 *fiche...ar chét*
150 *cóica...ar chét* or *trí cóicait*
152 *dáu coicat ar chét*
180 *ochtmoga...ar chét* or *nói fichit*
200 *dá cét* (or *cethra coecait*)
210 *deich ar dib cetaib*
400 *cethir chét*
1000 *míle*
2000 *di míli*
5000 *coic míli*
10000 *deich míli*
12000 *di míli déc* or *dá sé míle*
100000 *cét míle*
1000000 *míle míle*

Numerals.

230. The inflexion of *dá* two will be found in the Declension paradigmata. Besides *dá* there is a form *dáu, dó* for use without any substantive. Three is thus declined:

	Masc.	Fem.	Neuter.
N.	trí	teoir, teora	trí (aspirating)
G.	trí n-	teora n-	trí n-
D.	trib	teoraib	trib
A.	trí	teora	trí (aspirating).

In the same way *cethir*, Fem. *cetheoir, cetheora*, Neuter *cethir* (aspirating) besides a form *cethri, cethre* for all genders and cases.

231. The tens are masculine and are declined like *cara* § 134: *fiche* 20, Gen. *fichet*, Dat. *fichit; tricha* 30, Gen. *trichat*, Dat. *trichit* or *trichait* and in the same way the succeeding decimals.

232. *cét* is a neuter stem in *a* (§ 110), *míle* a feminine stem in *ia* (§ 115).

233. Ordinal numbers.

1	cét- (in comp.), cétne	10	dechmad
2	tánise, ala	11	óinmad...déac
3	tris, tress- (comp.)	12	ala...déac, ind ala...déac
4	cethramad	13	tris...déac
5	cóiced	14	cethramad...déac
6	sessed	20	fichet
7	sechtmad	23	tris...fichet (Gen. of the Card.)
8	ochtmad	47	sechtmad...cethorchat
9	nómad	50	cóicetmad.

In the year 565 *isin choiciud bliadain sescat ar ccccc (cóic cétaib)*.

VII. Numerals.

234. Numeral substantives.

	(a) for persons.	(b) for things.
1	*óinar* M. one person	
2	*días* F. two persons	*déde* duality
3	*triar* three persons : three men	*tréde* triad
4	*cethrar*	*cetharde*
5	*cóicer*	
6	*seser*	
7	*mór-seser, -feser*	*sechthe*
8	*ochtar*	
9	*nónbar*	
10	*dechenbar*	*deichthe*

The adverbial dative singular is particularly often used with the possessive pronoun: *meisse móinur* I alone; *a triur* they... by threes, three of them and so on.

235. Multiplicative expressions are formed by the preposition *fo, fa* (under) with the cardinal numbers: *fo dí, fa dí* twice, *fo thrí, fo ocht, fo deich, fo ocht fichet* (genitive of the Cardinal number) vicies octies, *fo choic sechtmogat* septuagies quinquies, *óinfecht, oenecht* once (*fecht* time).

236. Distributives are expressed by prefixing the pronoun *cach* each, *cach óen* singuli, *cach dá* bini, *cach trí* terni, and so on.

VIII.

PREPOSITIONS.

237. Prepositions governing the dative are:

do, du (asp.) to
di (asp.) of, Latin de
ó, úa (asp.) from, Latin a
a ass out of, Latin ex

co n- with
re n- ria n- before
íar n- after

fíad Latin coram
oc near, Latin apud
ís under
ós over.

238. Prepositions governing the accusative are:

co to, Latin ad
la by, with, through
fri towards
tri through

tar, dar over, Latin trans
sech Latin praeter, ultra
cen (asp.) without
imb, imm (asp.) around, Latin circa

eter Latin inter
echtar Latin extra
ol on account of
amal as.

239. Prepositions governing both dative and accusative:

ar (asp.) before, for
i n- Latin in

fo (asp.) under
for upon.

240. Nominal prepositions, which govern the genitive:

ar chiunn } before
ar chenn
i n-agid towards
do éis behind, after
tar éis, ési after, for

íar cúl
for cúlu
i n-dead, -diaid } after
i n-degaid
dochum n- to

} behind,

timchell around
dáig, fo dáig
fo, im dágin } on account
fo bith   of.
fo bithin

VIII. Prepositions.

241. *Fiad, oc, is, ós, la, cen, echtar, ol, amal* of the above prepositions (§ 237—239) do not occur in composition with verbal forms. *Co* ad and *ó, úa* from, are not completely ascertained. The following are only preserved in composition: *ad-* Latin ad; *aith-, aid-* (*ath-, ad-*) again, Latin re-, iterum; *ind-, inn-* Gothic *and-, od-* Gothic *ut-*.

242. Some prepositions have in composition an additional form in *m: com-* beside *co n-; iarm-* beside *iar n-; rem* for *re n-; tairm-, tarm-* for *tar; tremi-, trimi-, trem-* for *tri; sechm-* for *sech*. The extended form interchanges with the simple form: *conaitecht* (*con-aith-techt*) petivit, *comtachtmar* petivimus. Cf. *iarom* postea, *riam* antea.

Of *fri* there appears in composition beside the older form *frith-* an augmented form *friss-, fress-: frescsiu* expectation, for *fres-acsiu* (§ 54), *fris-racacha* speravi (*fris-ro-ad-cacha*).

243. In Old Irish as in the older periods of other languages the verbs were often compounded with more than one preposition: *ad-chon-darc* conspexi (*aith-con*); *im-di-bnim* circumcido; *adoparar* offertur (*aith-od-berar*, § 73). In many cases these prepositions are blended with one another, and are commonly only distinguishable when a pronominal object (§ 201) or one of the particles *ro* and *do* (§ 251) has intervened between them. In case of blending the preposition *do* has an initial *t*. The following frequently occur: e.g.

tair-, ter-, tar-	from	*do-air-, -ar-*
taith-, ted-, tad-	,,	*do-aith-, -aid-*
tess-	,,	*do-ess-*
tó-, tu-	,,	*do-fo-*
tór-, tuar-, tur-	,,	*do-for-*
timm-	,,	*do-imm-*
tin-	,,	*do-in-*
tind-	,,	*do-ind-*
tetar-	,,	*do etar-*

Prepositions. 67

tód-, túad-	from	do-od-
diud-, (tiud-)	„	di-od-
faith-, fath-	„	fo-aith-
fód-, fúad-; túad-	„	fo-od; do-fo-od-
do-fuis-, tuis-	„	do-fo-ess-
immó-	„	imm-fo-
iarmó-	„	iarm-fo-.

244. These blended forms may again be compounded with other prepositions: *túarascbat* proferunt from *túar* (*do-for*)-*as-gabat*; *teccomnocuir* accidit, from *ted* (*do-aith*)-*com-nacuir*.

245. In composition and union other phonetic occurrences are to be noticed.

(*a*) Assimilation of contiguous consonants: *ad-chíu*, *at-chiu* video (*aith* or *ad?*), perf. always *acca*; *at-bail* and *epil* interit; *frecart* respondit for *frith-gart* beside *fris-gart*; *adgládur* appello, beside the inf. *accaldam*; *atreba* habitat, for *ad-treba*; *cunutgim*, architector, for *con-ud-tegim*; *forócrad* indicatus est, for *fo-ro-od-garad*; *tuasulcud* resolutio, for *do-fo-od-salciud*; *teccomnocuir* accidit, for *do-aith-com-nacuir*; *éirge* surrectio, for *ess-rige*.

(*b*) Dropping of vowels: *aisndís* exponere, for *as-indís*; *tecmallad* colligere, for *do-aith-com-allad*; *frecndirc* præsens, for *frith-con-dirc*.

(*c*) Dropping of consonants: *tairngert* promisit, for *do-air-con-gert*; *coimthecht* convoy, protection, for *com-im-thecht*; *dochoimmarraig* spoliavit, for *do-chom-imm-ar-raig*.

246. Sometimes that preposition of a double composite which is especially important for the sense, is placed once again at the beginning: *comtherchomrac* congregatio, for *com-do-air-com-rac*, *húatuasailcthæ* absolutum, for *úad-do-fo-od-sailcthæ*; *asréracht* surrexit, for *ass-ro-ess-racht*; so also *ess-éirge* resurrectio, besides *éirge* (i.e. *ess-rige*) with obscured preposition.

VIII. Prepositions.

247. The preposition *do* receives the tenuis in initial sound not only in union with other prepositions, but also in close association with a radical syllable: *toimlim, tomlim* consumo, besides *domelat* consumunt; *tabur, tabraim, taibrim* I give, besides *dobiur; tarat* dedit, besides *dorat; tic* venit, for *do-ic; tanac* veni, for *do-anac*. In the infinitive, where the union of preposition and verb is irresolvable, the tenuis also appears invariably: *tomailt* consumere, *tabairt* give, *tochimm* stride (cf. § 77, *doching* he strides).

247[b]. The same occurs often with the particle *do* in its union with pronominal suffixes (§ 251), especially when preceded by the preposition (not the conjunction) *co n-* which then loses its *n* before the following tenuis: *cotob sechaim* I hinder you, for *con-do-b-sechaim, coscuim* I blame; *cotagart* convocavit cos, for *con-da-gart*, pres. *congairim; cutanméla* he will grind us up, for *con-do-n-méla*, pres. *comlim* I grind up.

IX.

VERB.

248. The Old Irish has three conjugations ("series" in the Grammatica Celtica) the forms of which correspond severally to the Latin third, first and fourth conjugation. The distinction between the conjugations fades in the onward course of time more and more.

249. Paradigms of fourteen distinct forms of tense and mood can be set forth all of which however are not formed in any single verb.

1 Present Indicative
2 Present Conjunctive
3 Imperative
4 Second Present
5 Present of habit
6 T-Preterite
7 S-Preterite
8 Reduplicated Future
9 Reduplicated Second Future
10 B-Future
11 B-Second Future
12 S-Future
13 S-Second Future
14 Perfect

In addition some less well established forms are found which are exhibited § 304 et seq.

250. The second present answers in use to the Latin imperfect indicative and imperfect conjunctive. The second future answers to the French conditional. The perfect has a

preterite signification. Most verbs form only one preterite and a future, derivative verbs (in the II. and III. conjugations) only the S-preterite and the B-future. These two tenses have, in Old Irish, also made their appearance in radical verbs by the side of other forms of their kind.

251. An untranslatable particle *no*, *ro* frequently stands before the verbal form. The verbal particle *no* precedes the present indicative, the second present, the present of habit, and the future. *Ro* precedes the preterite, the conjunctive present, the future, the second present when it is used as imperfect conjunctive. *Ro* further gives a preterite signification to the present indicative, and to the present of habit and sometimes gives the signification of the Latin futurum exactum to the present conjunctive in subordinate sentences. The verbal particle *do* is used less precisely. In the older language it is often used merely as a support for an enclitically affixed pronominal object (§ 202), and in this function it must be distinguished from the preposition *do* which forms compound verbs.

252. The particle *ro* is in Old Irish very often placed between the prepositions or between the preposition and the verbal form of the compound verb, but this is not done when a negative (*ni*, *ná*, *nád*) or the interrogative particle *in* precedes the verb: *for-ro-chon-gart* præcepit, present *for-con-gur; durairngert* he prophesied, for *do-ro-air-con-gert*, cf. *tairngire* prophecy; *fodaraithmine* (qui) id memoret, for *fo-(for-?)da-ro-aith-mine*, cf. *for-aith-minedar* deponent memorat, *for-aith-met* memoria; *as-ru-bartatar* dixerunt, beside *asbert* dixit; *at-ro-threb* habitavit, later *ro aittreb; dorolgetha* remissa sunt, for *do-ro-lugetha*, present *doluigim* remitto; *doreilced* for *do-ro-léced* (preterite passive), present *dolécim* I leave, relinquish; *torchair* he killed, for *do-ro-chair; foracab* reliquit, for *fo-ro-aith-gab*, present *fácbaim* relinquo, *arna érbarthar* ne dicatur, for *ess-ro-berthar*, present *asbiur* dico; *atraracht* surrexit, for *aith-ro-ass-racht* beside *asréracht*, § 246.

253. The passive has, with the exception of the preterite the same tenses as the active. A deponent flexion resembles the passive form as in Latin. All tenses of the active voice are represented in the deponent except the second tenses. The deponent verb which in Old Irish already frames active forms as well, gradually disappears altogether as a peculiar verbal class, but deponent forms enter into the usual active flexion. This happens most often in the conjunctive present and in the third person singular of the S-preterite. In Old Irish the perfect active and the T-preterite have already a deponent flexion in the plural.

254. The present indicative and present conjunctive, the S-preterite, and the future have two sets of forms in the active voice. Forms (formæ conjunctæ) with a shorter termination appear if the verb is compounded or when the verb is preceded by one of the particles *no, ro (coro* that) *do, ni, nad*. Forms (formæ absolutæ) with a longer termination, on the other hand, appear when the verb stands by itself. Even in Old Irish in the first person singular of the present indicative this difference is not carried out thoroughly. Modern Irish has only the absolute flexion in the present and in the future, but in the preterite which is usually preceded by *ro* or *do*, the conjoined form only is preserved.

This distinction between conjoined and absolute forms may also be observed in the passive and deponent.

255. The flexion of the five first tenses (§ 249), those which may in the widest sense of the word be called present forms, may be taken together. Paradigms: Conjugation I. *berimm* I carry, *do-biur* I give, Conjugation II. *carimm* I love, Conjugation III. *lécim* I leave *(dolléciu), dollécim* I set free, throw. As to the distinction of absolute (abs.) and conjoined (conj.) see § 254.

IX. Verb.

Active.

	I		II		III	
	abs.	conj.	abs.	conj.	abs.	conj.

1. Present Indicative.

		I abs.	I conj.	II abs.	II conj.	III abs.	III conj.
Sg.	1	berimm	dobiur	carimm	no charu	lécimm	dolléciu
	2	beri	dobir	cari	no chari	léci	dolléci
	3	berid	dobeir	carid	no chara	lécid	dolléci
	rel.	beres		caras		léces	
Pl.	1	bermme	doberam	carmme	no charam	lécme	dollécem
		bermmit		carmmit		lécmit	
	2	berthe	doberid	carthe	no charid	lécthe	dollécid
	3	berit	doberat	carit	no charat	lécit	dollécet
	rel.	berte		carate		lécte	

2. Present Conjunctive.

		I abs.	I conj.	II abs.	II conj.	III abs.	III conj.
Sg.	1	bera	dober	cara	coro char	lécea	dolléc
	2	bere	dobere	care	coro chare	léce	dolléce
	3	berid	dobera	carid	coro chara	lécid	dollécea
	rel.	beras		caras		léces	
Pl.	1	bermme	doberam	carmme	coro charam	lécme	dollécem
	2	berthe	doberid	carthe	coro charid	lécthe	dollécid
	3	berit	doberat	carit	coro charat	lécit	dollécet
	rel.	berte		carate		lécte	

3. Imperative.

	I		II		III	
	Sing.	Plur.	Sing.	Plur.	Sing.	Plur.
1		beram		caram		lécem
2	beir bir, berthe	berid	car carthe	carid	léic lécthe	lécid
3	berad	berat	carad	carat	léced	lécet

4. Secondary.

1	no berinn	no bermmis	no charinn	no charmmis	dollécinn	dollécmis
2	no bertha	no berthe	no chartha	no charthe	dollécthea	dollécthe
3	no bered	no bertis	no charad	no chartis	dolléced	dolléctis

5. Present of Habit.

| 3 | no berend | | no charand | | no lécend | |

Active. 73

256. In the II. Conjugation instead of *-imm, -i, -id, -it*, gradually *-aim, -ai, -aid, -ait*, are more and more regularly written, especially after a broad vowel in the preceding syllable: *caraim* I love, *molaim* I praise, *scaraim* I separate, *comalnaim* I fulfil, *adcobraim* I desire, *biathaim* I nourish, *techtaim* I have.

257. In the III. Conjugation on the other hand the slender vowel of the flexion-syllable enters more and more regularly into the preceding syllable: *léicim* I leave (§ 255), *dolléicem* we leave; *álim, no áiliu* I implore, *báigim* I fight, *guidim* I ask, *loiscim* I burn, *fodailim* I divide, *áirmim* I count, *suidigim* I set, *ainmnigim* I name.

258. In this tendency to the assimilation of vowels the verbs of the I. Conjugation join the II. Conjugation or the III. Conjugation, so that in Modern Irish only these two conjugations appear to exist. *gabaim* I take, *maraim* I stay, *canaim* I sing, *tíagaim* I go, *gonaim* I wound. On the other hand: *saigim* adeo, *fodaimim* I endure, *dligim* I deserve, *cingim* I step, *lingim* I leap. Old Irish, moreover, is not always consistent.

259. The doubled *m* of the absolute flexion in the 1 sg. and pl. is commonly written single. Before terminations with consonantal initial sound the suppression of the thematic vowels does not occur, in cases where too great an accumulation of consonants would result: *predchimme* praedicamus (II.).

260. Compound verbs even in Old Irish have frequently in 1 sg. present the form in *-im: for-chanim* beside *for-chun*, doceo, *for-chon-grimm* beside *for-con-gur* praecipio, *fo-daimim* patior, *dollécim* I leave, I throw, *atchim* gloss on *ateoch* I ask (*ad-teoch*), 3 *ateich*. In Middle Irish in the I. Conjugation forms also appear with terminal *u*, as in the II. and III. Conjugations: *tongu* for an older *tong* I swear (for *do-fong*?). Some verbs in *t* of the I. Conjugation are irregularly formed in the 3 sg. of the conjoined flexion: *do-diat* sistit, 1 *do-diut* sisto,

74   IX. Verb.

tad-bat demonstrat, pass. sg. 3 *tad-badar* demonstratur, *tin-fet* inspirat, *do-in-fedam* inspiramus, *tin-feth, -fed* aspiratio.

261. In the I. Conjugation all types of the Latin III. Conjugation are again found: *alim* I bring up (pret. § 266, f. § 284), *congarim* I call together, *frecraim* 1 answer (for *frith-garim* pret. § 266, fut. § 277), *atbail* he dies (§ 266, fut. § 277), *fodaimim* I suffer (pret. § 266, perf. dep. § 349, fut. § 277), *maraim* I remain (fut. § 277), *saigim* I seek for, *gabim* I take (pret. § 271, fut. § 277), *canim* I sing (perf. § 290, fut. § 275) as Latin *ago, alo*.

melim I grind (pret. § 266, f. § 277), *celim* I conceal (pret. § 266, fut. § 277), *rethim* I run (perf. § 295), *cunutgim* I build (perf. § 295), *cuintgim* I ask, I demand (pret. § 266, fut. § 287), *nigim* I wash (perf. § 295, fut. § 287), *ithim* I eat (fut. § 287), as Latin *rego, tego*.

orcaim I kill (§ 284), *gonaim* I kill (perf. § 295, fut. § 280), like Latin *molo*.

tiagaim I go (fut. § 285), *riadaim* I drive, as Latin *dico*, Greek στείχω.

ibim I drink, *sessaim* I stand (dep. § 336, pret. § 340), as Latin *bibo, sisto*.

ad-grennim I pursue (perf. § 295, fut. § 287), *fo-gliunn, -glennim* I learn (perf. § 295), *cingim* I go (perf. § 295, fut. § 288), *lingim* I jump (perf. § 295, fut. § 288), *bongaim* I break (pret. § 266, fut. § 287), *ticim* I come (§ 247, perf. § 299, fut. § 287, 284), as Latin *prehendo, pingo;* *aingim* protego sg. 3 (conjoined) *no ainich* (pret. § 266, fut. § 286, inf. § 370) is unique in its kind.

lenim adhæreo (perf. § 300, fut. § 276), *glenim* adhæreo (perf. § 298, fut. § 276), *renim* I give (perf. § 300, fut. § 276), *crenim* I buy (perf. § 298, fut. § 310), *benim* I strike (perf. § 296, fut. § 310), *clunim* I hear (perf. § 301, fut. § 280), *sernim* consero, as Latin *lino, cerno*.

262. In the II. Conjugation there are:

(a) Denominative verbs (pret. § 269, fut. § 282) like the Latin *laudo*, Greek τιμάω: *biathaim* I nourish, from *biath* food; *adcobraim* I desire, from *accobor* will, desire; *marbaim* I kill, from *marb* dead.

(b) Radical verbs like the Latin *domo*, *sedo*: *molaim* I praise (pret. § 269, fut. § 282), *scaraim* I separate (pret. § 269, fut. § 277), *in-sádaim* jacio.

263. In the same way there are in the III. Conjugation:

(a) Denominative (pret. § 269, fut. § 282), like the Latin *custodio*, Greek ἀλλάσσω, φυλάσσω: *áirmim* I count, from *áram* number; *cumachtaigim* potior, from *cumachte* might, *cumachtach* mighty; *foillsigim* I reveal, from *follus*, *foillsech* manifest, *sudigim* I set, from *sude* seat; *ailigim* muto, from *aile* alius.

(b) Radical verbs like the Latin *fodio*, Greek τείρω, τάσσω: *gudimm*, *no guidiu*, I ask (perf. § 290), *scuirim* I loosen (pret. § 269), *scuchim* discedo (perf. § 297), *no ráidiu* I speak (pret. § 269), *tibim* I laugh (pret. § 269), *rigim* I stretch (perf. § 295).

264. To the III. Conjugation also belong the verbs: *ciim* I see (§ 54, perf. § 295, fut. § 276) and *gniim* I do (pret. § 273, fut. § 277), with their compounds, e.g. *adchíu*, *déccu* I see, *dogníu* I make, *fogníu* I serve. The conjunctive of *dogníu* is noteworthy: sg. 1 *dognéo*, 2 *dogné*, 3 *dogné*, pl. 1 *dognem*, 2 *dogneid*, 3 *dognet*. Cf. *bíu* I am.

264ᵇ. The verb *gudimm* I ask, varies between the III. and I. Conjugation: *no guidiu* rogo III., *nosn-guid* rogat eos I.

264ᶜ. The radical syllable of certain verbs is in many forms difficult to recognise:

Root *av*: *con-ói*, *for-com-ai* servat, imperat. *com-id* servate, counted in the Grammatica Celtica as of Conjug. I., but the 3 pres. pass. *for-dom-chom-aither* servor (§ 329) shows it to belong to the III. Conjugation.

IX. Verb.

Root *sav*: *no soi-siu* avertis, *do-soi* convertit, *co ru thói* convertitur, *do-soat* convertunt, pass. *imme-soither* quo convertitur (Ml. 61ᵃ) III.; *tintúuth* (*do-ind-south*) interpretatio, translation.

Root (*p*)*ent*: *con état* assequuntur, pass. *ni étar* non invenitur; *do-éit*, *téit*, it, adit, imperat. sg. 3 *taet toet* (for *taeted*, cf. § 64), he shall go, come, pl. 2 *táit* (for *taitid*) come, pret. (or perf.?) *dotháet, tothóet; fris-tait* (for *-taitet*) they go against, fut. § 287; *tuitim* I fall (*do-fo-do-étim*, § 54), fut. § 287.

Root *enc*: *ticim* (for *do-icim*) I come, *ricim* (for *ro-icim*) I reach, *con-icim* I am able, fut. § 287, 284, perf. § 299.

6. T-PRETERITE.

265. The letter *t* is joined immediately to the root. The plural in the 1st and 3rd person has a deponent flexion (cf. the perfect § 290). Paradigm: *as-biur* dico.

Sg. 1	*asruburt*	Pl. 1	*asrubartmar*
2	*asrubirt*	2	*asrubartid*
3	*asrubert, -bart*	3	*asrubartatar*.

266. In the same way the following verbs of the I. Conjugation the radical syllable of which terminates in *r, l, c, g*, or a vowel, form their preterite.

Present.	Past 3 Sg.	Present.	Past 3 Sg.
atbail (sg. 3),	*atrubalt* mortuus est;	*cuintgim*,	*conaitecht* quaesivit;
alim,	*alt* educavit;	*toraig*,	*toracht* venit;
celim,	*celt* celavit;	*arutaing*,	*arutacht* restauravit, refecit;
gelim,	*gelt* depastus est;		
tomlim,	*dorumalt* consumpsit;	*bongim*,	*bocht* broke, harvested; *topacht* beat off;
frecraim,	*frisgart* respondit;	*no anich*,	*anacht* protexit;
airimim,	*arroét* accepit;	*iarmafoich*,	*iarfact*, *iarmifoacht* quaesivit;
doemim,	*do-r-ét* velavit;		
daimim,	*ro dét* passus est;	*inchosig*,	*inchoisecht* significavit;
dinim,	*dith* suxit;		
orcim,	*ro ort* delevit;	*doindnaich*,	*doindnacht* tribuit.
éirgim,	*éracht* surrexit;		

Isolated preterites of this species are further: *atbáth* mortuus est; *siacht, ro-siact, riacht* pervenit.

267. The *u* in the 1 sg. is not always evident: *dorét* defendi (pres. *doemim*), *conaitecht* quaesivi; and in 2 sg. the *i* is not always evident: *comtacht-su* quaesisti; in the 3 sg. in Middle Irish, forms in *i* are also found: *birt* gave birth to, *atrubairt*. In the plural forms the *a* in the radical syllable is not regularly employed: *asbertatar* dixerunt; in the 3 pl. an active flexion also now and then occurs *ad-ro-bartat* obtulerant, *geltat* pasti sunt, *conaitechtat* quaesierunt.

268. In the later language the T-preterite passes into the flexion of the S-preterite: sg. 1 *tormaltus* consumpsi, 2 *do-r-argertais-sui* promisisti (*tairngire* promise, for *do-air-con-gaire*), pl. 3 *atbertsat* dixerunt: Modern Irish *dubhras* dixi; *ro geltsat* they fed; *atbathsat* they died (Old Irish *atbathatar*); *altsat* they educated.

7. S-PRETERITE.

269. The S-preterite, like the B-future (§ 282), is chiefly found in verbs of the II. and III. Conjugations. The denominative verbs are limited to this preterite. The letter *s* is joined to the present-stem.

	II		III	
	conj.	abs.	conj.	abs.
Sg. 1	*ro charus*	*carsu*	*dollécius*	*lécsiu*
2	*ro charis*	*carsi*	*dollécis*	*lécsi*
3	*ro char*	*caris*	*molléic*	*lécis*
Pl. 1	*ro charsam*	*carsimme*	*dollécsem*	*lécsimme*
2	*ro charsid*	(*carste*)	*dollécsid*	(*lécste*)
3	*ro charsat*	*carsit*	*dollécset*	*lécsit*.

270. For *caris* frequently *carais* is found, and in the same way *scarais* secessit and so on; for *dollécius* often *dollécus*, and so also *imrordus* for *im-ro-radius* cogitavi.

271. Among verbs of the I. Conjugation in Old Irish *ro gabus* cepi, present *gabim* ought to be mentioned here. In Middle Irish, and in the later language, the S-preterite is a common form in many other verbs of the I. Conjugation. As to the formation of the T-preterite and of the perfect on the analogy of the S-preterite see § 268 and § 303.

272. The 3rd sg. present which has become preterite by the prefixing of *ro* must be distinguished from the 3rd sg. of the conjunctive flexion: preterite *ro-chreit*, pres. *ro chreti* credidit, *ro rigi* he stretched out.

273. The preterite of *do-gníu* facio exhibits irregular appearances: sg. 1 *dorignius*, 2 *dorignis*, 3 *dorigni*, *dorigéni*, *dorigenai*, pl. 1 *dorigénsam*, 2 *dorigénsid*, 3 *dorigénsat*. (Cf. § 312.)

274. In the 3 sg. a deponent flexion is often found: *ro charastar* instead of *ro char*, *ro suidigestar* instead of *ro suidig*, posuit.

8 and 9. REDUPLICATED FUTURE WITH CONDITIONAL.

275. The radical syllable is (*a*) retained, (*b*) after thrusting out of its vowel, contracted with the syllable of reduplication to one syllable with *é* (§ 75). This form of future is followed in Old Irish especially by those verbs, the radical syllable of which has a terminal sound in *r*, *l*, *m* or *n* (cf. the S-future § 285). Paradigms: of (*a*) *canim* Latin cano, *for-chun* I teach (perf. *cechan* § 290); of (*b*) *berimm* I bear, *do-biur* I give (pret. *burt* § 265).

8. FUTURE.

	conj.	abs.	conj.	abs.
Sg. 1	*forcechun,*	*cechna, cechnat*	*dobér*	*béra, bérat*
2	*forcechnae,*	*cechnae*	*dobérae,*	*bérae*
3	*forcechna,*	*cechnid* rel. *cechnas*	*dobéra,*	*bérid* rel. *béras*
Pl. 1	*forcechnam,*	(*cechnimmi*)	*dobéram,*	*bérmmi, -mit*
2	*forcechnid,*	(*cechnithe*)	*dobérid,*	*bérthe*
3	*forcechnat,*	*cechnit* (rel. *cechnite*)	*dobérat,*	*bérit* rel. *bérte.*

Active.

9. CONDITIONAL (SECOND FUTURE).

Sg. 1	*cechninn*	Pl. *cechnimmis*	Sg. *bérinn*	Pl. *bérmmis*
2			*bértha*	*bérthe*
3	*cechnad*	*cechnitis*	*bérad*	*bértis.*

276. Forms with (*a*) retained radical syllable and reduplication:

ni didemam non patiemur, *fodidmat* patientur, perf. dep. *damar*, pres. *fo-daimim* I;

gignid nascetur, perf. dep. *génar*, pres. dep. *gnaither* gignitur III (§ 336);

gegna I shall kill, perf. *gegon*, pres. *gonaim* I;

no gigius rogabo, pl. 2 *gigeste, ro gigsed* petierit, imperat. *ni gessid* nolite precari;

adcichitis they would see, perf. *acca*, pres. *adchíu* III;

dogega eliget, perf. *doróigu* elegit, pres. *togaim* (root *gus*) I;

asririu impendam, perf. *asrir*, pres. *asrenim* I;

lilit adhaerebunt, perf. *lil*, pres. *lenim* I;

no giuglad adhaereret, perf. *ro giuil*, pres. *glenim* I;

fo-chichur I shall throw, fut. sec. sg. 3 *fochichred* with *r* for *rr* from *rd*, if it belongs to *focheird* he throws (§ 295), with which it stands together L. U. p. 70ᵃ, 4.

To which a reduplicated S-future (§ 288) may be added.

277. As (*b*) *dobér, béra* are formed:

méraid manebit, pres. *marim* I;

frisgéra respondebit, pret. *frisgart*, pres. sg. 3 *frisgair* I;

scérmait discedemus, pret. sg. 3 *scarais*, pret. *scarim* II;

conscéra destruet, pres. *coscraim* II;

atbéla morietur, pret. *atrubalt*, pres. sg. 3 *atbail* I;

ebela educabit, perf. sg. 3 *ebail*, pres. *eblim*;

nad cél quod non celabo, pret. *ro chelt*, pres. *celim* I;

toméla consumet, pret. *dorumalt*, pres. *tomlim* I;

dogén, digéon faciam, pret. *dorignius*, pres. *dogníu* III;

etir-genat experituri sunt, pres. *itar-gninim* sapio prudentia; *cossénat* contendent, pres. *cosnaim*;

du-em-sa protegam, *duéma* vindicabit, pret. *dorét* velavit;

fodéma patietur beside *fodidmat* patientur, perf. *damar*, pret. *dét*, pres. *fodaimim* I;

nod lemad who would dare it, pres. dep. *ru-laimur* audeo III;

gébas qui capiet, pret. *ro gabus*, pres. *gabim* I.

278. The flexion of this future recalls the conjunctive of the present. The 1 sg. of the conjoined flexion has not this conjunctive type, e.g. *forcechun* (formed as in the indic. present *dobiur, dobur*); *asririu* impendam deviates also in the 3 sg. *asriri* appendat (cf. § 210).

279. By its flexion, the future without reduplication *doreg, raga*, veniam, belongs to this formation:

	conj.	abs.	condit.
Sg. 1	*doreg*	*rega, riga, ragat*	*doreginn*
2	*dorega*	*rega, raga*	*rigtha*
3	*dorega*	*ragaid*, rel. *ragas*	*do ragad*
Pl. 1	*doregam*	*rigmi, regmait*	
2	*doregaid*	*rigthi*	
3	*doregat*	*regait*	*na rachdais*

The oldest form is that with *e* in the radical syllable; instead of it may be found *i* or *a*, the latter under the influence of the conjunctive *a* of this form. If it is found occasionally written *doréga, rígad* (with a long vowel), this is a leaning towards *dobéra*.

280. The formation mentioned under (*a*) disappears in the progress of time. Old Irish even displays *fodéma* beside *fodidma* patietur, *géna* beside *gegna* I shall kill; *forchanub* (B-future § 282) beside *for-cechun* docebo. Also addition of the character of the B-future can in isolated cases be proved: *ririub* for Old Irish *ririu* vendam; *con cechlafat* audient with the fut. dep. *ro-chechladar* § 346. So also under form (*b*) the Old Irish *bérat* feram gives origin to Modern Irish *béarfad*.

Active.   81

281. Most Old Irish futures with *é* have changed this character to *eó* in the later language, e.g. Modern Irish *eibeólad* I shall die, pres. *eiblim* (Old Irish sg. 1 *atbél*, pres. sg. 3 *atbail*), *coiseónad* I shall defend, pres. *cosnaim*, *coingeobad* I shall hold, pres. *congbhaim* (a composite verb from Old Irish *gabim* capio), *freigeórad* I shall answer, pres. *freagraim*. The verbs in *-igim* and other denominatives have in a remarkable way followed this form: *maireóbhad* I shall kill, pres. *marbhaim* (from Old Irish *marb* dead), *ceingeólad* I shall tie, pres. *ceanglaim* (from Old Irish *cengal*, cingulum), *foillseóchad* I shall show, pres. *foillsighim* (from Old Irish *follus* apertus).

10 AND 11. B-FUTURE WITH CONDITIONAL.

282. This form occurs like the S-preterite (§ 269) especially in the II. and III. conjugations. The denominatives are confined to this future. It takes its name from the analogy to the Latin *amabo*, of which the characteristic is traced back to the root *bhū*.

The character *b* or *f* is affixed to the present-stem.

10. FUTURE.

	II		III	
	abs.	conj.	abs.	conj.
Sg. 1	*carfa, -fat,*	no *charub*	*léicfe, -fet,*	*dolléiciub*
2	*carfe,*	no *charfe*	*léicfe,*	*dolléicfe*
3	*carfid,* rel. *carfas,*	no *charfa*	*léicfid,* rel. *lécfes,*	*dolléicfea*
Pl. 1	*carfimme, -mit,*	no *charfam*	*léicfimme, -mit,*	*dolléicfem*
2	*carfithe,*	no *charfid*	*léicfithe,*	*dolléicfid*
3	*carfit,* rel. *carfite,*	no *charfat*	*léicfit,* rel. *léicfite,*	*dolléicfet*

11. CONDITIONAL (SECOND FUTURE).

Sg. 1	*carfinn*	Pl.	*carfimmis*	Sg. 1	*léicfinn*	Pl.	*léicfimmis*
2	*carfetha*		*carfithe*	2	*léicfetha*		*léicfithe*
3	*carfad*		*carfitis*	3	*léicfed*		*leicfitis*

283. The otherwise suppressed thematic vowel of the present remains before the characteristic of the future, when

I. G.   6

its suppression would lead to too great an accumulation of consonants. Behind the retained vowel, *b* instead of *f* appears as characteristic of the future: *predchibid* prædicabit; *folnibthe* regnabitis; *do-sn-aidlibea* visitabit eos, pres. *do-da-aidlea* II. adit eam.

284. The B-future is often used by the side of other futures: *ni aicfea* non videbit, beside *ad-cichitis*, pres. *adchiu;* *geinfes* qui nascetur beside *gignid* (§ 276). It is also and more and more in Later Irish formed from verbs of the I. conjugation: *do-icfa, ticfa* veniet beside the S-future, *tis* veniam, pres. *ticim* I come; *arom-fo-imfea* accipiet me, pres. *ar-fo-imim* accipio, *nodn-ailfea* educabit eum, pres. *alim;* *oirgfid* interficiet (also S-preterite *oirgset* devastaverunt beside the T-preterite *ro ort* § 266), pres. *orgim orcim* § 67; *dot-emfet-su* vindicabunt te (Ml. 112ᶜ), cf. § 277.

12 AND 13. S-FUTURE WITH CONDITIONAL.

285. This future has very often a conjunctive sense. Like the reduplicated future it is almost exclusively formed of verbs of the I. conjugation and especially those verbs the radical syllable of which has for terminal sound a guttural, a dental, or an *s*. The letter *s* joins this terminal sound immediately and assimilates it to itself (§ 54). The method of writing in median sound varies between *ss* and *s*. In the later language this future disappears. Paradigms: *tiagaim* I go, *for-tiagaim* I help.

	12. FUTURE.		13. CONDITIONAL.
	conj.	abs.	
Sg. 1	*fortías,*	*tíasu*	*téssinn, tíassainn*
2	*fortéis,*	*tési*	*tíasta,*
3	*fortéi, -té,*	*téis*	*téssed, tíasad*
Pl. 1	*fortiasam,*	*tésme, -mit*	*tíasmais*
2	*fortésid,*	*téste* (i)	*téste*
3	*fortíasat,*	*tésit*	*téssitis, tíastis.*

286. The 3 sg. of the conjoined flexion has in some instances also lost the radical vowel: *do-air, tair* veniat (*tair* also as 2 sg. come), 3 pl. *tairset*, perf. sg. 3 *tairnic* (for *do-air-*

anic, § 299); *con-éit* indulgeat, 1 pl. *com-etsam*, pres. sg. 3 *com-etig* I; *ro ain* protegat, 3 pl. *ro ainset*, pres. sg. 3 *no anich* I; *ar na dich, dig* ne veniat, 2 sg. *co n-dechais* that thou comest, 2 pl. *mani digsid*, preterite *dechaid* (§ 302).

287. The following are further safe examples of the S-future (cf. § 320 and § 343):

no tes effugiam, pres. *techim*, perf. § 295;

cu dusésa (for *sés-sa*) ut persequar, pres. sg. 3 *do-seich;*

inchoissised significaret, pres. sg. 3 *in-chosig*, pret. § 266;

acht conetis if thou only prayest, pres. *cuintgim*, pret. § 266;

dufi vindicabit, pres. sg. 3 *dofich;*

co du-di (vel *co midithir*) Gloss on ut inducat Ml. 35ᶜ, pres. conj. sg. 3 *do-da-decha* Hy. 5, 81 (?);

iarmid-oised (for *joised*) who would ask after it, pres. sg. 3 *iarma-foich*, pret. § 266;

cia rosme although we reach, pres. pl. 3 *ni rochet;*

doindin tradet, *doindnisin* traderem, pres. *do-ind-naich*, pret. § 266;

adnaissi sepelies, pres. sec. passive *adnaicthe* sepeliebatur, inf. *adnacul;*

co tora ut veniat, pres. sg. 3 *toraig*, pret. 262;

ro sia veniat, pret. *ro siacht* § 266;

do-fu-thris-se vellem, *dúthrais* optabis, pres. sg. 3 *dúthraic* vult (cf. § 79), perf. dep. § 349;

immechoimairsed he would ask, pres. pass. sg. 3 *immechomarcar*, perf. dep. § 349;

condarias (sg. 1) Gloss on quæ alligare compellor Ml. 21ᵇ, pres. *con-riug*, ligo, cf. § 288;

corrius until I come, *ro is, ris-sa* assequar, pres. *ru icim*, 3 *ric*, perf. *ro anac, ránac* § 299;

co ti donec veniat, pl. 3 *co tissat*, pres. *ticim*, perf. § 299;

conis poteris, *ma chotísmis* si id possemus, pres. sg. 3 *con-ic*, perf. dep. § 347;

comuir attinget, *comairsem* attingemus (pres. *com-air-ic-*);

fuirsitis they would find, past pass. *furecht* inventum est;

ni dérsid ne descrueritis, pres. *ni derig* non amittit;

nochon erus non surgam, *ass-éirset* resurgent, pres. *éirgim*, pret. *as-réracht* § 266;

atresat surgent, pres. pl. 3 *atregat*, pret. *atracht* § 266;

dlessaind I would deserve, pres. *dligim;*

dofonus-sa lavabo, pres. *do-fo-nug* (*nigim*), perf. § 295;

condesat exquirent, pres. *con-daig* quaerit;

ni sáis ne adeas, pres. *saigim;*

ro sasat dicent, pres. sg. 3 rel. *saiges;*

toissed he would swear, *ma fris-tossam* si abjuraverimus, pres. *tong* juro;

fulós sustinebo, *amal fundló* as he will bear it, pres. sg. 3 *fo-loing* (cf. § 288);

nad fochomolsam quam non sustineamus, perf. *fo-coim-lactar* pertulerunt;

co chotabosad-si ut vos comminueret (for *con-dob-bosad*), pres. *com-boing* confringit, pret. *bocht* § 266;

arutais-siu reficies, pres. sg. 3 *arutaing*, past § 266;

ni cuimsimmis we should not be able, pres. sg. 3 *cumaing;*

fum-ré-se he will aid me, pres. *cid fo-ruith* succurro.

in-restais invadere nitebantur Ml. 37ᵈ, pres. *inréith* vastat (cf. § 354ᵇ);

istais they would eat, pres. *ithim;*

fotimdiris suffias, pres. *fotimdiriut* suffio;

fris-tait opponunt (§ 264ᶜ), *coni frithtaised* ne opponeret;

toethsat, totsat they will fall, *dofoethsad* he would fall, *con-*

dositis (for *dothsitis*?) ut caderent, pres. *tuitim* I fall (for *do-fo-thitim*, § 264ᶜ);

co n-dárbais ut demonstres, *don-aid-bsed* that he would show, pres. sg. 3 *du-ad-bat* demonstrat, pass. *tad-badar;*

docói veniet, perf. *dochóid, -chúaid* § 301;

atchous nuntiabo, perf. *atchúaid* exposuit § 301;

don fe he may lead us, pres. *fedim, imme-fedat* circumferunt;

im-roimset peccabunt, perf. dep. *imme-ru-mediar* (read *-medair*) peccavit § 349;

co ingriastais ut persequerentur, pres. sg. 3 *in-greinn*, perf. § 295.

288. Some few verbs are known to exist in an S-future with reduplication:

co-riris-siu ligabis, with sg. 1 *conda-rias* § 287, perf. *reraig* § 295, pres. *con-riug;*

silsimi-ni caedemus, perf. sg. 3 *selaig* (for *seslaig*) § 295;

fo-lilsat sustinebunt, beside *fo-losat*, pres. *fo-loing, fulaing* tolerat;

cichset he would go, pres. *cingim* I, perf. *cechaing* § 295;

memais, commema will fall, break, pl. 3 *com-mebsat* (for *memsat*), perf. sg. 3 *memaid* § 295 (*maided* clades).

co tarblais thou shalt leap, perf. *tarbling, leblaing*, pres. *lingim* (cf. § 45).

The following are less certain: *ní chaemais* non poteris, *ni caemsat* non poterunt, with *ni cuimsin* non possem, pres. *cumaing* potest.

289. In Old Irish there are no S-futures with retained radical terminal sounds. The forms which seem such are either errors or may be otherwise explained. Instead of *hona cumachtaigset* quo non sunt potituri (Z.² p. 1094 to p. 462, 2) the MS. has *hona cumachtaigfet* (Ml. 28ᵃ, 12, ed. Ascoli); *foruraithminset* (Gloss on meminisse Z.² p. 468, Stokes Goid.² p. 26) is an S-pret.

14. PERFECT.

290. The perfect never occurs in denominative verbs. Most perfects are formed from roots with an intermediate *a*. Three types may be distinguished : (*a*) the radical syllable has a short *a*, and reduplication is either present or dropped ; (*b*) the radical syllable has a long *a* in the singular (whether it has long *a* also in the plural is questionable), reduplication is dropped; (*c*) the radical syllable and the syllable of reduplication are fused into a single syllable with *é*. Paradigms : *canim* I cano, *gudim* III oro, *aith-gnim* II cognosco.

	(a)	(b)	(c)
Sg. 1	*cechan*	*ro gád*	*aithgén*
2	*cechan*	*ro gád*	*aithgén*
3	*cechuin*	*ro gáid*	*aithgéuin, -géoin*
Pl. 1	*cechnammar*	*ro gadammar*	*aithgénammar*
2	*cechnaid*	*ro gadaid*	*aithgénaid*
3	*cechnatar*	*ro gadatar*	*aithgénatar*

291. The first and second persons singular are distinguished by the addition of the augmenting particles *sa* and *su* : *cechan-sa* cecini, *cechan-su* cecinisti. The flexion in the pl. 1 and pl. 3 is deponent (cf. the T-past § 265); but isolated forms like *gegnait* occiderunt (L. U. p. 23^b, 36) are found beside *gegnatar* sg. 1 *gegon*, pres. *gonaim*. In the pl. 2 a deponent form gains ground also in Middle Irish. Old Irish *tancaid* venistis (§ 299), Middle Irish *tancaibar*, Modern Irish *tángabhar*. In isolated cases absolute forms (§ 259) occur in the plural : *cachnaitir* cecinerunt, Older Irish *cechnatar, tair-cechnatar* vaticinati sunt ; *bátir* beside *bátar, ro bátar* fuerunt; *memdaitir* they broke ; *femmir* we slept (§ 295).

292. Those perfects which are formed as (*a*) *cechan* have often lost the reduplicative syllable, either without a trace, or after the *e* in the same had changed the preceding particle *ro* to *roi* (§ 19): *for-roi-chan* praedixit and many others. Some perfects exhibit no trace whatever of the reduplication : *ad-chon-darc* vidi, *do-chóid* venit (§ 302).

Active. 87

293. The vowel of the reduplicative syllable is *e*, rarely *a*: *fris-racacha* speravi, by blending and assimilation from *ro-ad-cecha;* later also *cachain* cecinit, *tathaim* quievit.

294. The perfect is formed directly from the root: variation according to the conjugation of the present does not exist. Perfects such as: *lil* adhaesit, *dedaig* oppressit, prove that the nasal of the presents *lenim* adhaereo, *dengaim* opprimo, does not belong to the root. However the median nasal sound has generally passed into the perfect form in radical syllables in *nd, nn,* in all examples.

295. The following are further examples of perfect forms which join the paradigms (*a*) *cechan:*

fo-roi-chlaid effodit, *rocechladatar* suffoderunt, imperative passive *cladar.*

dessid consedit, *indessid* insederat Ml. 20ª, pl. 3 *desetar; in-destetar* insiderunt, Ml. 58ª (root *sad*).

arob-rói-nasc despondi enim vos (for *ar-fob-*), 3 *ro nenaisc,* pres. *fo-naiscim* I.

gegon interfeci, 3 *gegoin, geoguin,* pres. *gonaim* I, fut. § 280.

fiu he slept, pl. 1 *femmir,* 2 *febair,* 3 *feotar,* pres. sg. 3 *foaid* (§ 56).

do rertatar they ran, pres. *rethim,* fut. § 287.

memaid broke, pl. 3 *memdatar, mebdatar, corraimdetar,* fut. § 288.

fochart I threw, 3 *fochairt,* pl. *fochartatar,* pres. *fo-cheird* he throws (cf. § 276).

taich confugit (Ml. 32ᵇ, written *taích*), pl. 3 *tachatar,* pres. *techim,* fut. § 287.

ad-roi-thach supplicavi, pres. *ateoch* precor.

ro selach I beat (for *seslach*), pret. passive *ro slechta* destructi fuerunt, fut. § 288.

foselgatar illiverunt, pres. *fo-sligim* delino.

reraig porrexit, pres. *rigim*.

con-reraig ligavit, pres. *con-riug* ligo, fut. § 288.

fonenaig purificavit, pres. *do-fo-nug* lavo, fut. § 287.

ro senaich stillavit (for *sesnaig*), S-preterite sg. 3 *snigis*.

lelgatar (*i. lomraiset* L. U. p. 57ᵇ, 19), pres. *ligim* lingo (?) (B. of L. in the same text reads *fogeltat*).

do ommalgg (*om-* ?) mulxi, pres. *bligim* § 41.

conrotaig extruxit, pres. *cunutgim* (for *con-ud-tegim*).

rom ebail me educavit, *rott eblatar* te educavęrunt (L. U. p. 123ᵇ, 124ᵃ), pres. *eblim*, fut. § 277.

in-roi-grann persecutus sum, *ad-roi-gegrannatar* persecuti sunt, pres. pl. 3 *in-grennat*, fut. 287.

roe-glaind didicit, pres. *fo-gliunn* disco.

ro-sescaind he sprang, pres. *scinnim*.

sescaing esiluit, pres. *scingim*.

cechaing he went, pres. *cingim*, fut. § 288.

leblaing he leaped, pres. *lingim* § 45, fut. § 288.

do-sephainn pepulit, pl. 3 *do-sephnatar, do-roiphnetar, tafnetar*, pres. *do-sennim* (§ 56), *toibnim*.

dedaig oppressit, pres. *dingim*, pl. 3 *for-dengat* opprimunt.

combaig confregit (beside *bocht* § 266), pres. sg. 3 *com-boing*, fut. § 287.

focoimlactar pertulerunt, pres. *fo-loing* sustinet, fut. § 287.

fris-racacha speravi, *acca, conacca* vidi, pres. *ad-chiu, acciu* video, *fris-aicet* opperiuntur, fut. § 284 and § 346.

do-ro-chair, torchair cecidit, pl. 3 *do-ciuchratar* (L. U. p. 54ᵃ, 5) *do-ro-chratar torchratar*, pres. *arin-chrin* interit, pl. 3 *hóre arinchrinat* quia intereunt.

296. From roots with *a* as terminal sound are formed: *bebe* mortuus est (cf. § 303), *nachim rind-ar-pai-se* quod me non reppulit, pl. *innarpatar* (cf. § 303), present *ind-ar-benim, immirera* profectus est, present *im raim* (used of going to sea.)

Active.

297. Of the same formation as (*b*) *ro gád* I prayed, pres. *gudimm* III, is *ro scaich, scáig* praeteriit, pres. *scuchim* III. discedo.

298. To (*c*) *adgén* cognovi belong of active forms:

ar-ro-chér redemi, sg. 3 *do-rad-chiúir* redemit, pres. *crenim* emo, *taid-chur* redemtio.

ro giuil adhaesit, pres. *glenim* adhaereo (fut. § 276).

ro taisfebin demonstravit, pres. *tais-fenat* demonstrant.

299. The perfect *anac* (Skr. *ánamça*), *do anac, tanac* I came, is sui generis, present sg. 3 *tic*, pl. 3 *tecat;* *ro anac, ránac* I reach, present sg. 3 *ric*, pl. 3 *recat*.

Sg.	1 *tánac*	Pl.	1 *táncammar*
	2 *tánac*		2 *táncid*, later *táncaibar*
	3 *tánic*		3 *táncatar*.

Other compounds are: *tairnic* (*do-air-anic*) accidit (future § 286); *imma-com-arnic* (*air-anic*) *dóib* they got together, pres. *imm-aircet* (for *-air-icet*) conveniunt.

300. Perfects from roots with *i:*

lil adhaesit, pl. 3 *leltar*, pres. *lenim*, fut. § 276;

rir dedit, *as-rir* vendidit, pres. *as-renat* reddunt, fut. § 276;

cich ploravit, pres. *ciid* plorat, pl. 3 *ciit*.

301. Perfects from roots with *u*:

do-choad veni, 3 *dochóid, chúaid,* pl. 3 *dochótar, dochúatar*, fut. § 287;

ad-chúaid exposuit, pl. 1 *ad-cóidemmar* tractavimus;

do-rói-gu elegit, *doroegu, doráiga*, pl. 3 *do-roi-gatar*, pres. *to-gu* eligo (root *gus*), fut. § 276;

ro bá fui, 3 *ro bói, ro bái, rabi, bu*, pl. 3 *bátar*, pres. *bíu* (root *bhū*);

ro chúala audivi (§ 74), 3 *ro chuale, chúala*, pl. 3 *ro chualatar*, pres. *clunim* (root *clu*).

302. The perfect *fúar* inveni is probably to be dismembered into *fu-ar* (*fu* preposition), cf. *frith* inventum est, perf. pass. § 328; 3 *fúair*, pl. 1 *fúarammar*, 3 *fúaratar*.

The following is inflected like a perfect: *lod, dollod* I went, 2 *dollot* (with suffixed *t* § 205), 3 *luid, dolluid*, pl. 1 *lodomar*, 3 *lotar, dollotar*, cf. however the infinitive *dula, dul* to go.

With *dochúaid* ivit (§ 301) the following are not to be confounded: *dechad, deochad, dodeochad* ivi, 2 *dodeochad*, 3 *dechuith, dechaid, dodeochaid*, pl. 3 *dechatar, tuidchetar*, but pl. 1 *dodechommar* irregular (cf. the future § 286).

303. In Later Irish the old perfects are very often changed according to the analogy of the S-preterite, or are replaced by the same: *tanacus* I came, sg. 2 *tanacais* (§ 299); *dochúadus* I came (§ 301); *cia ro tóipniset* gloss on *ce dosefnatar* although they hunted him (§ 295); *leblingsetar* they leaped, *tar-blingis* he leaped, pres. *lingim* (§ 295); Modern Irish *ro chonnarcas* I saw, Old Irish *con-darc*. So also *bebais* he died, for the Old Irish *bebe* (§ 296); *co ro innarbsat* reppulerunt (§ 296), *lilis* adhaesit, for Old Irish *lil*, *cichis* ploravit, for Old Irish *cich* (§ 300).

FURTHER TENSE-FORMS.

304. Stokes in his treatises on the Old Irish verb (Beiträge zur Vergl. Sprachf. VI. VII.) was the first to note certain sporadic and in part not completely determined tense-forms. Complete paradigms cannot be set forth.

305. B-preterite (l.c. VII. 31). Serglige Conculand 35 *feraib* interchanges with *ferais* he gave. In the same way *anaib* he remained, beside *anais*; *bruchtaib* vomuit, beside *brúchtis*. Sg. 2 *ma ro sellaib* i. *ma ro sillis* if thou hast seen Fél. July 4.

306. D-past (l.c. VII. 17) is up to the present established in only a few and somewhat uncertain examples: *damdatar* (*i. forodmatar*) passi sunt, occurs Fel. Oct. 15 in three MSS. and Fel. Prol. 32 (*i. ro damsat*) in two MSS. (perhaps transposed from *dadmatar*, § 80).

Active. 91

307. U-preterite (l. c. VII. 54) will perhaps have to be acknowledged: *riadu* S. C. 31, 12 from *ríadaim* I go; *fuacru* Hy. 5, 9 she announced, belonging to *fócair* (*fo-od-gair*) indicat. Cf. Old Gaulish ειωρου, ieuru, fecit, allied to Old Irish *iúrad* factum est.

308. T-future (l. c. VII. 28). Established examples are: *atbert* dicam, *bertait* they will carry off Sc. M. 4; and with obvious adaptation to the reduplicated future (§ 277): *mértait* they will remain (L. U. 36ᵃ, 6) beside *mérait*, *gébtait* capient (L. U. 56ᵇ, 26) beside *gébait*, *taitnébtait* they will seem (L. U. 36ᵃ, 6). In the same way with adaptation to the B-future (§ 282) *césfaitit* they will suffer, and *betit* they will be (Beitr. VII. 35).

Gabtait they take Fled Bricrend 15 is noteworthy in the narration after the present *atafregat* they rise, cf. § 309.

309. Preterite in -*ta* (l. c. VII. 27) seems to be established in *sénta* benedixit with the gloss *i. bennachais i. ro sénastar* Hy. 5, 38; *dobretha* dedit T. E. 5, F. B. 38; *alta* educavit CC. 3 Eg. beside *alt*. To this class also belongs *bentaiseom* he beat L. U. p. 127ᵃ, 4, pl. 3 *bentatar* ibid. p. 64ᵃ, 32, beside *benais*.

310. The forms designated aorist by Ebel (Gram. Celt.² p. 447) and by Stokes (l. c. VII. 7) may partly be so considered from an Indo-germanic point of view, but in Irish as far as they have a conjunctive sense, are allied to the reduplicated future, except that they are wanting in the syllable of reduplication:

ni ria ne vendat, pl. 3 *ni riat* with conjunctive flexion, whilst *as-ririu* impendam contrary to the ordinary rule forms 3 sg. *as-riri* (§ 278), perf. *as-rir* dedit, pres. *as-renim*, *érnim;*

ni cria ne emat, pres. *crenim*, perf. § 298;

forms belonging to *dofuibnim* (*do-fo-*) succido, *etirdibnim* (*etir-di*), compounds from *benim* caedo: fut. sg. 3 *dorodba* succidat, pl. 3 *co eter-dam-dibet-sa* ut me interficiant Ml. 44ᶜ, fut. sec. sg. 3 *co dufobath* ut (omnem.. spem) incideret Ml. 35ᶜ, *oldaas itir-n-da-di-bed* than that he should kill them Ml. 45ᶜ;

pass. fut. sg. 3 co *dufobither* ut succidatur, *co itirdibither* ut perimatur;

forms belonging to the perfect *bebe* mortuus est (§ 303), fut. sec. sg. 3 *nom-baad* that one might die Ml. 23ᵈ, pl. 3 *nom-batis* that they might die.

311. Certain forms belonging to the present *do-gniu* with a sense in part conjunctive-future, in part preterite are not yet made clear in every respect. They contain the particle *ro* between the preposition and the verbal form and this is so closely united with the latter, that the *g* of the same has disappeared before the *n*, according to the general law as to internal sound: sg. 1 *sechichruth dondrón* quomodocunque id fecero, 2 *act dorronai* modo feceris; sec. sg. 3 *duronad* fecisset. Of these forms the 1 sg. *dorón* probably stands for a prehistoric *do-ro-gn-(o)*.

In the preterite all the following occur side by side:

	(a)	(b)	(c)
Sg. 1	*dorignius* feci		*dorónsa* (Fel. Prol. 269)
2	*dorignis*		*dorónais*
3	*dorigni*	*dorigéni*	*doróni*
Pl. 1		*dorigénsam*	
2		*dorigénsid*	
3		*dorigénsat*	*dorónsat*

Cf. the preterite passive § 327. The forms (a) *dorignius* and (c) *dorónsa* (for *do-rónus-sa*) are probably not essentially distinct, whereas *dorigéni* calls to mind the future formed with reduplication *dogén* faciam.

Passive.

312. The passive has special forms for the third person only. As to the formation of the remaining persons see § 329. Paradigms of the present form: I *berim* I bear, II *carim* I love III *lécim* I leave.

Passive.

	I		II		III	
	abs.	conj.	abs.	conj.	abs.	conj.

1. PRESENT INDICATIVE.

Sg. 3 *berir,* *doberar* *carthir,* *no charthar* *léicthir,* *dolléicther*
Pl. 3 *bertir,* *dobertar* *caritir,* *no charatar* *lécitir,* *dolléciter.*

2. CONJUNCTIVE PRESENT.

Sg. 3 *berthir,* *doberthar* *carthir,* *ara carthar* *léicthir,* *ara léicther*
Pl. 3 *bertir,* *dobertar* *caritir,* *ara caratar* *lécitir,* *ara léciter.*

3. IMPERATIVE. 4. SECOND PRESENT.

	I	II	III	I	II	III
Sg. 3	*berar*	*carthar*	*léicther*	*no berthe*	*no charthe*	*no léicthe*
Pl. 3	*bertar*	*caratar*	*léciter.*	*no bertis*	*no chartis*	*no léictis.*

313. For *-ir, -thir, -tir* are also found *-air, -thair, -tair*: *dlegair* I debetur, *derbthair* III adprobatur. The suppression of the thematic vowel before the termination is not used, especially when the suppression would lead to too great an accumulation of consonants: *fo-éitsider* III subauditur; *du-fui-bniter* I succiduntur (pres. act. *benim*); *ar na tomnathar* II ne putetur (pres. dep. *do-moiniur*); *canitar* I canuntor.

314. The form in *-ar* of the I conj. seems also to occur as 3 sg. of the conjoined flexion: *nom berar ferar,* but e.g. *tiagar eatur* (without preceding particle) is imperative. The conjunctive form is clearly distinguished from the indicative form by *do-gníu* III facio and *bíu* III sum: 3 sg. ind. *dognither* fit, *i m-bither* in quo quis est, conj. *ma dugnether* si fit, *cia bethir* though one is (cf. § 264).

5 AND 6. REDUPLICATED FUTURE WITH CONDITIONAL.

315. Paradigms: *berim* I bear, *do-biur* I give:

	FUTURE.	CONDITIONAL.
Sg. 3	*dobérthar,* abs. *bérthir*	*bértha*
Pl. 3	*dobértar,* abs. *bértir*	*bértis.*

316. The verbs which are set forth § 275 of course form this future, e.g. *eter-scértar* separabuntur, pres. *etar-scarim* II; 3 sg. *géntir, dogéntar* fiet, pres. *gníim, dogníu* facio; *dofuisémthar* procreabitur, pres. *do-fuisim* I generat (for *do-fo-es-sim*); *furaithmenter* dignus memoria ducetur (? ducitur Ml. 17ᵇ), pres. dep. *for-aith-minedar* III memorat.

317. Reduplicated futures without contraction of reduplication and radical syllable into one syllable with *é* (§ 276) are rare: *asrirther* reddetur, pres. *as-renim; focichertar* ponetur, pres. *fo-cheirt, -cheird* ponit.

With *dorega, ragaid* ibit is the passive *doragthar, rigthir, ragthair* ibitur. Cf. *co dufobither* § 310.

7 AND 8. B-FUTURE WITH CONDITIONAL.

318. Most verbs of the II and III conjugation have this form in the passive as in the active. Paradigms: *carim* II I love, *lécim* III I leave.

FUTURE.   CONDITIONAL.
II
Sg. 3 *carfidir*, conj. *ni carfider*   *carfide*
Pl. 3 *carfitir*, conj. *ni carfiter*   *carfitis*.
III
Sg. 3 *léicfidir*, conj. *dolléicfider*   *léicfide*
Pl. 3 *léicfitir*, conj. *dolléicfiter*   *léicfitis*.

319. For *-fidir* are also found: *-faidir, -fithir* and (especially after a double consonant) *-ebthir, -ibthir;* for *-fider* are also found: *-faider, -fedar* (*-bedar*), *fither*, and (especially after a double consonant) *-abthar, -ebthar, -ibther:* *gairmebtair* vocabuntur from *gairmim* voco; *ailebthair* educabitur from *alim* educo; *ni for-brisbedar* non obruetur Ml. 51ᵇ.

9 AND 10. S-FUTURE WITH CONDITIONAL.

320. Paradigm *dligim* I mereo:

FUTURE.   CONDITIONAL.
Sg. 3 *ro dlestar*, abs. *dlestir*   *dlesta*
Pl. 3 *ro dlesatar*, abs. *dlesitir* *dlestis*.

Passive. 95

321. The verbs mentioned in § 287 for the S-future active have this passive form, e.g.:

duindnastar tribuetur, pres. *do-ind-naich* I tribuit;
adnastar sepelietur, *adnacul* sepelire;
doformastar, tormastar augebitur, pres. *tormaig* I auget;
ad-riastar (§ 21) alligabitur, pres. *ad-riug* I alligo;
for-diassatar opprimentur, pres. *for-dengat* I opprimunt;
co n-dárbastar ut demonstretur, pres. *du-ad-bat* I demonstrat;
du-n-diastae Gloss on deduci permissus sit Ml. 45^c;
accastar, du-ecastar cernetur, pres. *ad-chíu, déccu* III cerno.

322. The flexion of the S-future recalls in the active the indicative present of the I. conjugation. Likewise in the passive, for in the 3 sg. forms in *-ar* are found beside those in *-tar: dufiastar* (Ml. 27^c) and *co dufessar* (Ml. 32^c) ut vindicetur, pres. *do-fich* I ulciscitur; *co festar* ut sciatur, and *dia fessar* si sciatur, perf. *fitir* scit (§ 351); *adfessar* nuntiabitur, pres. *ad-fíadaim;* *coni messar* ut nihil estimetur Ml. 42^d, fut. dep. *miastir* judicabit, pres. *midiur* judico; *do-thíasar* eatur, pres. *do-thíagaim.*

323. Forms with reduplication also have been proved to exist: *rirastar* ligabitur in *cotan-rirastar-ni* obligemur (§ 331), pres. *con-riug* I; *folilastæ* would be borne, pres. *fo-loing* I sustinet; *atat-chigestar* videris (§ 331), pres. *ad-chíu* video; *fortut brágit bibsatar* L.U. p. 125, pres. *bongaim* I break?

11. PRETERITE.

324. The characteristic of the preterite passive is *t* which is either joined immediately to the root or to the present stem. Paradigm: *dobiur* I I give, *carim* II I love, *lécim* III I leave.

	I	II	III
Sg. 3	*dobreth*	*ro charad*	*ro léced*
Pl. 3	*dobretha*	*ro chartha*	*ro lécthea.*

IX. Verb.

325. Instead of the *breth* in *dobreth* other composite verbs have *-bred, -brath, -brad: asrobrad* dictum est, *ad-ropred* oblatus est (*ad-ro-od*), preterite active *asrubart* dixit, *adopert* obtulit; in the same way: *dorairngred* promissum est (*do-ro-air-con-gred*), *forruchongrad* praeceptum est, pret. act. *dorairngert* promisit, *forcongart* praecepit, pres. *for-con-gur* praecipio. In these cases the radical syllable has taken the form *bre, bra* (cf. Skr. bhri), *gre, gra*. In the same way *eblim* I bring up (fut. § 277, perf. 295) forms *eblad, rom-eblad-sa* educatus sum (§ 329); sg. 3 *toimled*, pl. 3 *ro tomlithea* consumpti sunt (L.U. p. 34ᵇ, 19), pres. *tomlim;* while from *alim* educo *ro alt* educatus est, pret. active *ro alt* § 266.

326ᵃ. *cht* comes from a radical guttural and *t:*

airecht was found, pres. pass. *air-ecar* I invenitur, perf. act. *arnic, tarnic* § 299;

furecht was found, pres. act. *fo-ric* I (i.e. *fo-ro-ic*) invenit, perf. sg. 3 *fornic* (for *fo-ranic*), fut. § 287.

huare ro slechta quia destructi fuerant, perf. act. *ro selaig;*

lase forruillecta postquam illita sunt (for *fo-n-ru-slecta*); pres. *fo-sligim* I delino;

ro-adnacht was buried, pres. sec. pl. 3 *no adnaictis* I they were burying, fut. § 287, inf. *adnacul;*

ro-ort was killed, pl. 3 *ro orta*, pret. act. *ro ort* § 266, pres. *orgaid* I caedit, inf. *orcun*.

326ᵇ. *ss, s* (§ 54) come from a radical dental or *s* and *t:*

ro fess scitum est, pl. *ro fessa*, perf. dep. *fetar* scio (§ 351), inf. *fiss;*

ro clas, fo-class was dug, imper. pass. sg. 3 *cladar* I, perf. act. *fo-roichlaid* effodit § 295;

do-chúas itum est, perf. act. *do-chóid, -chúaid* he went, *ad-chúas* nuntiatum est, perf. act. *ad-chúaid* nuntiavit;

fo-cress was thrown, pres. act. *fo-cheird* I he throws, perf. *fo-chart* I threw (*focress* with the formation of the radical syllable as in *do-breth* § 325);

ro-chloss was heard, pres. dep. *cloor* audio (root *clus* § 52);

ad-chess, accas visum est, pl. *atchessa*, pres. act. *ad-chiu* III, perf. *acca* vidi, fut. *ad-cichset* (root *cas* § 264).

326°. A radical nasal before *t* disappears with compensatory lengthening (§ 74):

ro chét cantus est, pl. *ro chéta*, pres. act. *canim* I, perf. *cechan;*

do-reiset profusus est (for *do-ro-es-set*), pres. act. *do-esmet* I profundunt, fut. pass. § 316 (root *sem*);

ro-goet, gaet was wounded (§ 74), pres. act. *gonim* I, perf. § 295, fut. § 280.

326ᵈ. In such verbs as *benim* caedo, *renim* do (§ 261) the nasal does not belong to the root, the characteristic of the preterite passive is directly united to the vowel terminal sound of the same: sg. 3 *imm-ruidbed* in *immum-ruidbed* circumcisus sum § 329, pres. *im-di-bnim* circumcido; pl. 3 *aní asatorbatha* id ex quo ejecti sunt (for *as-an-do-fo-ro-batha*), pres. *do-fui-bnim* succido; pl. 3 *ro ratha* are granted, pres. *renim* I give.

327. Most verbs of the II. and III. conjugation, especially all denominative verbs, affix the character *t* to the stem of the present: *ro erbad* commissum est, pl. *ro airptha*, pres. *erpimm* (§ 35) committo; *ro nóibad* sanctificatus est, pres. *nóibaim* II (*nóib, nóeb* holy); *doratad* datum est, pl. *dorata* (§ 64), preterite act. *doratus* dedi; *ro fóided* missus est, pl. *ru foitea, roitea*, pres. *fóidim* III; *du-rolged, -roilged* remissum est, pl. *dorolgetha, derlaichta*, pres. *do-luigim* III; *ro sudiged* positus est, pres. *sudigim* III (*sude* seat). In the same way is formed *ro gníith, ro gníth* factum est, pl. *cain ro gnata* (read *gnatha*) bene acta sunt Ml. 39ᵃ, pres. *gníim* III; *do-rigned* factum est, pres. *do-gníu*, and with another formation *do-rónad* factum est, pl. *dorónta* (§ 311).

IX. Verb.

328. Certain verbs of the I. conjugation have the *t* not immediately joined to the root: *ro-gabad* captus est, pres. *gabim* I capio; *foracbad* relictus est (for *fo-ro-aith-gabad*), pres. *fácabaim, fácbaim* (*fo-aith-gabaim*) relinquo; pl. *dorurgabtha* sunt prolata (for *do-ro-for-gabtha*); *ro coscad* correptus est, inf. *cosc* (for *con-sech-*).

So also perhaps *doroigad* electus est Ml. 123ª, perf. act. *do-rói-gu* elegit, pres. *togu, togaim* (root *gus* § 52), yet it is questionable whether the present belongs to the I. conjugation. The following are isolated forms: *frith, fofrith* inventum est, pl. *foritha*, perf. act. *fúar* inveni § 302.

THE FIRST AND SECOND PERSONS IN THE PASSIVE.

329. In order to express the first and second persons, the proper pronoun is prefixed in its enclitic form to the 3 sg. united to a particle or if the verb is a compound to a preposition (cf. § 201). Paradigms *nom berar* feror from *berim* fero, *immumruidbed* circumcisus sum, preterite (§ 326ᵈ) from the compound *im-di-bnim* circumcido (*benim* caedo):

Sg. 1 *nom berar-sa*	*immum-ruidbed*
2 *not berar-su*	*immut-ruidbed*
Pl. 1 *non berar-ni*	*immun-ruidbed*
2 *nob berar-si*	*immub-ruidbed.*

On -*sa*, -*su* &c. § 193.

330. In the same way the remaining tenses of the passive: *nob crete* credebamini (secondary present), pres. act. *cretim* III credo; *nom linfider-sa* complebor, pres. act. *linaim* II compleo; *nib iccfither* non salvabimini, pres. act. *iccaim* II salvo; *co dobemthar-si* defendamini (fut.), fut. act. *du-ema* vindicabit.

331. The pronoun is also united to the particle *do*, intercalated with this between preposition and verb: *atamroipred* consecratus sum Ml. 44ᶜ, pres. *adopuir* offert (§ 35), *cotobsechfider* instituemini, inf. *cosc* (that is *con-sech*) instituere; *cotan-rirastar-ni* obligemur (§ 323), pres. *con-riug* ligo; *atatchigestar* videris (for *ad-dot-chichestar*), pres. *adchiu* video.

Deponent.

332. In Modern Irish the independent pronoun in its accusative form is placed after the verb, e.g. *molaim* II I praise, *moltar mé* I am praised:

Sg.	1 *moltar mé*	Pl.	1 *moltar inn* or *sinn*
	2 *moltar thú*		2 *moltar ibh* or *sibh*
	3 *moltar é*		3 *moltar iad.*

DEPONENT.

333. The deponent flexion is found in all three conjugations, especially often in denominative verbs of the III. conjugation. The three conjugations are not everywhere marked by distinct forms. On the use of the deponent forms cf. § 253. Paradigms Conj. I *sechur* sequor, II *labrur* loquor, III *midiur* judico:

PRESENT INDICATIVE.

	I	II	III
Sg. 1	*sechur*	*labrur*	*midiur*
2	*sechther*	*labrither*	*mitter*
3	*sechethar*	*labrathar*	*midethar*
abs.	*sechidir*	*labridir*	*mididir*
Pl. 1	*sechemmar*	*labrammar*	*midemmar*
2	*secchid*	*labrid*	*midid*
3	*sechetar*	*labratar*	*midetar*
abs.	*sechitir*	*labritir*	*miditir.*

PRESENT CONJUNCTIVE.

	I	II	III
Sg. 1	*secher*	*labrar*	*mider*
2	*sechther*	*labrither*	*mitter*
3	*sechethar*	*labrathar*	*midethar*
abs.	*secchidir*	*labridir*	*mididir*
Pl. 1	*sechemmar*	*labrammar*	*midemmar*
2	*sechid*	*labrid*	*midid*
3	*sechetar*	*labratar*	*midetar*
abs.	*sechitir*	*labritir*	*miditir.*

334. The conjunctive forms predominate in use. They often stand in a relative position without any preceding particle: *intí labrathar* is qui loquitur; *cruthaigedar* (Gloss on *plasmantis*) qui format. The 2 pl. has only an active form in Old Irish; the later deponent forms in *-bar, -bair* seem only to occur in a preterite sense. In the 1 pl. there are also absolute forms in *-mair, -mir*.

In the place of *-ur* is also found *-or*, and *-ithir* instead of *-idir*, and *-edar, -adar* instead of *-ethar, -athar*, cf. § 319. In Middle Irish the 1 sg. in *-or, -ur* is used in a conjunctive sense: *con acor* ut videam, *co ro acilliur* ut appellem.

335. In the 2 sg. in particular, but also in the 3 sg. conjunctive occur noteworthy forms in *-ra, -thera, -thre*: sg. 2 *nit ágara* be not afraid S. C. 40; *dia n-accara* cum videris L. Breac p. 47^b, 41; *atchithera* quos videas L. Breac 43. Examples of such forms are found in the pieces for reading I, 49. Stokes was so kind as to give me the reference to most of them in a letter.

Sg. 3 *dianus faccara* cum eum viderit L. Breac 69^b, 28; *mada findara in cach* "if every one knows or finds out" Sench. M. III p. 12, 23; *num sichethre* sequatur me Cod. Cam. (Z.^{2} p. 1005). For similar forms in the S-future see § 344.

336. Verbs which have more or less consequent deponent forms:

adgládur I appello, 3 *ad-gladathar*, conj. sg. 1 *co ro acilliur* ut appellem (§ 334), past § 339, fut. § 346, pass. pres. sg. 3 *adgládar*, inf. *accaldam*;

águr, adagur I timeo, 3 *ni agathar*, conj. sg. 2 *ni aigther* ne timeas, *nit ágara* § 335, fut. § 341, inf. *aigthiu*;

cloor I hear, conj. sg. 2 *con dam chloither-sa* ut audias me Ml. 21^b, 3; *ro dam cloathar* qui me audiat, fut. § 346;

clunim I hear, 3 *nís cluinethar* non audit, conj. sg. 3 *ro dom cluinedar* qui me audiat, perf. § 301, pass. pres. sg. 3 *ni cluiner* (later *cluinter*) non auditur;

ad-chíu, déccu III video, conj. sg. 1 *con acor, accur* ut videam (§ 334), 2 *dia n-accara, atchithera* (§ 335), 3 *con accadar* ut videat, pl. 1 *mani decamar* nisi attendamus, perf. § 295, fut. § 346 and § 288;

do-moiniur III puto, 2 *domointer*, 3 *do-aith-minedar* commonet, conj. pl. 1 *con der-manammar* ut obliviscamur, perf. § 347, pass. pres. sg. 3 *fur-aith-menter* (fut. § 316);

atluchur budi refero gratias, *do-atluchur* with *duthluchimse* III peto, *duthluchedar* postulat, pl. 1 *itlochamar* we thank, conj. sg. 1 *co datlucher* ut efflagitem, *cia fiu todlaiger-sa* quam justa postolem, past § 340, fut. *atluchfam buidi* gratias agemus, inf. *atlugud*;

ar-asissiur-sa innitor, *fo-sisiur* confiteor, 2 *an dun-er-issider-su* Gloss on adstante te Ml. 38ᶜ, 3 *assissedar* he stops, *lase ar-asissedar* cum fuerit innisa, pl. 1 *fob-sisimar-ni* we explain to you, 3 *ar-asissetar* innituntur, *fris-tair-issetar* obsistunt, *fosissetar* confitentur, conj. sg. 2 *fosisider-su* profitere, preterite § 340, fut. § 342, inf. *sessom, sessam* to stand, standing, *tairissem* (*do-air*) constantia;

gainethar generatur, *gnaither* gignitur, pl. 1 *ad-gainemmar-ni* regeneramur, 3 *gnitir* gignuntur, perf. § 349, fut. § 346;

do-cuiriur III ascisco, 3 *docuirethar*, pl. 3 *hi cuiretar* in quo ponunt, *imme-churetar* tractant, *ni er-chuiretar* non evertunt, conj. sg. 1 *cura dichuirer* Gloss on deleam, past § 340, fut. § 342;

dofuislim labo (*do-fo-es-salim*), 2 *tuislider* laberis, conj. sg. 3 *dufuisledar* Gloss on ut possit elabi (Ml.);

rolaimur III audeo, conj. sg. 1 *rollámar* ausim, perf. § 349, fut. § 277;

molim and *molor* II laudo, *ro molur* laudavi, 3 *no moladar*, fut. § 342, pass. pres. sg. 3 *no moltar*;

intsamlur, insamlur imitor, conj. 1 *insamlar*;

comalnaim II impleo, 3 *comalnathar*, pl. 3 *comalnatar* qui implent, conj. sg. 3 *arin chomalnathar* ut id expleat;

beoigidir vivificat, *cuimnigedar* qui reminiscitur, and other denominatives of the III conj. (preterite § 269 or § 338, fut. § 282 or § 341).

337. In the second present and in the imperative deponents have an active flexion: second present sg. 1 *atat-gladainn-se* cum te convenirem; *no arsissinn* inniterer Ml. 44ᵈ; *adagain-se* verebar Ml. 63ᵈ; sg. 3 *nachib mided* ne vos judicet; imper. sg. 2 *atlaigthe bude* refer gratias. The sg. 2 conjunctive

of the deponent is often used in an imperative sense : *fosisider-su* profitere ; *níis coirther* ne posueris eam.

3. S-PRETERITE.

338. The S-preterite is most often formed in verbs of the III. conjugation. Paradigms : *labrur* II loquor, *sudigim* III pono :

		II	III
Sg.	1	*ro labrasur*	*ro sudigsiur*
	2	*ro labriser*	*ro sudigser*
	3	*ro labrastar*	*ro sudigestar*
	abs.	*labristir*	*sudigistir*
Pl.	1	*ro labrasammar*	*ro sudigsemmar*
	2	*ro labrisid*	*ro sudigsid*
	3	*ro labrasatar*	*ro sudigsetar*
	abs.	*labrisitir*	*sudigsitir*

339. Here also side by side with the deponent forms the active forms are in use : *labrais* he spake, beside *ro labrastar*; *ro sudig* he put, beside *ro sudigestar;* *acallais* he accosted, beside *acallastar*, later *aicillestar* (following the III. conj. ?) The conjoined 3 sg. is particularly often used in deponent flexion, even in verbs which otherwise have only an active flexion : *ro gudestar* Gloss on *rodas gaid* he prayed them (perf.); *ro éirnestar* Gloss on *asrir* dedit (perf.), pres. *érnim* that is *as-renim* ; *ro charastar* Gloss on *carais* (Hy. 5). In Middle Irish a deponent form in *-bar, -bair* occurs : *doronsabair* fecistis (§ 291).

340. Examples of the S-preterite in the deponent verbs given § 333 are : *ro sechestar* consecutus est; *dia-ru-muinestar* quibus destinavit (Wb.) with *co-ménar* § 347 ; *atlaigestar* he thanked ; *fu-ro-issestar* confessus est (Ml.) ; *do-ro-churestar* exciverat.

4. B-FUTURE.

341. Deponent forms of this tense are much rarer than active forms and are used side by side with them. A futurum secundarium distinct from the active form is not extant. Paradigms : *águr, ad-agur* I timeo, *labrur* II loquor, *sudigim* III pono :

	III	II	I
Sg. 1	no śudigfer	no labrabar	adaichfer
2	no śudigfider		
3	no śudigfedar	no labrabadar	adaichfedar
abs.	sudigfidir		
Pl. 1	no śudigfemmar	no labrafammar	
2	no sudigfid	no labribid	
3	no śudigfetar	no labrafatar	aichfetar
abs.	sudigfitir		

342. As to the change between *f* and *b*, *b* is preferably in use when the thematic vowel is preserved before the characteristic of this future (cf. § 283).

Further examples are: *aratmuinfer-sa feid* te venerabor (Ml.), pres. *ar-muinethar feid* reveretur; *fosisefar* confitebor (Ml.); *do-cuirifar* citabo; *no molfar* laudabo (Wb.); *nud comálnabadar* qui eam implebit (Ml.). But on the other hand, e. g. *ni contuslifea* non elabetur (Ml.) in active form beside *tuislider* laberis.

5. S-FUTURE.

343. The S-future in the deponent, as in the active, has also a conjunctive signification. The conditional does not differ from the form used in the active. Paradigm *fetar* scio (§ 351);

Sg. 1	ro fessur	Pl. 1	ro fessamar
2	ro fesser, co fesara	2	ro fessid
3	ro festar	3	ro fessatar
abs.	festir	abs.	fessitir.

344. In the 2 sg. the form *fesara* occurs as *accara* in the conj. present (§ 335). *Fiasur, fiastar* occur for *fessur, festar*. The frequently occurring S-future of *midiur* judico is inflected exactly in the same way: sg. 2 *meser*, 3 *míastar*, abs. *miastir*, pl. 1 *messamar*, abs. *messimir*, 2 *con irmissid* ut intellegatis.

345. The following are examples from other verbs of this future (cf. § 287): pl. 1 *adglaasmar-ni* alloquemur, pres. *adgládur* (cf. § 346); sg. 3 *mi-dúthrastar* male optabit, 3 *ci dutairsetar* quamvis desideraverint, perf. § 349; sg. 2 *na imroimser* ne delinquas, 3 *ar na im-ro-mastar* ne delinquet, perf. *imme-*

ru-mediar peccavit § 349; sg. 1 *esur* edam, 2 *cen con essara* without thou eatest ScM. 3 (or for *fessara*?), 3 *cini estar* etsi non edit; *conisimar* poterimus, cf. § 287.

6. REDUPLICATED FUTURE.

346. The reduplicated future is of very rare occurrence in the deponent: (*a*) *cách rot chechladar* quisquis te audierit, probably belonging to *cloor* audio (§ 336), cf. § 280; *ata-gegallar-sa* alloquor eos, 3 *ata-gegalldathar* (*i. acaillfes*), *ata-geglathar* L. U. p. 19^b; pres. *adgládur;* sg. 3 *ad-gignethar* renascentur (L. U. p. 68^a, 2), pres. *ad-gainemmar* renascimur, cf. § 284; also perhaps *atchichither* thou wilt see (S. C. 40, cf. § 276);

(*b*) perhaps *fo-mentar* thou shalt expect Wb. 28^e and 30^c (Gloss on scito), pl. 2 *fo-menaid* (Gloss on ut observetis Wb. 7^b), all three forms taken as perfects in the Gr. Celt. p. 451; *co ar-mentar féid* (Gloss on ut revereatur) Wb. 31^c.

7. PERFECT.

347. The flexion only differs in the singular from the perfect active: for that in the plural has assumed the deponent flexion. Paradigms: (*a*) *coim-nacar* potui, pres. *con-ic* potest (fut. § 287 and § 345); (*b*) *do-ménar* putavi, pres. *do-moiniur* (fut. § 342 and § 346).

Sg.	1	*coimnacar*	*doménar*
	2		
	3	*coimnucuir*	*doménair*
Pl.	1	*coimnacmar*	*doménammar*
	2	*coimnacaid*	*doménaid*
	3	*coimnactar*	*doménatar*

348. The *i* of *coim* in (*a*) *coimnacar* is sometimes absent, e.g. in *teccom-nocuir* (for *do-aith-com-*) and *for-com-nucuir* accidit; whether it may be regarded as an after-effect of the syllable of reduplication as set forth in § 19 is not quite certain. The later *caomnagair* lavavit (cf. *nigim* I wash) allows also a *coim-* to be inferred in Old Irish.

A reduplication-syllable appears to occur only in *siasair*

sedit (i. *ro saidestar* Hy. 5, 1) Pl. 3 *siasatár* L. U. p. 64ᵇ, but in this instance seems to belong to the verbal stem.

349. Further examples of the perfect deponent:

(a) *ro lámair* ausus est, pres. *ro-laimur* audeo, fut. § 277;

dúthraccar optavi, 3 *du-fu-tharcair* voluit § 79, pres. *dúthraic* optat, fut. § 345;

imchomarcair he asked, pres. *imm-chom-airc* interrogat, fut. § 287, preterite pl. *imcomaircsetar* L. U. 25ᵇ, 13;

fo-ro-damar passus sum, pres. *fodaim* patitur, fut. § 277;

in tan imme-ru-mediar (read *-medair?*) cum peccavit, pl. 3 *inna hí imme-ruimdetar* eorum qui peccaverunt, fut. § 345;

do-ru-madir-si quæ fuerat emensus, cf. *tomus* mensura;

ro mídar judicavi, pres. *midiur*, fut. § 344;

(b) *ro génar* natus sum, pres. *ad-gainemmar* renascimur, fut. § 284 and § 346;

ro chéssar passus sum, pres. *céssaim* II patior.

350. The following isolated forms have been found: *ro génartar* nati sunt (Wb.); *ro lamratar* ausi sunt, cf. § 351.

351. Of a special form is: *ro fetar* scio, (fut. § 343), of the root *vid;* the *t* in *fetar* has perhaps originated in the same way as in *cretim* I believe (cf. Skr. *çrad-dadhámi*, Latin credo). Paradigm:

Sg. 1 *ro fetar*   Pl. 1 *ro fitemmar*
    2 *ro fetar*   2 *ro fitid*
    3 *ro fitir*   3 *ro fitetar*

The 2 sg. is given by *in fetar-su* scisne tu (O'D. Ir. Gram. p. 239). In the 1 sg. for *fetar* are found *fetor, fetur*, with transition to the flexion of the present. Later Irish has *feadarmar* for *fitemmar* (cf. § 250).

352. In Modern Irish deponent forms have been imported into: (1) the 2 sg. present and future active, (2) the plural preterite active of all verbs;

IX. Verb.

	Present.	Future.	Past.
Sg. 1	*molaim*	*molfad*	*do mholas*
2	*molair*	*molfair*	*do mholais*
3	*molaidh sé*	*molfaidh sé*	*do mhol sé*
Pl. 1	*molamaoid*	*molfamaoid*	*do mholamar*
2	*moltaoi*	*molfaidh*	*do mholabhar*
3	*molaid*	*molfaid*	*do mholadar.*

The 2 sg. in *-air, -fair* is not extant in Old Irish. The plural forms in the preterite have taken their starting point from the perfect. In Modern Irish the old S-preterite and the perfect are associated so as to form a new preterite of mixed character, with peculiar forms only in a few "irregular verbs."

Participles.

1. Perfect Passive Participle.

353. A perfect passive participle is formed by the suffix *-te* (*-tae, -ta*), after vowels *-the, -de*. This participle is inflected as the words in *e* treated of in § 115: *brethe, berthe* (§ 354ᵉ) brought, gen. *berthi*, dat. *berthu*; nom. *carthe* loved, *lécthe* left.

354ᵃ. The suffix *-te* is in most verbs which are not denominative, especially those of the I. conjugation, attached directly to the root as the *t* is in the preterite passive. Thus are formed with a guttural in terminal sound:

timm-orte compressus (cf. § 266), pres. sec. pass. *du-immaircthe* artabatur; *neph-frithortae* inlesum, Ml. 39ᵃ, inf. *frithorcun* offendere;

etar-fuillechta interlitus, pres. *fo-sligim* delino;

cuim-rechta alligatus, pres. *con-riug* ligo;

tórmachta auctus, pres. *do-for-maig* auget.

354ᵇ. With a dental terminal sound and *s*:

indrisse invasus, pl. nom. *ind indirsi* vastati; *ind-rid* invasio, pres. *ad-riuth* adorior, *rethait* currunt; *airndrisse* Gloss on erratam Ml. 138ᵈ, pres. pl. 3 *du-airnd-redat* pererrant (for *du-air-ind-*);

mese examinatus, pres. *midiur* judico;

inna n-impesse Ml. 49ᵇ Gloss on obsessorum, pres. *im-suidet* obsident.

claissi nom. pl. defossi, perf. *fo-ro-chlaid* effodit, § 295;

anat n-acailsi Gloss on interpellati, Ml. 48ᵃ, pres. *ad-gládur* alloquor, inf. *accaldam*;

tuicse electus, *togu* choice (root *gus*), perf. *do-rói-gu* elegit.

354ᶜ. With a nasal terminal sound:

neph-toimte unexpected, *toimtiu* opinion, pres. *do-moiniur* puto, perf. *do-ménar*;

erite susceptus, conj. pres. sg. 3 *air-ema* suscipiat;

cete, cantus, pres. *canim*;

con-goite conpunctus Ml. 58ᶜ, pres. *gonaim* vulnero.

354ᵈ. With vowel termination:

imdibthe circumcisus, pres. *im-di-bnim* circumcido (cf. § 261); *tóbaide* abscisus, pres. *do-fui-bnim* succido; *airdbide* interfectus, pres. *airdben* interficit (for *air-di-*);

foirbthe complete, perfectus, pres. pass. sg. 3 *for-banar*, *for-fenar* perficitur;

rithæ datus, pres. *renim* do (cf. § 261);

cloithe convictus Ml. 32ᵇ, pl. dat. *donaib—clothib* victis 67ᵇ, preterite sg. 3 *ro chlói* vicit 37ᵃ, pass. pres. sg. 3 *cloithir* involvitur 16ᵇ, *clóither* Gloss on vinci 30ᶜ (root *klu*);

in-clothi exauditi Ml. 48ᵇ, pres. *clunim* (§ 261).

354ᵉ. With *r* or *l* as terminal sound:

forngarti jussi, pres. *for-con-gur* praecipio.

Verbs like *berim*, *celim*, *melim* ought to have forms with *re*, *le* before the suffix (cf. § 325, § 361ᵉ and § 373): *brethe*, *brithe*, *inna in-chlidi* occulta Ml. 26ʳ.

Thus is explained the aspiration of the *t* in the form with transposition: *rem-eperthae* antedictus, pres. *epiur* dico; *ted-barthe* Ml. 47ᵃ; pres. *do-aid-biur* offero.

355. Aspiration has further extended itself to cases in which it is not legitimate: *frithorthai* adflicti Ml. 58ʳ beside

frithortae Ml. 39ᵃ (§ 354ᵃ); *foircthe* eruditus Ml. 35ᵈ, pres. *forchun* doceo, beside *cete* cantus § 354ᶜ. Cf. § 361ᶜ.

356. The tendency not to join the suffix directly to the radical syllable shows itself also in verbs of the I. conjugation, not only in: *gabim* capio, part. *gabtha, aur-gabtha*, but even in verbs such as *canim: don terchantu* prophetato Ml. 53 (Z.² p. 881), pres. *do-aur-chanim* sagio.

357. Especially noteworthy is *frescastae* expectatum (Ml. 68ᵃ), dat. *neph-frescastu* (Ml. 56ᵈ) gloss on insperata morte (further explained through *neph-toimtiu*, dat. of *toimte* § 354ᶜ), the participle of *fris-aiccim* I expect, hope (*ad-chíu* I see, § 264), perf. *fris-racacha* speravi. The *t* of the suffix is again introduced, for one might expect *fres-casse* from § 354ᵇ and from the analogy of *frescsiu* spes, gen. *frescsen* (suffix *-tiu*, gen. *-ten*, § 158). Similar phenomena are shown § 361ᵇ and 375ᵃ.

358. Participles of verbs of the II. conjugation: *neph-etar-scarthi* indivisa, pres. *etar-scaraim* separo; *tinolta* (§ 64) locata, pres. *do-in-ola* adplicat.

Of verbs of the III. conjugation:

cuirthe jactus, pres. *cuirim*; *indhule-loiscthi* holocausta, pres. *loiscim* uro; *foilsigthe* revelatus, pres. *foilsigim* manifesto; *suidigthe* positus, pres. *suidigim* pono; *fodailte* (§ 64), pres. *fodalet* distribuunt.

359. Sometimes this participle has the sense of Latin adjectives in *-alis, -bilis*, and it then comes in contact with the following participle in *-ti*: *rithe* venalis (§ 354ᵈ); *di-brithe* importabilis (§ 354ᵉ); *neph-icthe* immedicabilis, pres. *iccaim* II. I cure.

2. PARTICIPIUM NECESSITATIS.

360. In the same way a participium necessitatis is formed by the suffix *-ti* (*-ti*), after vowels *-thi, -di*. This participle is generally used predicatively in the nominative and rarely in other cases: *brethi, berthi* ferendus (§ 361ᵉ), *carthi, carthai* amandus, *lécthi* linquendus. The dative plural is the only case which has a separate ending and not the mere *-ti*: *adnachtib* condendis (cadaveribus).

Participles.

361ª. In radical verbs the suffix is directly attached to the radical syllable. Thus are formed (cf. § 354ª):

cuimrechti stringendus, pres. *con-riug* ligo;

cuintechti quaerendus, pres. *cuintgim*, preterite act. *conaitecht* § 266;

adnachti sepeliundus, preterite pass. *ro adnacht* sepultus est;
aichti metuendus, pres. dep. *águr* I am afraid of.

361ᵇ. With a dental or an *s* in terminal sound (cf. § 354ᵇ):

messi judicandus, pres. *midiur*;

fissi sciendum, preterite dep. *fetar* scio, § 351.

Here also after assimilation the *t* has been introduced anew (cf. § 357): *im-casti* considerandus with *imm-caisiu* circumspectio (pres. *imm-ad-chíu*); *tin-festi* gloss on flatilem Sg. 17ᵇ, *tin-feth* aspiratio, pres. sg. 3 *tin-fet* inflat (§ 260).

361ᶜ. With a nasal in terminal sound one might expect e.g. from *canim, ceti,* but *forcanti* intimandum (cf. § 356) and *foircthi* imbuendus only are extant (cf. § 355).

361ᵈ. With a vowel termination: *buthi* qui esse debet (Ml. 23ᶜ, 29ª).

361ᵉ. The aspiration of the *t* after a terminal sound in *r* e.g. in *eperthi* dicendum, is perhaps also here explained as in § 354ᵉ from older forms with *re, le: clethi* celandum Hy. 5, 71; *com-srithi* conserendum, pres. *ní sernat* non conserunt (verba) Ml. 31ª.

362. The suffix is not directly joined to the radical syllable: *gabthi* capiendus, pres. *gabim* I.; *sechidi* assequendus, pres. dep. *sechur* I. sequor.

Especially in verbs of the II. and III. conjugation:

moltai (§ 64) psallendum, pres. *molaim* laudo;

ersailcthi reserandus, pres. pass. sg. *arosailcther* aperitur (*air-od-*); *ailti* implorandus, pres. *ailim* precor; *móiti* (§ 64) gloriandus, pres. *moidim* glorior; *dénti* faciendum, pres. *dénim*.

110   IX. *Verb.*

INFINITIVE.

363. In Old Irish the infinitive is not sharply distinguished from the ordinary nomen actionis. The dative of such a noun with the particle *do* approaches pretty nearly the infinitive of other languages; *do breith* ferre, *do charad* amare, *do léciud* linquere. The variety of forms used as infinitives is very great, still they are preferably formed in the second conjugation in *-ad*, and in the III. conjugation in *-iud, -ud*.

364. Object and subject usually follow the infinitive, the first in the genitive, the last in the dative with *do: ro pad maith lim-sa labrad ilbelre dúib-si* esset acceptum mihi vos loqui multas linguas. The infinitive with *do* is also predicative when associated with a precedent substantive which according to the usage of the Latin language would be its subject or object. This substantive either stands absolute in the nominative or is dependent upon a word going before it: *asbert in ben friú..., cach fer díb a aidchi do fairi na cathrach*, the woman said to them that each of them should watch the town his night FB. 80; *ar is bés leo-som in daim do thúarcain* nam est mos apud illos, boves triturare; *atá i n-aicniud chaich denum maith ocus imgabail uilc do denum*, it is in the nature of each to do good and to avoid doing evil, Ml. 14ᶜ; *co carad chaingnimu du denum* that he liked to do good deeds; *ní cumcat aithirgi n-do denum* they cannot do penance Ml. 23ᵃ.

365. In Irish the possessive pronoun stands in the place where in other languages a substantival personal pronoun is used: *tair dum berrad-sa* come to clip me; *asbert fria muntir a breoad* he told his people to burn her. In the sense of the subject the possessive pronoun is especially used in intransitive verbs: *ro bo maith arrochtain and* it was good that she came there; *in tan atchuala a bith alachta* when (Mary) heard that (Elizabeth) was gravid.

366. There is not a peculiar passive form of the infinitive, but it is necessary sometimes to construe the usual infinitive as

a passive: *bá nar lée a lécud ocus dul día tig* she thought it a shame to be forsaken and to go home S. C. 44.

367. The conjunction of the preposition with the infinitive is very idiomatic: *iar n-atlugud buide do Dia* after they had given thanks to God; *ria n-dul......don cath recam in n-eclais* before we go into battle, we will visit the church; *bátar oc ól* they were drinking, *bátar inna sessom* they were standing.

368. Denominatives may have the noun from which they are derived as an infinitive:

iccaim II I cure, from *icc* salus, inf. *do icc* or *do iccad*;

rannaim II I divide, from *rand* part, inf. *do raind* and *do rannad*.

369. Radical verbs of the II. and III. conjugations form infinitive in *-ad* and *-iud*, *-ud* (§ 363).

anad remain, pres. *anaim* II;

molad praise, pres. *molaim*;

scarad secedere, pres. *scaraim* (§ 277);

lassad flame, pres. *lassaim*;

céssad suffer, pres. *céssaim*;

atlugud thank, pres. dep. *atluchur* III;

brissiud break, pres. *brissim*;

bádud dip, pres. *báidim*;

cuitbiud laugh at, i.e. *con-tibiud*, pres. *tibim* I laugh;

im-rádiud reflect upon, pres. *im-rádiu*;

snádud defend, pres. *snáidim*;

loscud burn, pres. *loiscim*;

oslogud open, pres. *oslaicim*.

370. Stems in *a* as infinitives:

cosc blame, dat. *do chosc*, *in-chosc* demonstrare, pres. *in-chosig* I significat;

ainech (and *anacul* § 380) protect, present *aingim* I, *non anich* protegit nos (cf. § 266, § 286);

tórmach increase, add, dat. *do thormuch*, pres. *do-for-maig* I auget (cf. § 321);

indlach findere, pres. *ind-lung* I findo;
fulach and *fulang* tolerare, dat. *do imm-folung* efficere, pres. *fo-loing* I sustinet;
rád speak, dat. *oc rád*, pres. *no rádiu* III loquor;
scor loosen, dat. *do scor*, pres. *scuirim* III;
cor ponere, dat. *do chor*, pres. *cuirim* III.

371. Stems in *i:*
guin wound, dat. *do guin*, pres. *gonim* I (cf. § 276, § 280, § 295).
eráil order, dat. *do eráil*, pres. *eráilim* III;
fodáil distribute, pres. *fo-dáli* III distribuit.

372. Stems in *ia:*
faire wake, dat. *do fairi*, pres. *fairim* III;
fuine cook, dat. *ic fune*, pres. *fuinim* III;
gude pray, dat. *do guidi*, pres. *guidim* III (cf. § 290);
urnaide expect, dat. *oc urnaidi*, pres. *ir-, ur-naidim* III;
nige wash, dat. *oc nigi*, pres. *nigim* III (cf. § 287, § 295);
ithe eat, acc. *ithi*, pres. *ithim* (cf. § 287).

373. Stems in *ti*, (*a*) the suffix is attached immediately to the root:
breith bear, pres. *berim* I; *tabairt* (cf. § 354ᵉ), also *tabart* (§ 124), pres. *tabur* I give; *epert* say, dat. *do epert*, pres. *epiur* dico (preterite § 265, fut. § 275);
mlith, blith (§ 41) grind, dat. *do blith*, pres. *melim* I;
tomailt eat, pres. *toimlim*, i.e. *do-melim* (§ 261);
cleith hide, conceal, pres. *celim* I; *di-clith, di-cheilt* (§ 354ᵉ) hide (§ 261).
gleith depasci, pres. *gelid* I depascitur (past § 266).

(*b*) The suffix is not joined immediately to the root:
saigid, in-saigid go for, dat. *do saigid* (and *do saichtin* § 375ᵃ), pres. *saigim, in-saigim* I (§ 261);
saigid disputare, pres. *saiges* I qui dicit (fut. § 287);
iarfaigid ask, pres. *iarma-foich* I quærit (preterite § 266, fut. § 287);

cuindchid, cuingid ask, demand, pres. *con-daig* I quærit (fut. § 287).

374ª. Stems in *-tu*. These are very numerous, for they include the infinitives in *-ad* of the second conjugation and the infinitives in *-ud* of the third conjugation, (1) in which the suffix is attached to the present-stem (cf. § 363 and § 369); (2) in which the suffix is directly joined on to the radical syllable:

fiss know, dat. *do fiuss* (contracted *dús*), *fetar* I know (§ 351, fut. § 343);

mess to judge, dat. *do mess*, pres. dep. *midiur* (perf. § 349, fut. § 344).

374ᵇ. Stems in *tā* seem to be:

techt go, dat. *do thecht*, pres. *tiagim* I; *im-thecht* ambulatio (acc. pl. *imthechta* Wb. 28ᶜ) with *im-tiagam* ambulamus Wb. 6ª (fut. § 285, past § 269);

tuidecht come, pret. *tuidchetar, do-dechatar* venerunt (§ 302).

375ª. Infinitives in *-tiu* in the nominative, *-ten* in the genitive (§ 152):

airitiu accipere, pres. conj. *air-ema* suscipiat (pret. § 266, fut. § 277);

fo-ditiu tolerare, dat. *do foditin*, pres. *fo-daim* I patitur (§ 261);

ditiu to protect, dat. *do ditin*, fut. *du-ema* vindicabit (pret. § 266, fut. § 277);

toimtiu think (*do-fo-mitiu*), dat. *do thoimtin*, pres. dep. *do-moiniur* III puto (perf. § 347, fut. § 342);

teistiu profundere, profusio, dat. *do thestin*, pres. *doesmet* profundunt (*do-ess-semet*);

tuistiu generare, creare, dat. *do thuistin*, pres. *dofuisim* generat (*do-fo-es-sim*);

acsiu to see, dat. *do acsin, aiscin* (§ 80), pres. *adchíu*; *déicsiu* to see, dat. *do décsin*, pres. *déccu* (§ 264);

clósi to hear, dat. *do chlósin* and with reintroduction of the *t, iar clostin* (§ 357), pres. dep. *cloor* audio (preterite pass. § 326ᵇ);

taidbsiu to show, dat. *do thaidbsin*, pres. pass. *do-ad-badar* demonstratur (fut. § 287);

epeltu to die, dat. *do epeltin*, pres. *atbail* perit (§ 261);
Acc. *sirtin* (beside *siriud*) to seek, pres. *sirim* III;
Dat. *do saichtin* (and *do saigid* § 373), pres. *saigim* I adeo;
tíchtu, tíchte to come, dat. *oc tichtain*, acc. *co tichtin* usque ad adventum, pres. *tic* venit (§ 261); beside dat. *tichtain* in a similar sense *tiachtain*;
Dat. *do riachtain* to come, preterite *riacht* venit § 266;
Acc. *torachtain* to come, pres. *toraig* I venit (past § 266): with *toracht* processus, successio (*do-fo-racht*), *tiarmóracht* sequence, pursuit (*do-iarm-fo-racht*) § 374[b].

In the same way *fortacht* help, to help, acc. *fortachtain* and *fortacht* (belonging to *techt* come, pres. *tíagaim?* cf. *fortíag* Gloss on conniveo Z.[2] p. 428), changes in flexion.

375[b]. Here also cases occur in which the *t* of the suffix has not been immediately united with the radical syllable (cf. § 356).

áigthiu to fear, pres. dep. *águr*; *do saigthin* adire beside *saichtin*;
Dat. *oc ferthain*, pres. *feraim fáilti* I bid welcome.
Dat. *do cantain* (beside *do for-cetul* § 380), pres. *canim* I.

375[c]. *Fóisitiu* confiteri, confessio, dat. *do fóisitin*, as infinitive to the present *fosisiur* confiteor (§ 336) is strange.

376. The infinitives in *mm, m* (suffix *mann* § 160) joined immediately to roots in *ng, nd, nt* (cf. § 76):

léimm to leap, dat. *do lémaim*, pres. *lingim* I (§ 261);
céimm to go, pres. *cingim* I; *tochim* to stride, pres. *do-chingim* I (§ 261);
in-greimm to pursue, dat. *oc ingrimmim*, pres. *in-grennim* I (§ 261);
foglimm, foglaim to learn, pres. *fo-gliunn* I, I learn (§ 261);
fordiuglaim to swallow, fut. *for-tam-diucuilset* me vorabunt Ml. 44[c], partic. *for-diucailsi* absorpti Ml. 50 r, cf. *fordiuglantaid* devorator.

tóthim, tuitim to fall, dat. *do thuitim*, pres. *tuitim* I (§ 264[c]);

béimm to beat, dat. *do béim*, pres. *benim* I (§ 261).

377. Infinitives in *-om (-am)* and *-em:*

cosnom, cosnam contendere, defendere, dat. *do chosnom*, pres. *cosnaim* I, fut. pl. 3 *cossénat* (§ 275), perf. sg. 3 *ro chosain;*

sessom, sessam to stand, dat. *ina sessom* standing (§ 367), pres. *sessaim*, cf. § 336;

gním to do, dat. *do gním*, pres. *gníim* III; *fognam* to serve, dat. *do fognam*, pres. *fo-gniu* (§ 264);

dénum, dénom, dénam to do, dat. *do dénom*, pres. *dénim* III.

These infinitives are declined like masculine *u* stems (gen. *gnímo, dénmo*, § 126), but other forms also appear analogous to feminine *a* stems (§ 110):

accaldam alloqui, dat. *do accaldam*, acc. *accaldim*, pres. dep. *adgládur* (§ 336);

sechem to follow, acc. *fri sechem* and *fri sechim*, pres. dep. *sechur* (§ 333);

cretem belief, to believe, pres. *cretim* III, is only feminine.

378. Infinitives in *n* (suffix *na, ni*) are rarer: *búain* to reap, dat. *oc búain*, pres. *bongaim* I break, reap (§ 261); *súan* sleep, to sleep, pres. *foaim* I sleep (§ 56).

379. Infinitives in *-un, -an* in the nominative (suffix *-ana*), some of which have a masculine and some of which have a feminine flexion:

orcun to kill, pres. *orcaid* I occidit; *es-orcun* caedere, dat. *oc esorcuin; túarcun* triturare, dat. *do thuarcuin*, pres. *do-fu-aircc* triturat (§ 67, § 284);

blegun to milk, dat. *do blegun*, pres. *bligim* I (perf. § 295);

lécun (and *lécud*) to leave, dat. *do lécun*, pres. *lécim* III;

imbresan altercari, lis, dat. *oc imbresun*, pres. *imfresna* II adversatur (*im-fres-sna*) belongs to § 370.

380. Infinitives in *l* in the nominative:

forcetul, forcital, n. to teach, doctrine (beside *do chantain* § 375), dat. *do forcetul*, pres. *for-chun, -chanim* I (§ 261);

intinscital to begin, beginning, pres. *intinscana* II incipit (*ind-do-ind-scana*, cf. § 246);

tindnacul tradere, traditio, pres. *do-ind-naich* distribuit (past § 266, fut. § 287);

adnacul to bury, grave, pres. sec. pass. *adnaicthe* (fut. § 287);

gabál and *gabáil* f. to take, dat. *do gabáil*, pres. *gabim* I (§ 261);

imdegail f. to guard, dat. *do imdegail*, pres. *im-dichim* vindico, sg. 3 *imdig*;

atmail to confess, pres. pl. 3 *ad-daimet*;

ticsál, imperat. sg. 3 *ticsath a chruich* Gloss on tollet crucem suam, Cod. Camar. (Z.² p. 1005).

381. Infinitives in *end*, *enn*. These appear to have taken origin from the Latin gerund: *legend* Latin *legere*, gen. *legind*, Lat. *legendi*, dat. *do legund*; *scribend* Lat. *scribere*, gen. *scribint*, Lat. *scribendi*, dat. *do scribund*; in the same way is formed *dílgend* exterminare, dat. *do dilgiunn*, to *do-lega* delebit Ml. 62ᵇ, *dilegthith* exterminator.

382. But all the forms designated infinitives in the preceding are equally well used as simple nomina actionis: *fortacht* help and to help, *imrádud* reflection and to reflect, *ól* draught and to drink (as infinitive to *ibim* bibo). The profusion of forms which are used as infinitives is not exhausted by those above given, for every nomen actionis may be so used. The form of the stem is hard to determine in *im-di-be* circumcisio, circumcidere, *tó-be* decisio, decidere, pres. *im-di-bnim*, *do-fui-bnim* and other compounds of *benim*, as also *dula*, *dul* to go, infinitive of *luid*, *do-luid* he went (§ 302).

VERB SUBSTANTIVE.

383. Four different roots serve for the substantive verb: (1) *as*, (2) *stā*, (3) *vel*, (4) *bhū*.

1. Root *as*.

384. Paradigms of the root *as*, present *amm* I am:

Sg. 1 *amm, am, im* Pl. *ammi*
   2 *at*   *adib*
   3 *is*, relative *as* *it, at*.

385. Also in impersonal flexion: *is mé* French c'est moi, *is tú* c'est toi, *is snisni* c'est nous, *is sissi* (also *it sib*) c'est vous. Stokes (Beiträge VII. p. 40 note) detects in *is-am* (also *is-im*), *is-at*, *bid-at* (I am, thou art, thou shalt be) another form of impersonal flexion, being formed by suffixing pronominal elements: but probably this *am, at* is the verbal "I am, thou art," and the whole formula an emphatic "it is that I am, it is that thou art, it will be that thou art." This view is corroborated by the *is it*, mentioned in O'Donovan's Ir. Gr. p. 162: *isit imda a locha* many are its lakes (literally "it is that are").

2. Root *stā*.

386. Paradigms of the root *stā*, indicative and conjunctive present. Usually composed *attá, atá ad tá* or *aith-tá* est, or *itá*, the latter being either identical with the former or *tá* with the relative *in-* ubi. Instead of the simple *tá* very often *dá* appears (cf. § 61), e.g. after the particles of comparison *ol, in (an): ol dáas, indás (andás)* quam est. The absolute forms placed in parenthesis are taken from O'Donovan's Grammar.

INDICATIVE PRESENT.

		conj.		abs.
Sg. 1	*itáu, atto, atu*	*ol dáu, dó*		(*táim*)
2	*itái, atái*	*ol dái*		(*táir*)
3	*itá, attáa, atá*	*ni tá*, rel. *ol daas, dás*	*taith*	(*tá sé*)
Pl. 1	*itaam, attaam*	*ni tam, dam*		(*tamaoid*)
2	*ataaith, ataad*	*ni tad, dad*	*tathi*	(*tathaoi*)
3	*itaat, ataat*	*ni tat*, rel. *ol date*		(*táid*).

IX. Verb.

CONJUNCTIVE PRESENT.

Sg. 1 *ni ta, conda* (ut sim)   Pl. 1 *ni tán, con-dán*
   2   2 *con-dath*
   3   3 *con-dat.*

387. Deviating indicative forms occur in *na-te, na-de* non est, *ca-te* quis est? ubi est? *ca-teet* quid sunt?

In like manner to this verb or to *amm* (§ 384) belong the remnants of the verbal forms in the following unions with the conjunctions *ce, cia* (with conj.) although, *má* (with conj.) if, *mani* if not, *co n-* that, and farther with *dian-* cui, *nan-* qui, quæ, quod non, *in-* ubi:

Sg. 3	*cid*	*mad*	*manid*	*conid*	*dianid (diant)*	*nand*	*inid*
	cesu	*masu*					
Pl. 2		*mad* (Wb. 9ᵃ)					
3	*cit*	*mat*				*nandat*	
	cetu	*matu*					
		matis					

From *conid* (?) with further suffix *condid* and *condib* ut sit are formed, the latter of which contains distinctly a form from *biu* (§ 389).

3. Root *vel*.

388. The root *vel* in Old Irish occurs only in the 3 sg. It governs the accusative and often answers to the French il y a: sg. 3 *fil (fail)*, relative *file*; conj. *fel*, also *feil*. The latter is also proved as a relative form after the neuter sg. The remaining persons are in Old Irish expressed impersonally: *con-dum-fel* ut essem, *nis fil* non sunt. But a personal flexion also comes into use: *ni filet (failet)* non sunt, *filet* qui sunt; and in Modern Irish *go bh-fuilim* that I am, 2 *go bh-fuilir*, 3 *go bh-fuil sé*, pl. 1 *go bh-fuilimíd*, 2 *go bh-fuiltí*. 3 *go bh-fuilid*.

4. Root *bhū**.

389. Paradigms of the root *bhū*. Almost in every tense there are two series of forms, which appear to be different according to the formation of the stem, as the Latin *fio* and

---

* Stokes identifies *biu* with Latin *vivo*.

Latin *fuam* or Skr. *bhavāmi*. The forms (*a*) of the first series have a stronger signification (to be = *existere*, versari): the forms (*b*) of the second series serve as a simple copula. The same distinction of signification may be observed in the perfect, although here the different forms seem not to be of different origin.

	PRESENT INDICATIVE.		CONJUNCTIVE PRESENT.			
	absolute	conjoined	(a) abs.	conj.	(b) abs.	conj.
s. 1	*bíu*	*no bíu*	*beo*		*bá*	
2	(*bii*) *bi*				*ba, bát*	*ni-bá, co m-ba*
3	*biid, bíth*	*ni bii, bí*	*beith*	*ni bé*	*bá*	*ni-b, ro-p, roi-b*
rel.	*biis, bís*		*bes*		*bas*	
pl. 1	*bimmi*	*ni biam*	*bemmi*	*ro bem*	*bami*	*co m-ban*
2		*no bith*	*beithe*	*ni beid*	*bede*	*arna bad*
3	*biit, bít*	*ni biat*	*beit, bit*	*ro bet*		*co m-bat*
rel.	*bíte*				*beta, bete*	

	IMPERATIVE.		SECOND PRESENT.		PERFECT.	
	(a)	(b)	(a)	(b)		
s. 1			*biinn*	*bin*	*bá, ba*	*rop-sa*
2	*bí*	*ba*		*ni-ptha*	*bá*	*rop-su*
3	*bíith, bíd*	*bad*	*bíth*	*béth, beth*	*bád, bad*	*bói, bái, búi ba, combo*
					robe, rabi	*ni bu, nib, rop*
pl. 1		*baan, ban*	*bimmis*	*bemmis*	*bámmar*	
2	*biid, bith*	*bad*		*bethe*	*baid*	
3		*bat*	*bítis*	*betis*	*comtis, roibtis*	*bátar, bátir robtar*

	FUTURE.				SECOND FUTURE.	
	(a) abs.	conj.	(b) abs.	conj.	(a)	(b)
s. 1	*bia*		*be*		*ni beinn*	
2	*bia*				*ro betha*	
3	*bieid, biaid*	*ro bia*	*bid*	*ni ba*	*no biad*	*bed, ro pad*
rel.	*bias*		*bes*			
pl. 1	*bemmit*	*ni piam*	*bimmi*			*bemmis*
2		*ni bieid, bied*				
3	*bieit, biait, beit*	*ni biat*	*bit*	*ro pat*		*robtis.*
rel.	*beite*		*beta*			

X.

PARTICLES.

1. NEGATION.

390. Negation in the principal sentence is expressed by *ni* (*nī*), in dependent and relative sentences *na, nach, nad* (*ná, nách, nád*). The negative generally stands first in a sentence and can only be preceded by a conjunction, or in a relative sentence by a preposition, and in an interrogative sentence by the interrogative particle. *Na* and *nach* are also used with the imperative and conjunctive in principal sentences. Neither ...nor: *ni...ná*.

391. For *ní, ni con* often occurs, and later *no co, nocho, nochon*, literally not that; the counterpart of which is the strong assertion *ni nad* non quin.

In the relative *nand* (*nant*) qui, quæ, quod non est, pl. *nandat* besides a pronominal element a verbal form is contained (cf. § 387).

2. QUESTION AND ANSWER.

392. The interrogative particle is *in* (*inn*) always with a retained nasal, but it is written *im* before *b*. In the indirect question *dús in* (*dús* for *do fiuss* ad sciendum) is used. "Why" is expressed by *ca, co;* "why not" by *cani* (*cain*), *cini*.

In the double question, the Latin utrum...an is expressed by *in...fa* (*ba*), and the Latin utrum...anuon or necne by *in...fanacc*. The rhetorical question is introduced by *inná, innád* or...not, Latin annon.

393. *Acc, aicc* as well as *naicc, natho, nitho* stand for no. In direct speech the affirmative particles *êm, ám* are often met with in the sense of surely, verily, in sooth.

3. CONJUNCTIONS.

394. Conjunctions of principal sentences copulative, disjunctive, adversative or causal are the following:

ocus, acus
is } and
sceo

dana, dono
cid, cit (cf. § 396) } also

no, ná or

immorro*
noch } but, yet
cammaib

act, acht besides, except, but
acht...nammá except only, but only
acht chena
arai, araide } however, yet

didiu hence
tra, thra
dino } thence, then

idón namely, Latin id est.
ar, air for
emith...emith as well as
im...im (for *imb, im-ba*)
im...fa (ba) } sive...sive
ce...ce, cid...cid

méit...méit, quantum...tantum, sicut...ita
ni hed a méit...act not only...but also
ni...na neither...nor.

395. Some conjunctions are almost invariably written in abbreviation in ancient MSS.:

ocus and: 7, abbreviation for Latin et,
no or: *l̄*, abbreviation for Latin vel,
idon namely: *.i.*, abbreviation for Latin id est,
immorro but: *im̄*.
dana dono, dino: *dā, dō, dī*. For the different marks of abbreviation in Old Irish, see Zimmer, Glossæ Hib. p. liii.

396. The following list includes the most important of those conjunctions which introduce a secondary proposition or a subordinate sentence:

(a) CONDITIONAL.

má Greek εἰ
dia n- Greek ἐάν, ὅταν
mani, main if not
cén (céin) co although not
cen má unless

(b) CONCESSIVE.

ce, ci, cia although
cid, cesu, ciasu quamvis sit
cit, cetu quamvis sint.

---

* There seems to be an old Irish form *immurgu*, e.g. in the poems of the Milan Codex (Goid.² p. 18, and p. 20).

X. Particles.

To *cen má* belong *cenmitha, cenmotha* save, except. On *cid, cit* cf. § 394 and § 387.

397.

(c) Temporal.

a n-, *in tan, in tain*} when
resiu before
iarsindi after

céin, céine so long as, whilst
ó since
co, co n-, con until
lase whilst that, through.

(d) Comparative.

amail, amal just as, as if

(e) Causal.

óir (úair), óre
fo bith, fo bithin
dég, déig, dáig } because cf. § 240
fo dáig, fo dagin
ol, ol suide

ol sodain
arindí
isindí
sech.

The sentence at the head of which these conjunctions are is a relative sentence. The relative pronoun is often omitted.

398. *Sech* should also be included among the causal conjunctions. The original sense is beyond that, besides that, but it is not rarely used in the sense of *quoniam, siquidem*.

The formula *sech is* has much the sense of the Latin *nimirum*. The form *sechib hé, sechip hé, sechi hé* without the remainder of the verbal form has much the sense of the Latin *quicunque*.

399.

(f) Final.

ara n-
co, con, co ro, corro, cor} that
arna, arnach, arnad
cona, conna, connach, coni} lest
ar dáig na

(g) Consecutive.

co, co n-
co ro, corro, cor} that, so that
cona, conna
connach} so that not
cen con without that.

If *ara n-* (that) comes to stand before a double consonant, *ari n-* appears instead of it: *ari m-bad* ut esset, cf. § 7.

400. It is very difficult to prove any distinction of meaning between the forms *co, co n-, con*. This conjunction answers to the German dass in declaratory sentences (negative *coni, cona, conna, connach*), and also to the German da at the head of principal sentences standing in the second place, to the German und da in simple narration, and lastly often stands at the head of a principal sentence before the verb, when it is apparently redundant (negative *ni con, no co, nochon* § 391).

4. PARTICLES USED AS PREFIXES.

401. To the list of particles which as prefixes modify the sense of a noun especially belong the privative particles *an-, in-, am-, es-, é-, di-*: *firén* just, *an-firén* unjust; *asse* easy, *anse* difficult; *gnáth* known, *in-gnad* extraordinary; *reid* smooth, *am-reid* uneven; *cara* friend, *es-care* enemy; *nert* strength, *é-nirt* weak; *cosmil* like, *é-csamil* unlike, different; *treb* dwelling, *di-thrub* desert (also a form with a nasal: *búaid* victory, *dim-buaid* discomfiture).

Whilst these particles not merely negative the sense of the nouns but give them a reverse sense, the noteworthy particles *neb-, neph-* answer in composition to a bare not (the German nicht) and often represent the negative before an infinitive: *tri neb-airitin lóge* through not taking reward; *neph-fodlide* indivisible; *neb-marbtu* immortality; *ní* something, *neph-ní* nothing.

402. The particles *su-, so-* and *du-, do-*, both causing aspiration (cf. § 96), express the sense of goodness and badness like the Greek εὐ- and δύσ-: *cruth* form, *so-chruth* beautiful, *do-chruth* ugly, later by transition into the *i*-declension *sochraid, dochraid* (cf. Latin deformis from forma). The same antithesis is expressed by the adjectives *deg-, dag-* and *droch-* (Sanskrit *druh*): *dag-gním* a good deed, *drog-gním* a bad deed.

The particle *mí* (causing aspiration) turns the meaning of a noun simply in malam partem: *gním* deed, *mí-gním* misdeed; *toimtiu* opinion, *mí-thoimtiu* evil feeling.

403. The particles *ro-*, *for-*, *ér-* have an intensitive sense: *ro-mór* too great, very great; *ro-cháin* very beautiful; *in ro-grad* the great love; *for-granna* very ugly; *for-derg* very red; *érchosmil* very like.

Dí- and *der-* are also used intensitively: *dí-mór* and *der-már* hugely great; but on the other hand *dí* (§ 401) is also privative as is *der-*: *der-óil* penuria, *for-óil* abundantia. This *der-* is also found in composition with verbs: *con der-manammar* ut obliviscamur, cf. *do-moiniur* puto § 336. In *arna der-gaba* ne deficiat, beside *dí-gbail* deminutio, the *der-* changes with *dí-* and appears, at least in this case, to be derived from *dí-ro*. This also appears to be the origin of the intensitive *der-* for besides *ó der-chóiniud* Gloss on abundantiori tristitia Wb. 14^d is also found *dero-chóinet* desperant 21^b (Z.^{2} 864).

ADDENDA.

1[b]. In Old Irish the long accent, especially as regards *i* and *u* is frequently expressed by doubling the vowel: *gniim* factum, *sciith* molestia, *rúun* mysterium. As *líi, li* is related to the Latin *livor*, and *clúu, clú* to the Sanskrit *çravas*, it is possible that the double vowel in certain words may have a certain etymological justification, but not always, as e.g. in *ríi* = Latin *rex*.

25[b]. In most pure and spurious diphthongs the long accent properly belongs to the first element, which, judging from the modern pronunciation, was in most cases the predominant vowel. But in MSS. the long accent often stands on the second element, even if this is only a vowel of infection (§ 18): *cián* long, *sciám* Latin schema, *coínid* he wails, *huáin* of us, *buáid* victory, for the more correct *cían, scíam, cóinid, húain, búaid*; *hi ceím* in gradum (nom. pl. *cémenn* § 162), *breíc* (acc. sg. of *brēc* mendacium), *buaíd* victory (gen. *búada* § 122), *baí* fuit, for the more correct *céim, bréic, búaid, bái*, and so perhaps also *taích* Ml. 32[b], 24 for *táich* (cf. § 295).

In many cases the decision is difficult. Probably the old forms *éonu* (§ 22, acc. pl. of *én* bird § 74) and *éoin* (nom. pl.) ought to be *eónu, eóin*. In the same way *ad-géuin* cognovit, *dor-raid-chíuir* quos redemit (3 sg. perf. § 298) should be *ad-geúin, dor-raid-chiúir*, but, on the other hand, the *eo* of the future, mentioned § 281, is written *eó* in the modern language, see O'Donovan's Grammar, p. 195. In the same way the *o* in the words *ceol* music, *seol* sail (which are already so written in Old Irish), predominates so that the writing *ceól*, *seól* cannot be disputed.

25ᶜ. The long accent is also met with over syllables in which two vowels which originally belonged to separate syllables coalesce to one syllable (cf. § 81). Originally in most such cases the first vowel may have predominated in the pronunciation. For Old Irish at any rate *ina díaid* after him (*dead* finis, Cymr. *diwedd*), *téora* f. three, *bíu*, *béo* living (§ 31), *fríu* towards them (*fri* for *frith*, § 174), *líu*, *léo* with them, appear to be more accurate than *ina diáid, teóra, biú, beó, friú, liú, leó*. The same is true as to *drúi* Druid, gen. *drúad*, dat. *drúid* and *druí, druád, druíd*. The Modern Irish *draoi* Druid is pronounced as with a short *u* and a long *i*.

25ᵈ. In the 1 and 3 pl. of the secondary tenses -*mais*, -*tais*, also appear for -*mís*, -*tís*. Here the written form is not correctly *déntáis* they would do, but *déntais*, for the *a* is in such cases only introduced in consequence of an existing or once existing broad vowel in the preceding syllable. Cf. § 254ᵇ.

25ᵉ. In Old Irish a long accent often appears over short vowels before a double consonant, especially before grouped or doubled *r, l, n*: *márb* dead, *lóndas* indignatio (Ml. 18ᵃ, 10 ed. Ascoli), *ánd* here (Ml. 26ᶜ, 2), *óll* amplus (Ml. 20ᵃ, 3). However this inclination to pronounce the vowel long in such words has been neither permanent nor consistently carried out, although it may have been repeated in different periods and dialects.

25ᶠ. In Middle Irish the sign of length is sometimes found in places where it has not been proved in Old Irish, e.g. over the heavy deponent terminations in -*ar*: 3 sg. *ro charastár* amavit, 1 pl. *do-deochammár* venimus, 3 pl. *asbertatár* dixerunt, 3 pl. *bátár* fuerunt. This lengthening seems to have come in under the influence of a secondary tone which requires consideration in Irish for words of several syllables.

Addenda. 127

25ᵉ. The chief accent was early thrown back from the termination of the word, as may be concluded from the mutilation of the syllables of flexion. But certain phonetic appearances demonstrate positively many cases in which it did not stand on the radical syllable. Cf. §§ 25, 42, 46, 60, 61, 62, 77, 81, 83, 108ᵇ, 247, 275, 286, 295, 300, 325.

25ʰ. In verse a short terminal vowel not unfrequently rhymes with a long syllable of a stem. For example in a poem of the Codex S. Pauli *cele* (socius) rhymes with *ré* (time), and *messe* (I) with *glé* (splendidus). Also Sc. 37, 15 *airgdidu* (dat. of *airgdide* silver) with *clú* (fame). From these and similar appearances it would be unsafe without further evidence to consider as long numerous terminal syllables which are never found in Old Irish prose with a long mark upon them.

207ᵇ. The possessive pronouns of the third person are in Old Irish (e.g. in the Milan Codex) very often found with a long mark: *á ainm* his name, *á n-íc* their salvation.

254ᵇ. The 1 and 2 pl. active of the absolute flexion are in Old Irish but slightly supported by MSS., and the same is true in later Irish of the past tenses, in which the absolute flexion comes gradually to be altogether disused. To judge from the existing material the oldest forms of the terminations are *-me* and *-mit* in the 1st and *-te* in the 2 pl.; present *bermme*, *bermmit*, S-past *carsimme* (*carste*), and so on; also in § 275 it ought to be (*cechnimme*), "*bérmme*." But, especially in Middle Irish and Modern Irish there are also forms in *-mi*, *-mai*, *-ti*, *-tai*, which Stokes has taken into his paradigms: *carstai* amavistis, *téstai* ibitis, *bérmai* feremus; the *a* in *-mai*, *-tai* is only introduced in consequence of a suppressed broad vowel before the termination especially when the preceding syllable contains no slender vowel, so *bérmai* for *bérammi*. In Modern Irish the *i* of this termination (probably under the influence of a secondary tone) is pronounced long, as is shown by O'Donovan, Gr., p. 219, *beirimíd* ferimus, *beirthí*, *beirthídh* (*dh* at the end is silent, cf. § 3) fertis. If the radical syllable contains a broad vowel *aoi* (i.e. a long *i* preceded by a slightly articulated dull vowel *ŭī*) has established itself in the termination, *molamaoid* we praise, *moltaoi* ye praise, *molfamaoid* we shall praise. Cf. p. 126, § 25ᵈ.

254ᶜ. From the ordinary formation of the relative of the 3 sg. in *-es, -as* there deviate: *file* qui est § 388, *teite* qui it, the relative form of *téit*, i.e. *do-éit* § 264ᶜ; to which may be added the perfect form *boie* qui erat (Goid.² p. 87, Book of Armagh).

But there also occurs a preterite *teite, teiti* he went, besides *téit*, without any relative signification. In the same way *luide* he went, with *luid* § 302. Stokes (Beitr. zur Vergl. Sprachforsch. VII. p. 40, 42) is inclined in such cases to separate a pronoun -*e*, -*i* sometimes as nominative, sometimes as dative or accusative: *leigth-i duillen* he threw a javelin; *geibth-i Loeg cloich* Loeg takes it, a stone; *is Cuchulainn cobarthe*, it is Cuculainn who would have helped him. Cf. § 205 et seq., but on the other hand there are the preterites ending in *-ta, -tha* § 309, to which perhaps some of these forms belong e.g. *budigthe* he thanked T. E. 14.

272ᵇ. Stokes has lately (Three Middle-Irish Homilies, Preface, p. ix) explained as of a particular imperfect form, though not expressly *ro chreti*, yet similar forms of verbs of the II conjugation, e.g. *ro labra* he spake, *ro scribai* he wrote, and especially (without *ro*) *adcobra* he would, Hy. 2, 45.

276ᵇ. A reduplicated future has also been proved in *carim* II amo: *ni con chechrat act ni bas tol doib* they will only love, what is their desire (Gloss on et erunt homines se ipsos amantes Wb. 30ᶜ, 2); as a rule it forms the B-future, § 282.

289ᵇ. Difficult to explain is *dudichestar (i. miastair i. huaid fesin)*, Gloss on ducetur in the clause gravis illi vita tristisque ducetur Ml. 30ᵈ. The future passive should be *du-diastar*, as is shown by *du-diastae* § 321 and *du-di* § 287.

PIECES FOR READING.

Pieces V., VI. have not hitherto been printed. The Echtra Condla Chaim was published by O'Beirne Crowe, Journal Arch. and Hist. Association, 1874, p. 118. The learner had better begin with the Old Irish sentences in I. Of the remaining pieces V. is especially easy, for IV. Hennessy's exact translation may be examined. Italics indicate the expansion of a contraction in the MS.

I.

SENTENCES FROM THE OLD IRISH GLOSSED MSS.

1. Ní mebul lemm precept soscéli (Wb. 1ᵇ).
2. Is uisse lóg a saithir do chách (Wb. 29ᵃ).
3. Is sí ar n-ires hi sin atá mor dechur etir deacht ocus doinacht (Ml. 26ᵇ).
4. Is triit dorolgetha ar pecthi duún (Wb. 26ᶜ).
5. Ni ru foraithmenair Duid isin t-salm so a n-durigni Abisolón fris (Ml. 24ᶜ).
6. Denid attlugud buide do Dia di cach maith dogní frib (Wb. 27ᵃ).
7. Sech ni coimnactar ar namit son fortanbristisni (Gloss on obprimi nequivimus Ml. 135ᵇ).
8. Ni bat litre nota aram cia scríbtair hi fers (Sg. 6ᵇ).
9. Amal fongníter ídil, síc fognither donaib ánib (Wb. 27ᵇ).
10. Na taibred cách úaib bréic imm alaile (Wb. 27ᵇ).
11. Gaibid immib a n-etach macc cóimsa, amal nondad maicc cóima (Induite vos ergo, sicut electi dei sancti et dilecti per viscera misericordiæ, benignitatem...Wb. 27ᵇ).
12. Attlugud boide do Dia di bar n-ícc trit-som (Wb. 27ᶜ).

13. Adib moga-si dano, atá far cóimdiu innim (Wb. 27ᶜ).
14. Is airi am cimbid-se hore no predchim in rúin sin (Wb. 27ᶜ).
15. Bid di bar n-ág-si ron bia-ni indocbál (Wb. 25ᵃ).
16. Is hé in tecttaire maith condaig indocbáil dia thigerni (Wb. 8ᵈ).
17. Ro bad bethu dom, dian chomalninn (Wb. 3ᶜ).
18. Ni riat na dánu diadi ar a n-indeb domunde (Wb. 28ᶜ).
19. Ni tairmthecht rechto, mani airgara recht (Wb. 2ᶜ).
20. Sech ni thartsat som ní comtachtmar-ni (Wb. 24ᵇ).
21. Berir do imchomarc uaidib (Wb. 31ᵈ).
22. Ar osailcther hires tri degním ; innarbar (read innarbanar) hires dano trí droch-gnimu (Ml. 14ᶜ).
23. Ceni tormastar ho méit is trom cenae ho aicniud ut sunt lapides (Ml. 20ᵃ).
24. Tairchechuin resíu forchuimsed (Wb. 4ᵈ).
25. Nob sóirfa-si Dia dinab fochidib (Wb. 11ᵇ).
26. Is glé lim-sa rom bia buáid (Wb. 11ᵃ).
27. Nachin rogba uáll (Wb. 15ᵈ).
28. Mani ro chosca som a muntir in tain bíis cen grád, ni uisse toisigecht sochuide do (Wb. 28ᵇ).
29. Is immaille ro scaich in bolc do blith ocus in t-immun do denam (Lib. Hy. 11ᵃ).
30. Dobert goiste imma bragait fadesin conid marb, huare nad n-digni Abisolón a chomairli (Ml. 23ᵇ).
31. Foillsigthir as n-isel in dóinacht iar n-aicniud, huare as in deacht fodaraithmine *ocus* no da fortachtaigedar (Ml. 25ᶜ).
32. Is hed dí (or dino) alligitime, scarad fri indeb in domuin ocus tol Dǽ do dénum (Gloss on non coronatur nisi legitime certaverit, Wb. 30ᵃ).
33. Is do thabirt díglae berid in claideb sin (Wb. 6ᵃ).
34. "Cia atagegalldathar" ol Sencha. "Atagegallar-sa" ol Triscoth (L. U. p. 19ᵇ).
35. Cid bec cid mar ind inducbál ó dia tar hesi denmo ind libuir, bith má de do buith dait-siu hi coimthecht oco (Sg. 2ᵃ).

36. Aní dodesta di chomalnad cæsta Christ dom-sa, is occa attóo; is héd di*no* desta di suidiu dul martre tar far cennsi (Wb. 26ᵈ).

37. Ató oc combáig friss im sechim a gníme et im gabáil desimrechte de, conroissinn cutrummus friss et congní-som frimsa oc suidiu (Wb. 26ᵈ).

38. Manid tesarbi ní di maith assa gnímaib in tain rombói etir tuáith is uisso a airitiu i n-æclis (sc. viduæ, Wb. 28ᵈ).

39ᵃ. Forcain som híc servos obidire et servire dominis arna érbarat domini robtar irlithi ar moge dúun resíu tised hiress robtar anirlithi iarum; ní áil tra in sin do epert ol se-som ar ni do forcitul anirlatad dodechuid (Wb. 27ᶜ).

39ᵇ. Arna ërbarthar roptar irlithi ar moge dún, con tanicc hiress, et it anirlithi iarum (Wb. 29ᵇ).

40. In tan forcomnacuir in gním so crochtha Crist *ocus* dodechuid temel tarsin gréin, asrubartatar fir betho: tiagar huáin dochum hI(ru)salem dús cid forchomnacuir indi ind inaim so, air is ingnad linn a n-adciam (Ml. 16ᵉ).

41. In tan tét a laithe di chiunn cosnaib gnimaib *ocus* cosnaib imnedaib gniter and, dotét iarum imthanu aidche tar hæsi co n-dermanammar-ni inna imned sin i m-biam isind laithiu tri chumsanad inna aidche dod-iarmorat (Ml. 21ᶜ).

42. Ba bés leu-som dobertis da boc leu dochum tempuil *ocus* no leicthe indala n-ái fon díthrub co pecad in popuil *ocus* dobertis maldachta foir *ocus* noircthe di*no* and o popul tar cenn a pectha ind aile (Tur. 110ᶜ).

43. A*mal* dotéit side do gabáil báignil in tan nád n-acastar et nád forchluinter, isamlid dorriga Dia do bráth in tain nád tomnibther a thíchtu (Wb. 25ᵇ).

44. Cia rud chualatar ilbélre et ce nus labratar, ni pat ferr de; is follus di*no* nanmá ar bríg labrad ilbélre (Wb. 12ᵈ).

45. In tan durairngert Dia du Abracham a maith sin, ducuitig tarais fadeissin ar ni robe nech bad huaisliu tar a toissed (Wb. 33ᵈ).

46. Is di lus bis forsnaib caircib dognither in chorcur buide (Tur. 115).

47. Isel fri art, tailciud fri gargg, cáith a uuair, cach óin dod-géna samlid bid reid riam cach n-amreid (Bern. 117ᵃ).

48. Is dosaidi-siu for hirubinaib co n-dárbais frecndarcus du fortachtae dunaib trebaib so dia soirad i. triub Effraim rl. (Ml. 209).

49. Frange esurienti panem tuum et egenos vagosque induc in domum tuum, et cum videris nudum cooperi eum et carnem tuum ne despexeris. A duine fíreoin ar Ísu roind do bairgin frisin m-bocht tabair cendsa ocus aigidecht don fairind recait a less. Dia n-accara nech cen etach tabair etach dó. Cid iat do charait fen atchithera i m-bochta airchis diib (Leabh. Breac p. 47ᵇ, 37 ; dia faccara nech cen etach imbe ibid. p. 67ᵇ, 21).

50. Caput Christi oculus Isaiæ frons nassium Noé labia lingua Salomonis collum Temathei mens Beniamín pectus Pauli unctus Iohannis fides Abrache. scs. scs. scs. dns. ds. sabaoth.— Cauir[1] ani siu cach dia im du chenn ar chenngalar iarna gabáil dobir da sale it bais ocus dabir im du da are ocus fort chulatha ocus cani du pater fo thrí lase ocus dobir cros dit sailiu for ochtar do chinn ocus dogní a tóirand sa dano U. fort chiunn.

51. (After another spell.) Focertar in so do grés it bois láin di uisciu oc indlut ocus dabir it béulu ocus imbir in da mér ata nessam do lutain it bélaib cechtar ái á leth (from the Cod. Sg. Z.² p. 949).

52. Ní taibre grád for nech causa a pectha no a chaingníma ar biit alaili and ro finnatar a pecthe resíu docói grád forru, alaili is iarum ro finnatar; berir dano fri laa brátha (Wb. 29ᵃ).

[1] Canir (Zimmer).

II.

Verse from the Codex Sangallensis.

The text is from Grammatica Celtica (ed. 2), p. 953, and Nigra, Reliquie Celtiche, i. p. 18 ff. Cf. Stokes, Beitr. zur Vergl. Spr. viii. p. 320; Irish Glosses, pp. 44, 62, 70.

1 Sg. p. 112:
Is acher in gáith innocht   fufuasna fairggæ findfolt
ni ágor reimm mora minn   dond laechraid lainn oa Lochlind.

2 Sg. p. 203:
Dom farcai fidbaidæ fál   fom chain lóid luin lúad nad cél
huas mo lebrán indlínech   fom chain trírech inna n-én.

3 Sg. p. 204:
Fomm chain cói menn medair mass   hi m-brot glass de dindgnaib doss
debrath n-om choim*m*diu cóima   cáin scríbaim*m* foroid...[1]

4 Sg. p. 229:
Gaib do chuil isin charcair   ni ro ís chluim na colcaid
truag in sin amail bachal   rot giuil ind srathar dodcaid.

[1] The two absent syllables are unfortunately illegible in the MS. The last word must be a rhyme to *doss*. *foroid* with the defective penultimate syllable of the verse may contain a rhyme to *cóima*. Cf. *indlinech ... trírech* 2, 2; *mass ... glass* 3, 1. Perhaps *fo'roida ross?*

III.

ECTRA CONDLA CHAIM MAIC CHUIND CHETCHATHAIG IN SO.
(L. U. p. 120.)

The same text is found in H. 2. 16 (T. C. D.) col. 399, ibid. col. 914, Egerton, 1783 (Brit. Mus.) and other MSS.

1. Cid día n-apar Art Óenfer? Ni *insa*. Lá ro bói Condla Ruád mac Cuind Chetchath*aig* for láim a athar i n-uachtor Usnig, co n-acca in mnaí i n-etuch anetarguaid na doch*um*. Asb*er*t Condla: "Can dodeochad a ben?" or so. "Dodeochad-sa" *for* in ben "a tírib beó áit inna bí bás nó peccad na imorbus. Domelom fleda buána can rithgnom, cáincomrac leind c*en* debaid. Síd mór itaam, conid de suidib nonn ainmnigth*er* ǽs síde." "Cia a gillai" ol Cond fria m*ac* "acailli?" úair ni acca nech in mnaí acht Condla a óenur. 2. Ro recair in ben:

(R.) "Adgladadar mnaí n-óic n-alaind sochen*eoil* nad fresci bas na sentaid ro charus Condla Ruád cotn-gairim do Maig Mell inid rí boadag bidsuthain rí cen gol cen mairg inna thír ó gabais flaith.

(R.) Tair lim a Condlai Ruáid muinbric caindeldeirg barr bude fordotá oás gnuís corcorda bidordan do rígdelbæ má chotum-éitís ní chrínfa do delb a hóitiu a haldi co bráth brindach."

3. Asb*er*t Cond fria druid, Corán a ainm side, ar ro chuálatár uili an ro rádi in ben cen co n-acatár:

(R.) "Not álim a Choráin mórchetlaig[1] mordanaig forb*ón*d dodom-anic as dom moó airli as dom moo cumachtu níth náchim thánic o gabsu flaith mu imchomruc delb nemaicside cotom-éicnigidar immum macc rocháin d'airchelad tre-thoath bandu dí[2] láim rígdai brectu[3] ban m-berir."

Do chachain iarom in druí *for*sin n-guth inna mná connach

---
[1] Gloss i. canas chetla.
[2] The first copy in H. 2. 16 has di*m*.
[3] The other MSS. have brechtaib.

cúala nech guth na mná ocus conna haccai Condla in mnaí
ond úair sin. 4. In tan trá luide in ben ass re rochetul in
druad dochorastár ubull do Condlu. Boi Condla co cend mís
mís[1] cen mir cen dig cen biád. Nir bo fíu leis nách tuára aile
do thomailt acht a ubull. Ní dígbad ni dia úbull cacha tomled
de *acht* bá ógslan beus. Gabais eólchaire íarom inní Condla
imon mnaí atconnairc. Allá bá lán a mí baí for láim a athar
im-Maig Archomnin inti Condla, *conn*-aca chuci in mnaí cétna
a n-asbert fris:

(R.) "Nallsuide[2] saides Condla eter marbu duthainai oc
idnaidiu éca úathmair. Tot-churethar bíi bithbi at gérat do
dáinib Tethrach ar-dot-chiat cach dia i n-dálaib t athardai eter
du gnathu inmaini."

5. Amal ro chuala Cond guth na mna, asbert fria muintir:
"Gairid dam in druíd atchíu doreilced a tenga di indiu." Asbert in ben la sodain:

(R.) "A Chuind Chetcathaig druidecht nís gradaigther ar
is bec ro soich for messu ar trág máir. Firién co n-ilmuinteraib
ilib adamraib motát-icfa a recht conscéra brichta druád tardechta ar bélaib demuin duib dolbthig."

Ba ingnad tra la Cond ni con taidbred Condla aithesc do
neoch acht tísad in ben. "In deochaid" ol Cond "fot menmain-siu a radas in ben a Condlai?" Asbert Condla "Ní
reid dam sech cach caraim mo dóini. Rom gab dano eolchaire
immon mnai." 6. Ro frecart in ben and-side, co n-epert in so:

(R.) "Tathut airunsur álaib fri tóind t'eólchaire oadib
    im loing glano condrísmaís ma róismais síd boadaig.

(R.) Fil tír n-aill nad bu messu do saigid
    atchiú tairnid in gréin n-gil cid cían ricfam rían n-
    adaig.

(R.) Is *ed* a tír subatar menmain cáich dotimchealla
    ni fil cenel and nammá *acht* mná *ocus* ingena."[3]

---

[1] The other MSS. omit the second mís.
[2] Over *nallsuide* is the gloss *i. uasal*.
[3] The stops and the division of the verses are according to the MS.

7. O tharnic dond ingin a haithesc, foceird Condla iar sudiu bedg uádib co m-boí isind noi glano, i. isin churach comthend commaidi glanta. Atconnarcatar uadib mod nad mod i. in fat ro siacht ind radairc a roisc. Ro raíset iarom in muir uádib *ocus* ni aicessa o sin ille ocus ní fes cid dollotar. A m-bátar *for* a n-imrátib isind airiucht co n-aicet Art chucu. "Is a oenur d'Art indiu" ol Cond "dóig ni fil bráthair." "Buádfocol an ro radis" or Coran "iss *ed* ainm fo*r*bia co bráth" Art Óenfer, conid de ro len in t-ainm riam o sin immach.

IV.

FOTHA CATHA CNUCHA IN SO.

(L. U. Facs. p. 41; translated by W. M. Hennessy, Rev. Celt. II. p. 86 et seq.).

1. Dia m-bói Cathair Mór mac Fedelmthi Firurglais m*aic* Corm*aic* Geltai Gáith irrigi Temrach ocus Cond Cétchathach hi Cenandos hi f*er*and rigdomna, boi drúi amra la Cathair, i. Nuadu mac Achi m*aic* Dathi m*aic* Brocain m*aic* Fintain do Thuaith Dathi a Bregaib. Boí in drui oc iarraid feraind il-Laignib for Cathair, ar ro fiti*r* co m-bad il-Laignib no beth a chomarbus. Dobe*ir* Cathair a thoga tíri dó. Iss *ed* ferand ro thog in drui i. Almu. Robi ro bo banceli do Nuádait[1] i. Almu ingen Becain.

2. Ro ch*um*taiged dún ocan druid and-sin i n-Almain ocus ro comled alamu dia sund cor bo ængel uli, ocus co m-bad de-sin no beth Almu fo*rr*i, dia n-ebrad:

Oengel in dun dremni drend   mar no gabad æl Erend
dond alamain tuc dia thig   is de ata Almu ar Almain.

Ro boí ben Nuádat i. Almu oc iarraid a anma do bith fo*r*sin cnuc ocus tucad di-si ind ascid sin, i. a ainm do bith fo*r*sin chnuc, ar is inti ro ad*n*acht iar tain, dia n-ebrad.

Almu rop alaind in b*en*   b*en* Nuadat moír m*aic* Aiched
ro cuinnig ba fír in dál   a ainm fo*r* in cnuc comlán.

[1] In the facsimile Nuádhait.

Pieces for Reading. 137

3. Bói mac sainemail oc Nuadait i. Tadg mac Nuadat. Ráiriu ingen Duind Duma a banchéli sidé. Druí amra dana Tadg. Tanic bás do Núadait ocus ro ácaib a dún amal ro bói oc a mac, ocus iss e Tadg bá druí do Chatbáir dar ési a athar. Bert Raíriu ingin do Thadg i. Murni Muncaim a ainm. Ro as gnoé móir in n-ingin i sin co m-bitís maic ríg ocus ro-flatha na Erend oc a tochra. Bói dana Cummall mac Trenmóir rígfennid hErend fri láim Cuind. Boi sidé dana cumma cháich oc iarraid na ingine. Dobreth Nuadó cra fair¹ ar ro fitir co m-bad tremit no biad scarad dó fri Almain. Inund mathair do Chumall ocus d'athair Cuind, i. do Fedelmid Rechtmar. Tic trá Cumall² ocus berid ar écin Murni for aithed leis ar ní thucad dó chena hí.

4. Tic Tadg co Cond ocus innisid dó a sarugud dó Chumall, ocus gabais fri grisad Cuind ocus oc a imdercad. Fáidid Cond techta co Cumall ocus asbert fris Ériu d'ácbáil nó a ingen do thabairt do Thadg. Asbert Cumall na tibred acht is cach ní dobérad ocus ni bád sí in ben. Fáidis Cond a amsaig ocus Urgrend mac Lugdach Cuirr rí Luagni, ocus Dáiri Derc mac Echach ocus Áed a mac (is fris-side atberthe Goll íar tain) do saigid Cummaill.

5. Tinolaid Cumall a socraiti chucu ocus doberar cath Cnucha etorro ocus marbtair Cummall and ocus curthir ár a muntiri. Dofuit Cumall la Goll mac Morna. Gonais Luchet Goll ina rosc cor mill a suil conid de rod lil Goll de, conid de asbert:

Áed ba ainm do mac Dáiri diar gǽt Luchet co n-áni
O ro gǽt in laigni trom airi con rate fris Goll.

Márbais Goll Luchet. Is de-sin dan ro bói fich bunaid eter maccu Morna occus Find. Dá ainm ro bátar for Dairi, i. Morna ocus Dairi.

6. Luid Murni iar sin co Cond, ar ro diúlt a athair di ocus nir leic cuci hí, ar ro bo torrach hí, ocus asbert fria mun-

---
¹ In the facsimile far.
² In the facsimile Chumall.

ti*r* a breoad ocus arai nir lam ammudugud fri Cond. Roi boi ind ingen oc a iarfaigid do Chund cinnas dogenad. Asbert Cond "Eirg" *for* se "co Fiacail ma*c* Conchiud co Temraig Mairci ocus dentar th'asait and," ar d*é*rfiur do Ch*u*mall be*n* Fiacla i. Bodball Bendron. Luid Condla gilla Cuind lei dia idnacul, co ranic tech Fiacla co Temraig Mairci. Ro f*e*rad fǽlti frisin n-ingin and-sin ocus ro bo maith arrochtain and. Ro hasaited ind ingen iar tain ocus b*er*t mac ocus dobreta Dem*n*i d'anmum dó.

7. Ailt*i*r in mac iar tain leo cor bo tualaing fogla do denom f*or* cac*h* n-æn rop escarait dó. Fuacraid da*na* cath nó comrac oenfir *for* Tadg *no* lanéraic a athar do thabairt dó. Asbe*r*t Tadg co tibred breith do ind. Rucad in bret ocus is si in breth rucad do, i. Almu am*al* ro bói do lecun do ar dilsi ocus Tadg dia facbail. Doronad amlaid ro facaib Tadg Almain do Find ocus tanic co Túaith Dathi co a f*e*rand duthaig fesin ocus ro aitreb i Cnuc Réin frisi raite*r* Tulach Taidg indiu, ar is uad-som raite*r* Tulach Taidg fria, o sin co sudi ; conid de-sin asb*er*t in so :

Cuinchis Find f*or* Tadg na tor   i C*u*mall mór do marbod
cath ca*n* chardi do cac*h*[1] dáil   *no* comrac oenfir d'fagbail.
Tadg uair nír tualaing catha   i n-agid na ardf*l*atha
ro facaib[2] leis ba loor do   mar ro boi uli Almo.

8. Docoid Find i n-Almain iar tain ocus ro aittreb inti ocus is sí ro bo dun arus bunaid dó céin ro bo beó. Doroni Find ocus Goll síd iar tain ocus doratad eric a athar o claind Morna do Find, ocus batar co sidamail noco tarla etorro i Temair Lúacra imman muic Slanga ocus im Banb Sinna mac Mailenaig do marbad, día n-ebrad :

Ar sin doronsatar síd   Find ocus Goll co*m*meit gnim
co torchair Banb Sinna dé   mon muic hi Temair Luacræ.

---

[1] Hennessy ca*n*.
[2] Facsimile ro fac.

V.

Fragment from the Irish Version of the Historia Britonum of Nennius (L. U. Facs. p. 3).

Gilla Caemgin, who died in 1072, is the reputed author of this version. See O'Curry On the Manners, &c. II. 222.

The British king Guorthigern having been cursed for an offence by the clergy, takes counsel with the Druids as to how he may build a fortress to defend him from his foes the Saxons. A suitable site is found, but the building materials collected each day vanish each night, and it is impossible to raise a firm structure. The Druids declare that the building must be cemented with the blood of a child without father. Such a miraculous child is found. The boy is told by the king what he is threatened with, and puts the pretended wisdom of the Druids to the test. Here begins the fragment. (The Irish version of the Hist. Brit. has been published at length in the Publications of the Irish Archæological Society by Dr Todd from a later MS., the readings of this fragment being given in the notes, 1848.)

1. "Acht chena" ol se "a rí failsigfit-sea fírinne duit-siu, ocus iarfaigim dona druidib ar thús cid atá i foluch fond erlar sa inar fiadnaise." Ro ráidset na druíd "Nochon étammar" ol siat. "Ro fetar-sa" ol se. "Atá loch usci and. Fegtar ocus claiter." Ro claided ocus frith in loch and. "A fathe ind ríg" ol in mac, "abraid cid atá immedon ind locha." "Ni etamar" or siat. "Ro fetar-sa" ol se, "atát da clárchiste mora and, inagid tagid ocus tucthar as." Ocus tucad as. "A druide" ol in mac, "abraid cid atá etir na clarlestraib út." Ocus ni etatar. "Ro fetar-sa" ol se "atá seolbrat and ocus tuctar as." Ocus frith in seol timmarcte etir na da chlárchiste. 2. "Abraid a éolcho" ol in mac, "cid atá immedon ind étaig út." Ocus ni ro recratar, ar ni ro tucsatar. "Atat dá crúim and" ol se,

".i. cruim derg ocus cruim gel. Scailter in t-étach." Ro scailed in seolbrat. Ro batar na di chruim ina cotlud and. Ro ráid in mac: "Fégaid-si in-dignet innosse na bíasta." Atraracht cách díb co araile co rabe cechtar de ic sroiniud araile ocus co rabatar ic imletrad ocus ic imithi ocus no innarbad in chruim díb araile co medón in t-iuil ocus in fecht n-aill co a imel. Dorónsat fa thrí fon innasin. In chruim rúad trá ba fand ar thús, ocus ro innarbad co himel ind étaig. In chruim taitnemach im*morro* ba fand fo déoid ocus ro teich isin loch ocus ro tinastar in seol fo chetoir.

3. Ro íarfaig in mac dona druidib: "Innisid" ar se, "cid follsiges in t-ingnad so." "Ni etamar" ar siat. "Dogen-sa" ar in mac "a follsigud dond ríg. Is é in loch flathius in domuin uile. Is é in seól do lathiusa a rí. Is iat na dá chruim na dá nert .i. do nert-su co m-Bretnaib ocus nert Saxan. Do nert-su in chruim ruad, is i ro innarbad ar thús don flathius. Nert Sachsan im*morro* in cruim gel ro gab in seól uile *acht* bec .i. ro gab inis Bretan *acht* bec. Coron innarba nert Bretan fo deoid íat. Tu-su im*morro* a rí Bretan eirg asin dún sa, ar ni chæmais a chumtac ocus sir innis Bretan ocus fógeba do dun fadéin." 4. Ro ráid in rí: "Cia do chomainm-so?" ol se. Ro recair in gilla: "Ambróis" ol se "mo ainm-se." Is é sein in t-Ambrois Gleotic rí Bretan. "Can do cen*el*?" ol in rí. "Consul romanach m'athair-se" ol se, "ocus bíd hé so mo dún." Ro leic Gorthig*ernd* in dun do Ambróis ocus rige iarthair inse Bre*tan* uile ocus tanic cona druidib co túascert inse Bre*tan*, i. cosin ferand dianid ainm Gunnis ocus ro chumtaig dún and i. Cær Gorthigernd.

VI.

Do cheli De *no* di clerech reclesa (LBr. Facs. p. 261ᵇ).

Dia m-bam fo mamm clerchechta   is uasal in bes
athaigem in noebeclais   da cec*h* trath[1] do gres.
In tan clomar in clocan   ni fu*r*ail in bes[2]
tocbam cride solma[3] su*a*s   telcem gnusi ses[4].
Canam p*ate*r ocus gloir   cach tairle[5] trist (.i. co lar)   5
sénam bruinne ocus gnuis   airrde cruchi[6] Cr*i*st.
[7]Arroisam ind ecla*i*s   slechtam co bo tri[8]
nis fillem glun imama[9] i n-dómnaigib[10] De bíí.
Celebram is cuindrigiu*m*m[11]   cen lobra cen lén
sruith in fer adgladamar   coimdiu nime nel.   10
Figlem legem irnaigtiu   cec*h* meit[12] a neirt
feib nunreafeaglat[13] (?)   ina glóir co teirt.
Teit cech gradh ria chomadus   feib dobeba coir
am*al* ainmnigter do cach   otha te*ir*t co nóin.
In t-oes graid don ernaigthi   don oiffrind co c*er*t   15
oes legind do f*or*cetul   feib rotnai[14] a nert.
In[15] ócaes don erlataid   feib ronta a tlí[16]
ar is diles do diabu*l* in[17] corp na déni ní.
Lubair[18] don oes anecnaid   do rer[19] clérig[20] chaid
soethar ecnadu na ghin   sæthar buirb na laim.   20
Celebrad cec*h* entratha[21]   la cech n-ord dogniam
tri slechtain[22] ria celebrad   a tri inna diaid.
Tua ocus díchratu   réthince[23] cen lén[24]
cen fodord cen imchomairb   dlegar da cech oen.

A British Museum MS. Additional 30,512, fol. 20ᵇ, gives the following readings:

[1] in cach trath.   [2] in cís.   [3] solam.   [4] sís.
[5] nachar tairli.   [6] chruichi.   [7] mar ro hissam inn ecclaiss.
[8] thrí.   [9] ni fillem gluine nammá.   [10] indomhnach.
[11] cuinrigein.   [12] cach immeit.   [13] feib na ree fégha lat.
[14] ata.   [15] indocbad.   [16] ind oibad dond humallóit: feib rotha a cl*í*.
[17] without in.   [18] ubar.   [19] reir.   [20] clerech.   [21] œn-.
[22] iii figli.   [23] raithinchi.   [24] chlén.

DICTIONARY.

A.

a (asp.) particle of the vocative.
a (asp.) his (M. N.).
a her (F.).
a, a n- their (plur.).
a, a n-, an who; conj. as.
a, ass out of; *ass, assa.*
Abisolón Absolon.
Abracham Abraham.
abraid, apar from *epiur, epur.*
aca, acca, accai, acatár, acastar from *adcíu.*
ro ácaib from *fácbaim.*
acailli see *adgládur.*
acher Latin *acer.*
Achi IV, 1, *Aiched* 2.
acht conj. except, Latin nisi; but; *acht chena* however.
adaig F. night.
adamra wonderful.
adcíu, adchíu, atchíu I see; *adciam, aicet; accai, acca, aca, acatár; accara, faccara, atchithera; acastar; aicessa.*
adgládur dep. I address, speak with anyone; *adgladadar, adgladamar, atagegallarsa, atagegalldathar;* Act. *acailli.*
adib from *am* I am.
adnacim I bury; *ro adnacht.*
Áed mac Dáiri IV, 4, 5.
ael lime.
áen, óen one (of all genders).
ǽrbarthar from *asbiur.*
áes, óes M. age, collectively the people; *oes legind* the readers (*fer legind* lector).
hǽsi s. *ési.*
ág battle I, 15.
aged face; *i n-agid* with gen. towards.
ágor dep. I fear.
ái s. *indala, cechtar.*
aicessa, aicet from *adcíu.*
aicned N. nature; *iar n-aicniud.*
aidche F. night.
aigidecht F. hospitality.
áil agreeable; *ní áil* I, 39[a].
aile, N. *aill* Latin alius.

ailim I rear; *ailtir*.
ainm N. name; *anma, d'an-munu, dá ainm*.
ainmnigim I name; *ainmnig-ter* VI, 14 read *ainmnigther*.
air, ar prep. before, for; *airi* therefore; *airun* III, 6?
air, ar conj. for.
airchelad III, 3, cf. *arcelim* aufero Sg. 9ᵃ, *arachela* vel *dogaitha* Gloss on quæ frustretur mentes eorum Ml. 31ᵃ; *airchellad* raptus Z² 868.
airchissim I have mercy; *airchissi* parcit Wb. 4ᵉ; *airchis*.
airde N. sign; *airrde* VI. 6.
airecht M. assembly.
airgarim I forbid; *mani airgara*.
airitiu F. reception.
airle F. counsel.
airunsur III, 6.
áit place.
aithed escape, elopement; *for aithed*.
aithesc N. answer.
aittrebaim I dwell; *ro aittreb, aitreb*.
álaib III, 6, cf. grian alaib (i. alaind) a delightful sun Fél. Sep. 3.
alaile Latin alius.
álaind lovely.
alamu IV, 2, *Alaun*? Latin alumen; *dond alamain*.

álde, áilde F. beauty.
álim I beg.
Almu ingen Becain IV, 1.
Almo, Almu now the hill of Allen, near Newbridge, Co. Kildare, Hennessy: *in Almain*.
am I am; *at, is, as* (*as n-isel* I, 31), *adib, it*.
amail, amal prep. and conj. as.
Ambróis Ambrosius, a name of the well-known prophet and magician Merlin, Cymr. Merddin Embrys, according to Nennius identical with a king Ambrois Gleotic, Cymr. Embrys Guletic.
amlaid, amlid thus; *is amlid* it is so, that...
amra wonderful, famous.
amsach from *amos* satellites, mercenary; *a amsaig* his soldiers IV, 4.
an pron. rel. see *a, a n-*.
and there, here, Grk. ἔνθα; *and-side, and-sin* Grk. ἐνταῦθα.
áne F. splendour, deliciæ.
áne Pl. divitiæ; *donuib ánib*.
anecnaid unwise.
anetargnaid wondrous.
aní Latin id quod.
anirlatu disobedience; *anirlatad*.
anirlithe disobedient.

Dictionary. 145

apar from *epiur, epur.*
ar, or, ol Latin inquit.
ar, air prep. before, for; *airi; ar sin* IV, 8 for *iar sin.*
ar, air conj. for.
ara n-, ar a n- conj. that, in order that; *ar na* that not.
ar n- our.
ár defeat.
arai conj. however.
araile Latin alius.
aram F. number.
Archommin see *mag.*
árd high; *ard-flaith.*
ar-dot-chiat III, 4, cf. *nim aircecha* "thou shalt not see me" Rev. Celt. II p. 490.
are M. temple (of head), *im du da are* I, 50.
arna conj. that not.
Art Óenfer Arturus Unicus (O'Flaherty Ogyg. p. 314).
arus dwelling IV, 8.
as from *am.*
ásaim I grow; *ro as* IV, 3.
asait delivery, parturitio; *ro hasaited* she was delivered IV, 6.
asbiur I say; *arna érbarat, ǽrbarthar; asbert, asrubartatar.*
ascid F. request IV, 2.
ass out of, forth, *a, ass.*
at from *am.*
atá, ató see *attóo.*

atberthe from *epiur.*
atchíu see *adcíu.*
atconnairc conspexit; *atconnarcatár.*
athaigim I visit; *athaigem* VI, 2.
athair M. father; *athar.*
atharda patrius, subst. patria III, 7.
atraracht surrexit.
attluchur with and without *buide* gratias ago; *attlugud buide.*
attóo, ató I am; *atá.*

B.

bachal M. "slave," cf. *bachlach* famulus.
baile M. place, town.
báigul, báegul M. danger; *báiguil.*
bairgen F. bread; *bairgin.*
Banb Sinna IV, 8.
banchéli F. wife.
bar n- your.
barr M. top, hair.
bas, bos F. hand; *it bais, bois.*
bás N. death.
bec little, few; *acht bec* all but.
Becan IV, 1.
bedg leap.
béim N. to beat, blow.
béist F. Latin bestia; *na bíasta.*
bél M. lip, mouth; *béulu, ar bélaib* before, towards.

I. G. 10

bélre N. speech.
ben F. woman; *mná, mnái, mnái n-, ban.*
béo living; *bii, bíi, bí.*
berim I bear, bring, bring forth; *berid, bert, berir.*
bés M. custom.
bethu M. life.
beus moreover.
biad N. nutriment, food.
bith M. world; *betho.*
bithbeo eternal; *betho.*
bíu I am; *bí, bíis, i m-biam, biit, dia m-bam, ni bat, ni pat; no beth, ni bád, co m-bad, ro bad, co m-bitis; ro bia, bith, bid; no biad; bói, bái, ro bo, cor bo, nir bo, nad bu, bá, ba, robe, co rabe, rop, bátar, co rabatar, robtar; do buith, do bith; feib do beba* VI, 13?
do blith from *melim.*
bo tri VI, 7 for *fo thri.*
Bodball Bendron Cumall's sister IV, 6.
boadag see *búadach.*
boc M. ram.
bocht poor.
bochta F. poverty.
boide see *buide.*
bois see *bas.*
bolc M. bag.
borb proud, saucy; *buirb.*
brage M. neck; *bragait.*
brat M. cloak; *hi m-brot.*

bráth M. judgment; *brátha, co bráth.*
bráthair M. brother.
brec pied.
bréc F. lie.
brectu III, 3 from *bricht,* read *brechtaib.*
Brega pl. the eastern part of Meath; *a Bregaib* IV, 1.
breo flame; whence *breoad* IV, 5.
Bretan Briton; *co m-Bretnaib.*
breth F. judgment.
bricht charm, spell; *brichta.*
bríg valor.
brindach III, 2?
Brocan IV, 1.
bruinne M. breast.
búadach victorious, lordly; *Boadag* III, 2, *Boadaig* 6.
búadfocol a good word III, 7.
búaid N. victory, triumph.
búan everlasting; *búana.*
bude, buide yellow.
buide, boide, F. thanks.
bunad N. origin, family: *fich bunaid* hereditary feud IV, 5, *arus bunaid* family seat IV, 8.

C.

cach, cech each (adj.).
cách every (subst.); *cáich.*
cacha how many III, 4.
caemais from *cumaing* potest.

cær the Cymric form of the Irish *cathir* town; Caer Gorthigernd V, 4.
cæsta, see *césad*.
cáid holy.
cáin beautiful.
cainel III, 2 for *cainnel*, Latin candela.
can ? whence ?
can for *cen*.
canim I sing; *fom chain, canas, canam, do chachain; cani* I, 50 seems to be the Latin cane.
cara M. friend; *carait*.
caruim I love; *ro charus*.
carcar Latin carcer; *isin charcair*.
carde F. peace; *can chardi*.
carric stone, rock; *forsnaib caircib*.
cath M. battle; *catha*.
cauir from *curim*.
ce, cia although.
cech, cach each (adj.).
cechtar ái, cechtar de each of two.
céin conj. so long as.
céle M. socius; *céle Dé* Culdée (a monk), *do cheli De*.
celebraim Latin celebro, (1) I celebrate, (2) I bid farewell; *celebram, celebrad*.
celim I conceal, I hide; *nad cél*.
cen prep. without; *cen co n-* without that.

Cenandos the town of Kells (Co. Meath) IV, 1.
cendsa F. mansuetudo.
cenél N. kind.
cend, cenn M. head; *cinn, fort chiunn; tét...di chiunn* he goes forth I, 41; *co cend mís* to the end of a month, *tar cenn* for.
cert M. right.
césad M. suffering.
cét- the first; *fochet-óir* straightway.
cét N. hundred; *Cét-chathach* see *Cond*.
cétal N. song; *cetla*.
cétna the first, the same.
chena adv. besides, else; *acht chena* however.
cia ? who ? what ?
cia conj. although; *cid* quamvis sit.
cían remote.
cid ? what ?
cid Latin velut I, 49; *cid... cid* be it...be it.
cimbid M. prisoner.
cinnas ? how ?
claideb M. sword.
claidim I dig; *claiter, ro claided*.
cland F. kin, posterity, clan.
clár M. table; *clár-chiste* flat chest; *clar-lestar* flat vessel.
clerchecht clergy, ecclesiastical condition; *clerchechta*.

clerech M. Latin clericus.
clocán M. bell.
cloch F. stone.
cloor dep. I hear; *clomar*.
clúm F. Latin pluma; *cluim*.
cnoc M. hill; *forsin chnuc*.
Cnoc Réin IV, 7.
Cnucha now Castleknock near Dublin.
co prep. to, after, Latin ad, is used in the formation of adverbs; *cosin; cuci, chuci, chucu*.
co n- prep. with; *cosnaib*.
co n- that, there (in conclusion).
cói cuckoo II, 3.
cóim pretiosus.
cóim dear (?); *maicc cóima* I, 11, *om choimmdiu cóima* II, 3.
cóima, cf. *caomha*, nobility O'Cl.
cóimdiu M. the Lord; *om choimmdiu* II, 3.
cóimas (?) benignitas (?); Gen. *cóimsa* I, 11.
coimnactar from *conicim* I can.
coimthecht M. to accompany, societas.
cóir just.
comadus VI, 13, cf. *comadas conveniens* Z.² 994.
comainm N. cognomen.
comairle F. counsel; *comairli*.
comalnaim I fulfil; *di comalnad*.

comarbus M. succession IV, 1.
combág F. contention, to contend; *oc combáig*.
comlaim I rub; *ro comled* IV, 2
comlán full, whole IV, 2.
commaide III, 7, cf. *maide* "a stick" (Corm. transl. p. 118)?
comméit of equal weight.
comrac M. meeting: *cáinchomracc benevolentia* Wb. 30ᵇ; *comrac óenfir* duel.
comtachtmar from *cuintgim* I beg, I demand.
comthend IV, 7, cf. *is tend mo chris est firmum meum cingulum* Z.² 954.
con conj. that I, 37, IV, 5, until I, 39.
Conchend IV, 6.
Cond Cetchathach Quintus Centimachus 121, rex Hiberniae 177—212 p. Chr. O'Flaherty, Ogyg. p. 313; *Cuind, do Chund*.
condaig from *cuingim* quaero.
Condla Rúad III, 1 et seq.; *a Chondlai*.
condrigim convenio, concurro; *cuindrigiumn* VI, 9; *condrísmaís* III, 6.
congniu cooperor; *congni*.
conid ut sit.
conna, connach conj. except, so that not.
conscéra from *coscraim* I destroy, I conquer.

consul Latin consul.
cor conj. that, so that; *co ro, co rabe, co rabatar.*
Corán III, 3, 7.
corcorda purple coloured.
corcur F. purple.
corp Latin corpus.
colcaid Latin culcita, flock bed.
Cormac Geltai Gáeth IV, 1.
coscim coerceo; *ro chosca* I, 28.
cot-gairim III, 2, from *con-gairim* I call.
cotlud M. to sleep, sleep.
cotom-éicnigidar from *com-éicnigim* cogo.
cotum-éitis from *con-éitgim*, *com-éitgim* indulgeo.
crínaim I vanish.
Críst Christ.
croch F. cross; *cruchi.*
crochad to crucify; *crochtha.*
cros Latin crux I, 50.
cruim F. worm.
cúala from *clunim* I hear; *cúalatár.*
cuci, chuci, chucu from *co* prep. to.
cuil corner, angle.
cuinchis IV, 7 from *cuintgim* I beg, I demand (with *for*).
cuindrech castigatio.
cuindrigium see *condrigim.*
cuingim I beg, demand; *condaig, cuinnig.*
culatha I, 50 "the back parts of the head" (Stokes Ir. Glos. p. 148).
cumachte N. might, *cumachtu.*
Cumall mac Trénmóir Finn's father, IV, 3 et seq., sometimes written *Cummall.*
cumma manner; *cumma cháich* IV, 3.
cumsanad M. to rest, rest.
cumtaigim I· build; *ro chumtaig, rochumtaiged;* inf. *cumtac* for *cumtach* V, 3.
curach boat.
curim, cuirim I put; *cauir* I, 50? *do chorastar* III, 4, *curthir.*
cutrummus M. similarity.

D.

-d- infixed pronoun.
da infixed pronoun I, 31.
da for *do* VI, 2, 24.
dá F. *dí* N. *dá n-* two.
dad I, 11, from *táu.*
dáinib from *duine.*
Dáiri Derc father of *Aed* IV, 4; *do mac Dáiri* 5, cf. *Morna.*
dál F. assembly; *ba fír in dál* IV, 2; *do cach dáil* IV, 7; *i n-dálaib* III, 4.
dam see *do.*
dano, dana conj. also.
dán M. gift; *dánu.*
dar see *tar.*
co n-dárbais I, 48, cf. *tadbat*

demonstrat; *do-ad-badar* demonstratur.
Dathe IV, 1, cf. *Túath Dathi.*
de, di prep. of, Latin de ; *de* thence ; *desin.*
de after the comparative, the Latin eo.
de see *cechtar.*
deacht F. Godbead.
déad end ; *fo déoid* at last V, 2; *inna diaid* after it VI, 2.
debaid F. dispute III, 1.
debrath n-om choimmdiu cóima II, 3 perhaps a form of oath, cf. Patrick's oath *dar mo debroth*, etymologically explained by *dar mo dia m-brátha* (Stokes Three Middle-Irish Hom. p. 26).
dechur N. difference.
degním for *deg-gním, deg-* good.
delb F. form; *delbœ* III, 2.
Demni IV, 6, one of Finn's names.
demon M. demon ; *demuin.*
déním I make, do ; *na déni, denid, dentar ;* inf. *denom, denam, denmo.*
deoch F. to drink, drink ; *cen dig* III, 4.
deochad veni; *deochaid* III, 5, cf. *dodeochad.*
fo déoid V, 2 see *déad.*
derg red.
dermanammar I, 41 from *dermoiniur* I forget.

dérfiur for *derbfiur* F. sœur germaine IV, 6.
desimrecht example; *desimrechte.*
desta for *testa* deest I, 36.
di, de prep. of, Latin de; *dinab, dit, dib, di.*
di see *do.*
dí see *dá.*
dia M. God; *dǽ, dé.*
dia day ; *cach dia* I, 50.
dia see *do.*
dia n- wherefore, conj. as, if.
diabul M. diabolus.
dianid cui est.
diade godlike ; *diadi.*
inna diaid VI, 22, see *déad.*
dichra fervent.
dichratu VI, 23.
dig see *deoch.*
digal revenge ; *diglae* I, 33.
digbaim I diminish, I lessen; *digbad.*
digni from *dogníu* I do, make.
diles proprius VI, 18.
dilse F. property ; *ar dilsi* IV, 7.
dino conj. namely, Latin ergo, igitur.
dindgna hill; *de dindgnaib* II, 3.
dithrub desertum I, 42.
diultaim I deny, refuse ; *ro diúlt* IV, 6, inf. *diltud* negatio Z.² 991.
do, du thy.

do, du prep. to, after; dative and infinitive particle; *don, dond, donaib, dona; dam, dom* (as *dom moó airli* III, 3 ?), *dún, dait, duit, dó, di, dia, dia n-*.

do verbal particle; *do chachain* III, 3; *do chorastar* III, 4; *do-d-esta* I, 36 ?

dobiur, tabur, doberim I give, I take; *dobir, dobeir; dobertis; dobert; dobérad; doberar; dobreta; dobreth*.

docoid, dochóid perf. he went; *docói*.

dochum prep. to; *ina dochum, na dochum*, to him III, 1.

dodcaid poor, unfortunate II, 4, cf. *dothchaid* poor (Corm. Transl. p. 51, 55); *dodcad* infelicitas Wb. 2b (Z.² 647).

dodeochad I came, am come; 2 sg. *dodeocoad*, 3 *dodechuid*.

dod-iarmorat for *do-d-iarm-foratad* I, 41, past pass. with infixed pronoun, to put after.

dodom-anic III, 3, from *tánac*.

dodom-chela III, 6, read *do-d-imchela* from *timchelaim* I surround, perambulate.

dofuit from *tuitim*.

dogáithim illudo, pellicio.

dogníu I do, make; *dogní, digni, dogniam, dignet; durigni; dogen; dogenad; dognither*.

doig verisimilis III, 7 (*doíg*).

dóinacht F. human nature.

dóini see *duine*.

dolbthach gen. *dolbthig* III, 5, from *dolbud* figmentum Wb. 4° (Z.² 352), cf. *doilbtheach*, sorcerer O'R.

dolécim, dollécim I leave, resign, release, throw; *doreilced* III, 5.

doluid, dolluid he went; *dollotar*.

doluigim remitto.

domelim, toimlim I consume; *domelom* III, 1.

dom-farcai II, 2 me cingit (Stokes).

domnach Sunday, *i n-domnaigib* VI, 8.

domun M. world; *domuin*.

domunde worldly.

Dond Duma IV, 3.

dorat he gave; *doratad*.

doreg I shall go; *dorriga*.

doreilced from *dolécim*.

dorolgetha I, 4, from *doluigim*.

doroni he made; *dorónsat; doronsatar, doronad*.

dosaidi-siu sedes I, 48.

doss thicket II, 3.

dothéit, dotét it, venit.

dremne rage; *dremni drend* IV, 2 ("of battle renown," Hennessy).

drend quarrel, battle IV, 2.

drochgním M. ill-deed; *drochgnimu*.

drúi M. druid, magus; *druád, druid, a druide, dona druidib.*
druidecht F. sorcery III, 5.
du, do thy.
dub, black; *duib.*
ducuitig juravit I, 45.
Duid David.
duine, dune M. person; pl. *dóini, do dáinib.*
dul inf. to go.
dún N. stronghold, arx.
durairngred I, 45 from *do-air-con-gairm, tairngrim* I promise.
durigni from *dogníu.*
dús (= *do fíus* ad sciendum) used to introduce an indirect question.
duthaig belonging, own IV, 7.
duthain transient; *et(er) marbu duthainai* III, 4, cf. *suthain* æternus.

E.

é he; *is hé, isse.*
ebrad from *epur.*
éc death; *éca.*
écen F. necessity; *ar écin.*
echtra, ectra expedition (O'D. Gr. 119), adventures (O'C. Mat. 589).
eclais, œclis Latin ecclesia.
écnaid wise; *ecnadu* VI, 20.
éd it; *is héd, ised, issed* (often contracted).

Effraim Ephraim I, 48.
éirgim I arise, stand up; *eirg.*
én M. bird.
én for *aen, áen* VI, 21.
Eocho gen. *Echach* IV, 4.
eola experienced; *a éolcho.*
eólchaire grief.
epiur I say; *epert, apar, atb(er)the, ebrad;* inf. *epert.*
éra "refusal" IV, 3.
éraic, eric F. indemnity, compensation for murder, Old H. G. *wëragëlt* IV, 7, 8.
Eriu Ireland; *Erend.*
erlár M. floor, pavimentum *fond erlar* V, 1.
erlatu M. obedience; *don erlataid* VI, 17; cf. *irlithe.*
ernaigthe F. prayer; *don ernaigthi* VI, 15; *irnaigtiu* 11.
escare M. enemy; *escarait* IV, 7.
dar ési after, behind IV, 3; *tar hœsi* I, 41; *tar hesi* for I, 35.
étach N. cloth, dress; *étaig, i n-etuch.*
nochon étammar see *fetar.*
etir, eter prep. between, under; *etorro.*

F.

fa thrí thrice, from *fo.*
fácbaim I leave, I give up, I abandon; *ro facaib, ro ácaib;* inf. *do facbail, d'ácbáil.*

fadéin self.
fadeissin, fadesin self.
fœlte F. joy, welcome.
fagbail see *fogbaim*.
fáidim I send; *fáidid, fáidis*.
failsigfit from *foillsigim*.
fairend F. crowd, people; *don fairind*.
fairggœ ocean II, 1.
fáith prophet, wise man; *a fhathe*.
fál hedge, enclosure II, 2.
fand weak.
far n- your.
fat length, extent III, 7.
fecht N. time (in sense of turn); *in fecht n- aill*.
Fedelmid Firurglas the father of *Cathair Mór; Fedelmthi* IV, 1.
Fedelmid Rechtmar Fedlimius Legifer 129, rex Hiberniæ 164—174 p. Chr. (O'Fl. Ogyg. p. 306).
fégaim I see; *fégha, fégaid, fegtar*.
feib how.
féin self; *do charait fén* thine own friends I, 49.
fer M. man; *fir*.
feraim fǽlti I give welcome; *ro ferad*.
ferand M. land; *feraind*.
ferr better; *ferr de*.
fers Latin versus; *hi fers* I, 8.
fes from *fetar*.

fesin self.
fetar I know; *fitir, nochon étammar, ni etatar; fes.*
Fiacail mac Conchind; Fiacla.
fiadnaise presence; *inar fiadnaise* before us.
fich feud IV, 5.
fidbaid forest, *fidbaidœ* II, 2.
figell, figil from Latin vigilia i. e. *frithaire* (watch) indicates certain prayers, cf. Stokes, Corm. Transl. p. 77; and *figlem* 1 pl. imperat. let us watch or let us say vigils VI, 11.
fil it is.
fillim I bend (the knee); *nis fillem*.
filliud flexio.
find white.
finnaim I find; *ro finnatar*.
Fintan IV, 1.
fir true.
firién just III, 5.
firinne F. truth.
Firurglas see *Fedelmid*.
fiu just, fit.
fled F. feast; *fleda* III, 1.
flaith F. lordship; *ardflaith, roflaith, flatha*.
flathius M. lordship; *do lathius*.
fo prep. under; *fon, fond; fot; fo chétóir* forthwith.
fochanim succino; *fom chain* II, 2.

focherdaim I put, throw; *fo-ceird* III, 7; *focertar* I, 50.
fochaid F. suffering; *dinab fochidib*.
focol word III, 7.
fodaraithmine I, 31 ? read *for-da-raithmine*.
fodord murmuratio VI, 24.
fogal F. spoliatio IV, 7.
fogbaim I find; *fogéba*.
fogniu I serve; *fognither, fogníter*.
foillsigim I show; *follsiges, failsigfit, foillsigthir;* inf. *follsigud*.
folach custodia, cover or concealment (Stokes, Corm. Trans. p. 77); *i foluch* V, 1.
folt hair.
for prep. upon; *forsin, forsnaib; foir, forri, forru, fort; for aithed* "in elopement" IV, 3 Hennessy.
for, or, ol inquit.
for-aith-muiniur I am mindful, remember; *foraithmenair* I, 5, cf. *fodaraithmine* I, 31.
forbia III, 7 fut. (cf. § 310) from *forbenim* perficio, *forfenar* consummatur, *forbe* completion, Grk. διατελέσει.
forbond III, 3 perhaps O'Reilly's *forbann* proclamation of an edict?
forbrissim opprimo; *fortanbristis* I, 7.

for-canim, -chanim, -chun I teach; *forcain*.
forcetal, forcital N. teaching; *do forcitul* VI, 16, infinitive of *forchun*.
forchluinim I hear; *forchluinter*.
forchomnacuir evenit; *forchuimsed* (cf. § 347).
fordotá III, 2 probably for *for-dot-tá* is upon thee.
foroid...II, 3?
fortacht help; *fortachtae*.
fortachtaigim I help; dep. *fortachtaigedar*.
fotha M. cause.
frecndarcus M. presence.
frecraim I answer; *ro recair, ro frecart, ro recratar*.
fresciu I wait; *fresci* III, 2.
fri prep. towards, against; *frisin n-, frim, friss, frib; fria, ria; frisi* IV, 7 for *frisa; frisside* say to anyone, separate from anyone, equal with anyone, and so on.
frith is found.
frithgnom M. preparation; *can rithgnom* III, 1.
fuacraim I announce; *fuacraid*.
fufuasnaim compound of *fuasnaim* I rave; *fufuasna* II, 1.
furail VI, 3 O'Reilly's *foráil* excess, superfluity, cf. *erail i. imforcraid* O'Dav. *erain*.

G.

gabim I take, seize; *gaib, gaibid; nachin rogba* I, 27; *ro gab, gabsu, gabais, no gabad;* inf. *do gabáil; gabais fri grisad* began to instigate IV, 4.

gæt from *gonaim.*

gáith, gáeth F. wind.

galar N. disease.

garim I call; *gairid.*

gel white; *oengel* all white; *gil.*

gérat III, 4, cf. *gerait i. mac bec, no beodha* "lively" *no glic* (skilful) *no anrud* (nomen secundi gradus poetarum Corm. O'Dav.) but translated "champion" by Stokes Fél. Prol. 90.

gilla M. servant; *a gillai.*

gin M. mouth.

giuil II, 4 from *glenim* adhaereo.

glain (or *glan*) glass; *glano* III, 6.

glan clean.

glanta III, 7 from *glanaim* I clean.

glass green.

Gleotic for Cymric *guletic*, later *gwledic princeps*, see Ambróis.

glé clear.

glóir Latin gloria.

glún N. knee.

gnáth known.

gníim I do; *gniter.*

gním M. to do, deed; *gníme, assa gnímaib.*

gnoé beautiful IV, 3, cf. Corm. Transl. p. 86.

gnúis F. face; *gnuis, gnusi.*

goiste noose.

gol shout.

gonaim I kill; *gonais; ro gæt.*

Gorthigernd Vortigern, king of Britain, who received the Saxons under Hengist and Horsa about A.D. 447.

grád N. grade, rank I, 28, 52; *oes graid* VI, 15.

grádaigim I love, with *nis gradaigther* III, 5.

grés memoria, *do grés* always.

grían F. sun; *tarsin gréin.*

grísad drive on, stimulate IV, 4.

Gunnis a district in the north of Britain V, 4.

guth M. voice.

H.

For words having *h* as initial sound see the same without the *h*.

hirubin Cherubim; *for hirubinaib* I, 48.

I.

i determinative particle, *in n-ingin i sin* this maiden.

i. contraction for *idon* namely.

i, hí she IV, 3, 6; acc. IV, 5.
i n-, hi n- prep. in; *isin, indi, inti, im, inar, it.*
iar n- prep. after; *iarna, iar sin, iar sudiu* thereupon; *iar tain* later.
iarfaigim I ask (with *do*); *ro iarfaig*; inf. *iarfaigid.*
iarom, iarum adv. thereupon.
iarraid seek, ask.
iarthar west, the western part; *iarthair.*
iat they.
ic prep. at V, 2, see *oc.*
icc to heal, cure.
idal M. Latin idolum; *idil* I, 9.
idnacul no doubt infinitive of *adnaicim* (originally I deliver, then I bury); *dia idnacul* to escort "her" IV, 6 Hennessy.
idnaide expectation; *oc idnaidiu* III, 4.
il much; *co n-ilmuinteraib ilib* III, 5; *il-bélre.*
ille adv. huc; *o sin ille* thence, hither III, 7.
im see *imm.*
imberim I carry about; *imbir* I, 51.
imchomairb VI, 24, cf. *comhairp* "emulation" O'Reilly, *comairb i. cominnairbe* O'Dav.
imchomarc salutation I, 21.

imchomrac coming together, battle; *mu imchomruc* III, 3
imdercad reproach, to reproach III, 3.
imel, imbel border.
imithe to devour one another; *ic imithi* V, 2, cf. *longud no ithi*, consuming or eating Ml. 118.
imletrad cutting one another, *ic imletrad* V, 2; cf. *letrad* hacking, cutting Corm. Transl. p. 105.
imm, im prep. about; *imman, immon, imon, mon; imbe, immib; immum, imma*; in composition *im-* often indicates reciprocity.
immach adv. out, forth; *osin immach* thenceforward.
immaig adv. without.
immaille together I, 29.
immedon adv. in the midst, midway between.
im(morro) conj. but.
immun M. hymnus.
imned N. oppression.
imorbus Old Irish *immormus* M. scandalum III, 1.
imrádiud M. counsel; *for a n-imrátib* III, 7.
imthanu change I, 41.
in interrogative particle III, 5.
in-dignet V, 2 for *a n-dignet.*

in, ind, in t- the § 171.
in sin οὗτος; *in so* τόδε.
inagid tagid V, 1, cf. *aigh i. eirigh ut est aigh taig í. tair doridhis i. eirigh go Cormac ocus tair doridhisi uadh* (*aigh* viz. arise up e.g. *aigh taig,* viz. return, viz. go to Cormac and come back from him); O'Dav. cf. also "*tagaidh*" come ye on, advance (O'Reilly).
ind inaim so at this time I, 40.
indala n-ái one of two I, 42.
indeb N. gain I, 18; 32.
indiu adv. to-day.
indlinech II, 2, super me libello interscripto (Stokes).
indlat wash; *oc indlut* I, 51.
indocbál, inducbál F. fame; *indocbáil.*
ingin F. maiden, daughter; *ingine, ingin, ingena.*
ingnad wondrous, wonder.
inid III, 2 ubi est, cf. § 387.
inis, innis F. island; *inse.*
inmain dear; *inmaini* III, 4.
inna in suo III, 2.
inna ubi non III, 1.
innarbenim pello, repello; *no innarbad, coron innarba* V, 2, 3; *innarbar* (read *innarbanar*) I, 22, *ro innarbad* V, 2.

innas M. condition, manner; *fon innasin* in this way, so.
inní see *intí.*
innisim I say; *innisid.*
innocht adv. to-night.
innosse adv. now V, 2.
insin, inso see *in sin, in so.*
intí (article with the determinative *i*) the, the well-known, *intí Condla* III, 4, acc. *inní Condla* ibid.
inund pron. idem, eadem, idem IV, 3.
ires, hires F. faith.
irlithe obedient.
irnaigtiu VI, 11, see *ernaigthe.*
Irusalem Jerusalem I, 40.
is and VI, 9.
isel low I, 31.
Isu Jesus.
itaam III, 1 from *itáu* § 386.

L.

la prep. by, with, through; *lasin, lemm, lim, linn, leind, leis, lei, leo, leu; lase* thereby; *ba ingnad la Cond* Conn was astonished; *la sodain* thereupon.
lá see *laithe.*
labrur dep. I speak; *ce nus labratar;* inf. *labrad.*
laechrad F. the warriors; *dond laechraid* II, 1.

in laigni trom IV, 5 "the heavy lance" Hennessy.
laithe, laa, lá N. day; *isind laithiu* I, 41.
lám F. hand; *láim, di láim; for láim a athar* beside his father III, 1; *fri láim Cuind* by the side of Conn IV, 3.
lámaim I dare; *nir lam.*
lán full; *láin.*
lann, lond rapidus, immitis, fierce; *lainn* II, 1.
lár M. floor, ground.
laxa, laxu Latin laxitas see *lén.*
lebrán M. libellus.
lécim, léicim I leave; *ro leic; no leicthe;* inf. *lecun.*
legim Latin *lego;* 1 pl. imperat. *legem* VI, 11; inf. *oes legind* lectores VI, 16.
lén VI, 9, 23, cf. *corp-len* bodily ease Stokes, Fél. Jun. 22, i. *corp sleman no laxu no sadaile.*
lenim I adhere; *ro len; ro lil.*
less commodum; ricim less with genitive I need.
leth N. side.
libur, lebor M. Latin liber; *libuir.*
litir F. litera; *litre.*
lobra F. infirmitas.
loch M. lake; *locha.*
Lochlind Norway II, 1.
lóg, lúach N. reward.

lóid song II, 2.
loiscim I burn; *loiscther.*
lon M. merle.
long F. ship.
loor enough.
lúad, liath swift.
lúad a speaking.
Luagni IV, 4, *Luagni Temrach* "a sept seated near Tara, in the present county Meath" Hennessy.
lubair work VI, 19.
Luchet IV, 5.
Lugaid Corr. IV, 4.
luid he went; *luide* III, 4.
lúta the little finger; *do lutain* I, 51.

M.

-m suffixed pronoun of the 1 sg. III, 3.
m' for *mo* my.
má conj. if III, 2, 6.
má see *móo.*
mac, macc M. son; *maicc.*
mag N. plain; *im-Maig Archommin* III, 4; *Mag Mell* the Elysium of the pagan Gaedel.
Mailenach, gen. *Mailenaig* IV, 8.
mairg woe, *cen mairg* III, 2.
maith good, the good.
maldacht F. maledictio; *maldachta* I, 42.

mámm servitus; *fo mamm* VI, 1.

mani conj. if not I, 19, 28; *manid* nisi sit I, 38.

mar conj. as, just as IV, 2, 7.

már, mór great.

marb dead; *marbu.*

marbaim I kill; *marbais, marbtair;* inf. *marbad.*

martir martyrium; *martre* I, 36.

mass beautiful II, 3.

mathair F. mother.

mebul F. shame.

medair "talk, discourse" O'Reilly; *medair mass* II, 3 parenthetic; a lovely conversation.

medón middle.

méit greatness; *imméit.*

melim I grind; inf. *do blith.*

mell, older *meld* agreeable.

menma mind; *menmain.*

menn clear II, 1, 3.

mér M. finger.

messu (comparative) worse.

mí month; *mís.*

millim I spoil, destroy IV, 5.

mír N. piece, bit.

mná, mnái from *ben.*

mo, mu my; *m'athair.*

mo, mos soon (before the future).

mod M. modus; *mod nad mod* by and by III, 7.

moga, moge from *mug.*

mon (*nuic*) IV, 8 for *imon.*

moó, moo, mó, mu comparative of *mór* III, 3.

mór, már great; *móra.*

mórchetlach having song (*mór*) great (*cétal*) III, 3.

mórdánach possessing great (*mór*) art (*dán*) III, 3.

Morna or *Dáire Derc* head of the Fenians of Connacht IV, 4, his son was *Aed* or *Goll mac Morna*, his descendants *maic* or *cland Morna* 5, 8.

motáticfa for *mo-dot-icfa* mox te adibit? III, 5.

mu, mo my.

mucc F. pig; *muic.*

mudugud destruction, to destroy.

mug M. slave; *moge, moga.*

muin nape III, 2; cf. i. *bráige* (neck) Corm. *Emain; muinél* collum; *Mun-caim* the fair-necked.

muir N. sea; *mora.*

munter, muinter F. family, followers; *muntiri, muntir, muinteraib.*

Murni Muncaim Finn's mother IV, 3.

N.

-n, -nn suffixed pronoun of the 1 pl. I, 7, 27; III, 1.

na not I, 10; IV. 4.

na (dochum) III, 1 for *ina inna*; VI, 20.

ná, na, nó or; *nad fresci bas na sentaid* III, 2; *ni róis chluim na colcaid* II, 4; *fuacraid...cath...for Tadg ná éraic a athar do thabairt dó* IV, 7.

nach not; *nachin rogba* I, 27; *náchim thánic* III, 3.

nách adjectival pronoun, any; *nách túara* III, 4.

nad, nád not (in relative and dependent sentences) III, 2, 6; *nad cél* II, 2; *in tan nad n-acastar et nad forchluinter* I, 43; *huare nad n-digni* I, 30; *mod nad mod* see *mod* III, 7.

nallsuide III, 4 with the gloss *i. uasal*, it is perhaps *ni allsuide* like *alltogu* Cod. S. Pauli V, 9; cf. also *all n-glaine* "a rock of purity" Fél. Jan. 6.

nama M. enemy; *namit*.

nammá adv. only; *nanmá* I, 44.

nech subst. some one; *ni...nech* no one; *do neoch*.

nél cloud.

nem N. heaven; *nime, innim*.

nemaiscide invisible (?) III, 3.

nert N. strength, might; *neirt*.

nessam superl. the nearest I, 50.

ni, ní not; *nir, nír* for *ni ro*; *nís* III, 5; *ni con* not III, 5.

ní something, with subsequent relative clause id (quod); *cach ní* all; *ni...ní, na...ní* nothing; *ani sin* this I, 50.

-ni augmentative particle of the 1 pl. I, 7, 15, 20, 41.

ni insa (ansa) not hard.

nith combat III, 3; *i. guin duine* (homicidium) Corm.

no, nu verbal particle (§ 251); *nonn ainmnigther* III, 1; *not alim* III, 3; *nob sóárfasi* I, 25; *nus labratar* I, 44; *no da fortachtaigedar* I, 31; *am(al) nondad* I, 11.

nó ship; *isind noi* III, 7.

nó or; *áit inna bí bas no peccad na immorbus* III, 1; IV, 7.

nochon not V, 1.

noco n- until IV, 8.

noéb, naeb holy.

nón Latin nona (nones); *co nóin* VI, 14 (the canonical hour).

not Latin nota sign; *nota* I, 8.

Núadu Cathir's druid; *Núadat, do Núadait* IV, 1.

nunreafeaglat VI, 12.

O.

ó, úa prep. from; oa Lochlind II, 1; ond; huáin; úaib, uad, oadib, úadib, uaidib; om; o sin immach thenceforward III, 7; o sin ille, o sin co sudi from there to the present III, 7; IV, 7.

ó conj. since.

óas, úas prep. over.

oc, ic prep. at, by; ocan, occa, occo; oc idnaidiu a waiting = exspectans III, 4; ato oc combáig sum certans I, 37.

óc young; óic; óc-aes VI, 17.

ócbad F. the young people.

óchtar, úachtar the upper part; i n-uachtor III, 1.

ocus, acus conj. and, usually represented in these texts in the MS. by the Latin et or by a contraction (§ 395).

óen, áen one.

óenar singleness; Condla a óenur Condla alone III, 1.

óenfer one man; comrac oenfir single combat IV, 7; Art Oenfer see Art.

óes see áes; oes graid VI, 15, legind 16.

ógslan quite safe III, 4.

oifrend mass; don oiffrind VI, 15.

óitiu youth III, 2.

ol inquit.

or inquit.

I. G.

ór, úar F. hour, time; ond úair sin III, 3; fo chet-óir straightway; hóre, húare, úair conj. because.

ord M. order VI, 21.

ordan, ordán honour III, 2.

orgaim, orcaim I kill; noircthe I, 42.

osailcim, oslaicim I open; o-sailcther I, 22.

ósin = ó sin, see ó.

otha from VI, 14.

P.

pater Our Father I, 50; VI, 5.

peccad M. Latin peccatum; pecthi, pectha.

popul Latin populus; popuil.

precept Latin preceptum, doctrine, to teach.

predchim praedico, I preach.

R.

R. III, 2 a frequent contraction for retoric.

radairc sight III, 7.

rádim, ráidim I say, call (with fri); ro rádi, radas; ro radis, ro ráid, ro raidset; rate IV, 5.

ráim I range the sea, row; ro raiset III, 7.

h úiriu IV, 3.

ranu. perfect of ricim.

rannaim I divide; roind I, 49.

ré N. time; ree, rea.

11

ré n-, ría n- prep. before.
recht N. or M. right, law; *rechto.*
Rechtmar see *Fedelmid.*
reclesa VI, cf. O'Reilly's *reiglios* F. a church, shrine.
reid light III, 5.
réimm run, to run, to travel.
renim I give, sell; *ni riat* I, 18.
resiu conj. before I, 24.
réthince, raithinchi VI, 23 cf. *roithinche* hilaritas Z.² 809.
rí M. king; *ríg, a rí.*
ria for *fria* VI, 13.
ría n- see *ré n-.*
riam adv. antea III, 7.
ríar F. voluntas; *do rer* (more correctly *réir*) according to wish, secundum.
riat from *renim.*
riccim (for *ro-iccim*) I reach; *recait, ricfam, ranic, ró-is* II, 4, *ro-isam* VI, 7, *roissinn*, I, 37, *ró-ismais* III, 6.
rígda royal; *rígdai.*
rigdomna royal heir IV, 1.
ríge sovereignty; *irrigi Temrach* IV, 1.
rígfennid IV, 3, "king warrior," (Hennessy) leader of the Fenians.
ro, ru verbal particle (§ 251); *rom gab* III, 5; *rom bia* I, 26; *rot giuil* II, 4; *rod lil* IV, 5; *rud chualatar* I, 44; *ro m-bói* I, 38; *co rabe* for *ro be; rop, roptar* for *ro bo, ro batar; cor, nir, díar* for *co ro, ni ro, día ro.*
rocháim very beautiful III, 3.
rochetul N. strong singing; *re rochetul* III, 4.
rochim, roichim I come, adeo; inf. *rochtain* IV, 6.
róed, raed gen. *raeda* forest.
rofaith title of nobility: the degree next to the king IV, 3.
rogba see *gabaim.*
ró-is see *riccim.*
Romanach Romanus.
ronta VI, 17, from *do-rónad?*
rosc M. eye; *roisc.*
ross forest.
rotha VI, 17, from *táim* § 386?
rotnai VI, 16, for *rontai* from *do-rónad?*
rúad red.
ruc tulit; *rucad* IV, 7.
rún F. secret; *rúin.*

S.

-sa augmentative particle of the 1st sg. *dodeochad-sa dom-sa, frim-sa, failsigfit-sea* V, 1.
sadaile F. ease.
saethar see *sáithar.*
saidim I sit; *saides* III, 4.
saigim I seek for, visit; inf. *do saigid.*

sainemail distinguished.
sáithar, sáethar, sóethar N. work, labour; *saithir.*
sale, saile sputum; *dit sailiu, da sale* I, 50.
salm M. psalm.
sárigim contemno, inf. *sarugud* IV, 3.
scáich præteriit I, 29, from *cuichim* discedo.
scailim I untie, scatter; explico *scailter, ro scailed.*
scaraim I separate (with *fri*); inf. *scarad.*
scríbaimm I write II, 3 *scríbtair* I, 8.
sé, se he, see *é,* or *se, for se, ol sesom* I, 39ᵃ.
-se augmentative particle of the 1 sg., see *-sa;* *am cimbid-se* I, 14.
sech prep. beside, beyond, past; conj. *sech ni* except, has not I, 7, 20.
sechur dep. I follow, pursue; inf. *sechem* F. *in sechim.*
sénaim I bless, I cross, *sénam* VI, 6.
Sencha I, 34.
sentu M. old age; *sentaid* III, 2.
seol M. sail, linen cloth V, 1, *in t-iuil.*
seolbrat M. linen cloth V, 1, 2.
ses 1, *co lar* (upon the ground) VI, 4, cf. *sís* deorsum.

-si augmentative particle of the 2 pl. *di bar n-ág-si* I, 15, 36; *adib moga-si* 13, 25.
sí she IV. 4.
siacht reached III, 7.
síat they.
síd peace.
síd F. the dwelling of the *síde* or fairies III, 1, 6; *áes síde* the fairies III, 1.
sídamail peaceful; *co sidamail* IV, 8.
side demonstrative pronoun, this, *a ainm-side* III, 3; IV, 3.
sin demonstrative pronoun, that *in claideb sin* that sword; *in n-ingin i sin* that girl; *in sin* that one, *de-sin* thence, *iar sin* thereupon; *and-sin* then, there.
sírim I seek.
siu see *so.*
slechtaim I kneel, Latin flecto; *slechtam* VI, 7.
sléchtain VI, 22 "genuflexions," Stokes, Corm. Transl. p. 77.
slemon, slemain smooth Latin levis, lubricus (Ir. Gl. 639).
so demonstrative pronoun *in gním so* this deed I, 40; *in so* τόδε.
-so -su augmentative particle of the 2 sg. *dait siu* I, 35; *fot menmain-siu* III, 5.
socheneoil noble III, 2.

sochuide F. a number, multitude.
sochraite F. army; *socraiti* IV, 5.
sodain demonstrative pronoun hoc; *la sodain* thereupon.
soethar see *sáithar*.
soichim I reach; *ro soich* III,5.
sóiraim, sóeraim I set free, *nob sóirfa*, inf. *soirad*.
solma swift VI, 4.
-som augmentative particle of the 3 sg. M. and the 3 pl.; *congni-som; ni thartsat-som; uad-som, leu-som*.
són pron. hoc.
sond, dia sund IV, 2, cf. *sonnad* and *sonnach* wall.
soscéle N. evangelium; *soscéli*.
srathar F. saddle II, 4.
sróinim I destroy, conquer; inf. *sroiniud* V, 2.
sruith VI, 10 senior, "dignified person," Stokes, Corm. Transl. p. 54.
súas up, upwards.
suba joy III, 6. In the ms. *subatar* is written in one word.
sude, suide N. seat.
sude, suide dem. pron. the, this; (commonly N.); *di suidiu* I, 36, *oc suidiu* 37, *iar sudiu* III, 7, *os in co sudi* IV, 7, *de suidib* III, 1.
súil F. eye.

sur III, 6, for *síur* sister? In the ms. *airunsur* is written in one word.
suthain everlasting III, 2.

T.

-t suffixed pronoun of the 2 sg.
tabur I give, *ni taibre, tabair, na taibred, tibred;* inf. *do thabirt, do thabairt*.
Tadg name of a druid IV, 3. *Tulach Taidg* IV, 7, *do Thadg* 3.
tagid V, 1 cf. *taig .i. tair doridhis* (O'Dav. p. 50).
taidbrim offero; *taidbred* III,5.
tair come III, 2, cf. § 286.
tairchanim I prophesy; *tairchechuin*.
tairle VI, 5, adeat, cf. *tarla*.
tairmthecht transgression.
tairnim I descend, lower; *tairnid* III, 6.
taitneinach shining.
tan F. time; *iar tain* after that IV, 2, *in tan* and *in tain* (with a relative clause following) whilst, as, when, I, 28, 40, 41, 43, 45.
tánic from *ticcim*.
tar, dar prep. over, Latin trans; *tarsin, tarais, tarfar cennsi* I, 36, 42; *tar ési* behind, after, for.
tarat, dorat he gave; *ni thartsat*.
tardechta III, 5?

tarla accidit IV, 8.
tathut see *táu*.
táu, tó I am; *tathut* tibi est III, 6; *itaam* ubi sumus III, 1, *amal nondad* I, 11.
tech N. house; *dia thig*.
techim I flee; *ro teich*.
techt messenger; *techta* IV, 3.
techtaire, tecttaire M. messenger.
teirt Latin tertia (terce, the canonical hour) VI, 12.
Temair Tara, the seat of the chief king of Ireland IV, 1; *Temrach*.
Temeair Lúachræ IV, 8 *Luachair* the old name of a district "between the counties of Limerick and Kerry." Hennessy.
Temair Mairci, co Temraig Mairci IV, 6.
temel darkness.
tempul templum; *tempuil*.
tenga tongue III, 5.
tesarbi I, 38 from *tesbuith*, deesse.
tét téit he goes I, 41.
Tethra i. *rí Fomóire* king of the Fomorians (a legendary race) *iter triunu Tethrach* "among Tethra's mighty men." Corm. Transl. p. 157, *do dóinib Tethrach* III, 4.
tiagaim I go; *tiagar* I, 40.
tibred see *tabur*.

tichtu F. coming.
ticcim, ticim I come; *tic; motáticfa* III, 5; *tised, tísad, tánic*.
tigerne M. Lord; *dia thigerni* I, 16.
timmarcte Latin complicatus V, 1 from *do-imm-urc* ango.
tinaim I vanish; *ro tinastar* V, 2.
tinólaim I assemble; *tinolaid*.
tir N. land; *tíri, a tírib*.
tlí VI, 17 read *clí*, strength (O'R.)?
tocbaim I lift; *tocbam*.
tochra, oc a tochra IV, 3 "were courting her" (Hennessy).
tochuiriur, docuiriur dep. ascisco (Z.² 873); *tot-churethar* III, 4 perhaps we should read *-churetar*.
toga see *togu*.
togaim I choose; *ro thog* IV, 1.
togu, toga choice.
tond, tonn F. wave, flood, *fri tóind* III, 6?
tóirand, tórand N. sign I, 50.
toisigecht F. leadership, guidance I, 28.
tomlim, toimlim I consume, *tomled* III, 4.
tomnibther I, 43 from a deponent *tomniur* (*to-* = *do-fo-* cf. *do-moiniur* puto) I expect.
tongaim I vow (*tar* by so and so); *toissed* I, 45.

tor IV, 7 cf. *tor .i. imat* (crowd) O'Dav.
torchair fell IV, 8.
tormastar see § 321.
torrach gravid.
trá, tra conj. now, but.
tráig strand.
tráth N. time, hour; *tratha*.
treb M. tribe; *truib, trebaib*.
Trénmór father of Cumall; *mac Trenmoir* IV, 3.
tre thoathbandu III, 3, perhaps " through heathen tricks."
tri (*trí* I, 22); *tre* prep. through, *tri chumsanad* I, 41, *trit* I, 12, *tremit* IV, 3.
trí three; *fo thrí* thrice I, 50, V, 2.
trírech song, hymn II, 2, cf. O'Curry on the Manners, &c. III, p. 388, Stokes Corm. Transl. p. 89.
Triscoth I, 34
trist VI, 5, Latin tristis?
trom heavy.
tú thou.
tua silence VI, 23.
tualaing peritus, gnarus IV, 7.
túare, túara F. food III, 4.
túascert the northern part V, 4.

túath F. people; *etir túaith* I, 38.
Túath Dathi IV, 1, 7.
tuc tulit, dedit IV, 2, *tucthar* V, 1, *tucad* IV, 3.
tucsatar V, 2 from *da-ucci, tucci* intelligit Z.^{a} 431.
tuitim I fall; *dofuit* IV, 5.
tulach F. hill.
Tulach Taidg IV, 7.
tús beginning, *ar thús* at first.
tu-su pron. thou.

U.

uachtor see *óchtar*.
úad, úadib, húain, úaib see *ó*.
úair, úare conj. because, see *ór*.
úall F. haughtiness.
úas, húas prep. over.
úasal noble, elevated; comparative *húaisliu*.
úathmar dreadful; *úathmair*.
ubull apple III, 4.
uile, ule whole, all.
uisse just.
Urgrend IV, 4.
usce, uisce, M. water, *usci, di uisciu*.
Usnech place in West Meath; *Usnig* III, 1.
út adv. there.

By the Translator.

AN ESSAY ON THE HISTORY OF MEDICINE IN IRELAND.

Founded on an Examination of some Manuscripts in the British Museum. St Bartholomew's Hospital Reports, 1875.

SMITH, ELDER, AND CO., LONDON.

THE LOSS OF THE CROWN OF LOEGAIRE LURC.

(Text and Translation with Vocabulary) from the Dindsenchas in the Book of Leinster.

ADLARD, BARTHOLOMEW CLOSE, LONDON, 1881.

UNIVERSITY PRESS, CAMBRIDGE.
October, 1892.

PUBLICATIONS OF

The Cambridge University Press.

THE HOLY SCRIPTURES, &c.

HEBREW.

A short Commentary on the Hebrew and Aramaic Text of the Book of Daniel, by A. A. BEVAN, M.A., Fellow of Trinity College. Demy 8vo. 8*s*.

GREEK.

The Old Testament in Greek according to the Septuagint. Edited by the Rev. Professor H. B. SWETE, D.D. Crown 8vo. Vol. I. Genesis—IV Kings. 7*s*. 6*d*. Vol. II. I Chronicles—Tobit. 7*s*. 6*d*. [Vol. III. *In the Press.*

The Book of Psalms in Greek according to the Septuagint. Being a portion of Vol. II. of the above work. Crown 8vo. 2*s*. 6*d*.

The Parallel New Testament Greek and English. The New Testament, being the Authorised Version set forth in 1611 Arranged in Parallel Columns with the Revised Version of 1881, and with the original Greek, as edited by the late F. H. A. SCRIVENER, M.A., D.C.L., LL.D. Crown 8vo. 12*s*. 6*d*. (*The Revised Version is the joint Property of the Universities of Cambridge and Oxford.*)

Greek and English Testament, in parallel columns on the same page. Edited by J. SCHOLEFIELD, M.A. *New Edition, with the marginal references as arranged and revised by* DR SCRIVENER. 7*s*. 6*d*.

Greek and English Testament. THE STUDENT'S EDITION of the above on *large writing paper*. 4to. 12*s*.

The New Testament in the Original Greek, according to the Text followed in the Authorised Version, with the Variations adopted in the Revised Version. Edited by the late F. H. A. SCRIVENER, M.A., D.C.L., LL.D. Crown 8vo. 6*s*. New Edit. Fcap 8vo. [*In the Press.*

Biblical Fragments from Mount Sinai, edited by J. RENDEL HARRIS, M.A. Demy 4to. 10*s*. 6*d*.

Notitia Codicis Quattuor Evangeliorum Græci membranacei viris doctis hucusque incogniti quem in museo suo asservat Eduardus Reuss Argentoratensis. 2*s*.

London: Cambridge Warehouse, Ave Maria Lane.

SYRIAC.

The Harklean Version of the Epistle to the Hebrews, Chap. XI. 28—XIII. 25. Now edited for the first time with Introduction and Notes on this version of the Epistle. By ROBERT L. BENSLY. Demy 8vo. 5*s*.

LATIN.

The Latin Heptateuch. Published piecemeal by the French printer WILLIAM MOREL (1560) and the French Benedictines E. MARTÈNE (1733) and J. B. PITRA (1852—88). Critically reviewed by JOHN E. B. MAYOR, M.A. Demy 8vo. 10*s*. 6*d*.

The Missing Fragment of the Latin Translation of the Fourth Book of Ezra, discovered and edited with Introduction, Notes, and facsimile of the MS., by Prof. BENSLY, M.A. Demy 4to. 10*s*.

Codex S. Ceaddae Latinus. Evangelia SSS. Matthaei, Marci, Lucae ad cap. III. 9 complectens, circa septimum vel octavum saeculum scriptvs, in Ecclesia Cathedrali Lichfieldiensi servatus. Cum codice versionis Vulgatae Amiatino contulit, prolegomena conscripsit, F. H. A. SCRIVENER, A.M., LL.D. Imp. 4to. £1. 1*s*.

The Codex Sangallensis (Δ). A Study in the Text of the Old Latin Gospels, by J. RENDEL HARRIS, M.A. Royal 8vo. 3*s*.

The Origin of the Leicester Codex of the New Testament. By J. R. HARRIS, M.A. With 3 plates. Demy 4to. 10*s*. 6*d*.

ANGLO-SAXON.

The Four Gospels in Anglo-Saxon and Northumbrian Versions. By Rev. Prof. SKEAT, Litt.D. One Volume. Demy Quarto. 30*s*. Each Gospel separately. 10*s*.

ENGLISH.

The Authorised Edition of the English Bible (1611), its Subsequent Reprints and Modern Representatives. By the late F. H. A. SCRIVENER, M.A., D.C.L., LL.D. Crown 8vo. 7*s*. 6*d*.

The Cambridge Paragraph Bible of the Authorized English Version, with the Text revised by a Collation of its Early and other Principal Editions, the Use of the Italic Type made uniform, the Marginal References remodelled, and a Critical Introduction, by the late F. H. A. SCRIVENER, M.A., LL.D. Crown 4to., cloth gilt, 21*s*.

THE STUDENT'S EDITION of the above, on *good writing paper*, with one column of print and wide margin to each page for MS. notes. Two Vols. Crown 4to., cloth, gilt, 31*s*. 6*d*.

London: Cambridge Warehouse, Ave Maria Lane.

HOLY SCRIPTURES.

The Lectionary Bible, with Apocrypha, divided into Sections adapted to the Calendar and Tables of Lessons of 1871. Cr. 8vo. 3s. 6d.

The Book of Ecclesiastes. Large Paper Edition. By the Very Rev. E. H. PLUMPTRE, late Dean of Wells. Demy 8vo. 7s. 6d.

(*See also pp.* 24, 25, *Cambridge Bible for Schools.*)

The Gospel History of our Lord Jesus Christ in the Language of the Revised Version, arranged in a Connected Narrative, especially for the use of Teachers and Preachers. By Rev. C. C. JAMES, M.A. Crown 8vo. 3s. 6d.

A Harmony of the Gospels in the words of the Revised Version with copious references, tables &c. Arranged by Rev. C. C. JAMES, M.A. Crown 8vo. 5s.

Wilson's Illustration of the Method of explaining the New Testament, by the early opinions of Jews and Christians concerning Christ. Edited by T. TURTON, D.D. Demy 8vo. 5s.

SERVICE-BOOKS.

A Classified Index to the Leonine, Gelasian, and Gregorian Sacramentaries of Muratori. By H. A. WILSON, M.A., Fellow of Magdalen College, Oxford. Demy 8vo. 5s. net.

Breviarium ad Usum Sarum. A Reprint of the folio edition by Chevallon and Regnault, Paris, 1531. Edited by F. PROCTER, M.A. and CHR. WORDSWORTH, M.A. Demy 8vo.

    Vol. 1. Kalendar and Temporale. 18s.

    Vol. 2. Psalter &c. 12s.

    Vol. 3. Sanctorale. With an Introduction, lists of editions from the papers of H. Bradshaw, and complete Indexes. 15s.

    The three volumes together, £2. 2s.

Breviarium Romanum a FRANCISCO CARDINALI QUIGNONIO editum et recognitum iuxta editionem Venetiis A.D. 1535 impressam curante JOHANNE WICKHAM LEGG. Demy 8vo. 12s.

The Greek Liturgies. Chiefly from original Authorities. By C. A. SWAINSON, D.D., late Master of Christ's College. Cr. 4to. 15s.

The Pointed Prayer Book, being the Book of Common Prayer with the Psalter or Psalms of David, pointed as they are to be sung or said in Churches. Royal 24mo, cloth, 1s. 6d.

The same in square 32mo. cloth, 6d.

London: Cambridge Warehouse, Ave Maria Lane.

Wheatly on the Common Prayer, edited by G. E. CORRIE, D.D., late Master of Jesus College. Demy Octavo. 7s. 6d.

The Cambridge Psalter, for the use of Choirs and Organists. Specially adapted for Congregations in which the "Cambridge Pointed Prayer Book" is used. Demy 8vo. cloth, 3s. 6d. Cloth limp cut flush, 2s. 6d.

The Paragraph Psalter, arranged for the use of Choirs by the Right Rev. B. F. WESTCOTT, D.D., Lord Bp. of Durham. Fcp. 4to. 5s.
The same in royal 32mo. Cloth, 1s. Leather, 1s. 6d.

The Homilies, with Various Readings, and the Quotations from the Fathers given at length in the Original Languages. Edited by G. E. CORRIE, D.D., late Master of Jesus College. Demy 8vo. 7s. 6d.

Two Forms of Prayer of the time of Queen Elizabeth. Now First Reprinted. Demy Octavo. 6d.

THEOLOGY.

Sayings of the Jewish Fathers, comprising Pirqe Aboth and Pereq R. Meir in Hebrew and English, with Critical Notes. By C. TAYLOR, D.D., Master of St John's College. [*New Edition. Preparing.*

The Palestinian Mishna. By W. H. LOWE, M.A. Royal 8vo. 21s.

Chagigah from the Babylonian Talmud. A Translation of the Treatise with Notes, etc. by A. W. STREANE, B.D. Demy 8vo. 10s.

Psalms of the Pharisees, commonly known as the Psalms of Solomon, by H. E. RYLE, B.D. and M. R. JAMES, M.A. Demy 8vo. 15s.

The Witness of Hermas to the Four Gospels. By C. TAYLOR, D.D. Master of St John's College, Cambridge. Fcap. 4to. Buckram. 7s. 6d. Net.

Fragments of Philo and Josephus. Newly edited by J. RENDEL HARRIS, M.A. With two Facsimiles. Demy 4to. 12s. 6d.

The Rest of the Words of Baruch: A Christian Apocalypse of the year 136 A.D. The Text revised with an Introduction by J. RENDEL HARRIS, M.A. Royal 8vo. 5s.

The Teaching of the Apostles. Newly edited, with Facsimile Text and Commentary, by J. R. HARRIS, M.A. Demy 4to. 21s.

A Collation of the Athos Codex of the Shepherd of Hermas. Together with an Introduction by SPYR. P. LAMBROS, PH.D., translated and edited with a Preface and Appendices by J. ARMITAGE ROBINSON, B.D. Demy 8vo. 3s. 6d.

London: Cambridge Warehouse, Ave Maria Lane.

The Philocalia of Origen. The Greek Text edited from the Manuscripts, with Critical Apparatus and Indexes, and an Introduction on the Sources of the Text. By J. ARMITAGE ROBINSON, B.D.
[In the Press.

Theodore of Mopsuestia's Commentary on the Minor Epistles of S. Paul. The Latin Version with the Greek Fragments, edited from the MSS. with Notes and an Introduction, by Professor H. B. SWETE, D.D. Vol. I., containing the Introduction, and the Commentary upon Galatians—Colossians. Demy Octavo. 12s.

Volume II., containing the Commentary on 1 Thessalonians—Philemon, Appendices and Indices. 12s.

The Acts of the Martyrdom of Perpetua and Felicitas; the original Greek Text now first edited from a MS. in the Library of the Convent of the Holy Sepulchre at Jerusalem, by J. RENDEL HARRIS and SETH K. GIFFORD. Royal 8vo. 5s.

The Diatessaron of Tatian. By J. RENDEL HARRIS, M.A. Royal 8vo. 5s.

TEXTS AND STUDIES: CONTRIBUTIONS TO BIBLICAL AND PATRISTIC LITERATURE.

Edited by J. ARMITAGE ROBINSON, B.D., Fellow and Assistant Tutor of Christ's College.

Vol. I. No. 1. The Apology of Aristides on behalf of the Christians. Edited from a Syriac MS., with an Introduction and Translation by J. RENDEL HARRIS, M.A., and an Appendix containing the chief part of the Original Greek, by J. ARMITAGE ROBINSON, B.D. Demy 8vo. *[Reprinting.*

No. 2. The Passion of S. Perpetua: the Latin Text freshly edited from the Manuscripts with an Introduction and Appendix containing the Original Latin Form of the Scillitan Martyrdom: by J. ARMITAGE ROBINSON, B.D. 4s. Net.

No. 3. The Lord's Prayer in the Early Church: with Special Notes on the Controverted Clauses; by F. H. CHASE, B.D., Christ's College. 5s. Net.

No. 4. The Fragments of Heracleon: the Greek Text with an Introduction by A. E. BROOKE, M.A., Fellow of King's College. 4s. Net.

London: Cambridge Warehouse, Ave Maria Lane.

Vol. II. No. 1. **A Study of Codex Bezae:** by J. RENDEL HARRIS, M.A. 7s. 6d. Net.

No. 2. **The Testament of Abraham.** By M. R. JAMES, M.A., with an Appendix containing Translations from the Arabic of the Testaments of Abraham, Isaac and Jacob, by W. E. BARNES, B.D. 5s. Net.

The following are in course of preparation:

No. 3. **The Rules of Tyconius:** freshly edited from the MSS., with an examination of his witness to the Old Latin Version: by F. C. BURKITT, M.A.

No. 4. **Apocrypha Anecdota:** containing the Latin Version of the Apocalypse of Paul, the Apocalypses of the Virgin, of Sedrach, of Zosimas, &c.: by M. R. JAMES, M.A.

No. 5. **The Homeric Centones:** by J. RENDEL HARRIS, M.A., University Lecturer in Palaeography.

No. 6. **The Curetonian Syriac Gospels:** re-edited with a new translation into English: by R. L. BENSLY, M.A., Lord Almoner's Reader in Arabic.

Tertullianus de Corona Militis, de Spectaculis, de Idololatria with Analysis and English Notes, by G. CURREY, D.D. Crown 8vo. 5s.

Sancti Irenæi Episcopi Lugdunensis libros quinque adversus Hæreses, edidit W. WIGAN HARVEY, S.T.B. Collegii Regalis olim Socius. 2 Vols. Demy Octavo. 18s.

Theophili Episcopi Antiochensis Libri Tres ad Autolycum. Edidit Prolegomenis Versione Notulis Indicibus instruxit GULIELMUS GILSON HUMPHRY, S.T.B. Post Octavo. 5s.

Theophylacti in Evangelium S. Matthæi Commentarius. Edited by W. G. HUMPHRY, B.D. Demy Octavo. 7s. 6d.

M. Minucii Felicis Octavius. The text newly revised from the original MS. with an English Commentary, Analysis, Introduction, and Copious Indices. By H. A. HOLDEN, LL.D. Cr. 8vo. 7s. 6d.

S. Austin and his place in the History of Christian Thought. Being the Hulsean Lectures for 1885. By W. CUNNINGHAM, D.D. Demy 8vo. Buckram, 12s. 6d.

Works of Isaac Barrow, compared with the original MSS. A new Edition, by A. NAPIER, M.A. 9 Vols. Demy 8vo. £3. 3s.

London: Cambridge Warehouse, Ave Maria Lane.

Treatise of the Pope's Supremacy, and a Discourse concerning the Unity of the Church, by I. BARROW. Demy 8vo. 7s. 6d.

Select Discourses, by JOHN SMITH, late Fellow of Queens' College, Cambridge. Edited by H. G. WILLIAMS, B.D., late Professor of Arabic. Royal Octavo. 7s. 6d.

Pearson's Exposition of the Creed, edited by TEMPLE CHEVALLIER, B.D. 3rd Edition revised by R. SINKER, D.D. Demy 8vo. 12s.

An Analysis of the Exposition of the Creed, written by the Right Rev. Father in God, JOHN PEARSON, D.D. Compiled by W. H. MILL, D.D. Demy Octavo. 5s.

De Obligatione Conscientiæ Prælectiones decem Oxonii in Schola Theologica habitæ a ROBERTO SANDERSON, SS. Theologiæ ibidem Professore Regio. With English Notes, including an abridged Translation, by W. WHEWELL, D.D. Demy 8vo. 7s. 6d.

Lectures on Divinity delivered in the University of Cambridge. By JOHN HEY, D.D. Third Edition, by T. TURTON, D.D., late Lord Bishop of Ely. 2 vols. Demy Octavo. 15s.

Cæsar Morgan's Investigation of the Trinity of Plato, and of Philo Judæus. 2nd Ed., revised by H. A. HOLDEN, LL.D. Cr. 8vo. 4s.

Christ the Life of Men. Being the Hulsean Lectures for 1888. By Rev. H. M. STEPHENSON, M.A. Crown 8vo. 2s. 6d.

SYRIAC AND ARABIC.

Lectures on the Comparative Grammar of the Semitic Languages from the Papers of the late WILLIAM WRIGHT, LL.D. Demy 8vo. 14s.

The History of Alexander the Great, being the Syriac version of the Pseudo-Callisthenes. Edited from Five Manuscripts, with an English Translation and Notes, by E. A. W. BUDGE, Litt.D. Demy 8vo. 25s.

The Chronicle of Joshua the Stylite edited in Syriac, with an English translation and notes, by W. WRIGHT, LL.D. Demy 8vo. 10s. 6d.

Kalīlah and Dimnah, or, the Fables of Bidpai; with an English Translation of the later Syriac version, with Notes, by the late I. G. N. KEITH-FALCONER, M.A. Demy 8vo. 7s. 6d.

The Poems of Beha ed din Zoheir of Egypt. With a Metrical Translation, Notes and Introduction, by the late E. H. PALMER, M.A. 2 vols. Crown Quarto.
    Vol. I. The ARABIC TEXT. Paper covers. 10s. 6d.
    Vol. II. ENGLISH TRANSLATION. Paper covers. 10s. 6d.

London: Cambridge Warehouse, Ave Maria Lane.

SANSKRIT AND PERSIAN.

Maḳála-i-Shakhsí Sayyáḥ ki dar Kaziyya-i-Báb Navishta-Ast (a Traveller's Narrative written to illustrate the Episode of the Báb). Persian text, edited, translated and annotated, in two volumes, by E. G. BROWNE, M.A., M.B. Crown 8vo. 15s. net. Vol. II. (containing the Translation and Notes) separately, 10s. 6d. net.

The New History (Tarikh-i-Jadid), a circumstantial account of the Bábí movement in Persia from its first beginnings till the death of the Founder (A.D. 1844—1850), chiefly based on the contemporary history of Ḥájí Mirzá Jání of Káshán, translated into English and supplemented by original historical documents, plans and fac-similes, by EDWARD G. BROWNE, M.A., M.B. 10s. 6d. net.

Nalopákhyánam, or, The Tale of Nala; containing the Sanskrit Text in Roman Characters, with Vocabulary. By the late Rev. T. JARRETT, M.A. Demy 8vo. 10s.

Notes on the Tale of Nala, for the use of Classical Students, by J. PEILE, Litt.D., Master of Christ's College. Demy 8vo. 12s.

The Divyâvadâna, a Collection of Early Buddhist Legends, now first edited from the Nepalese Sanskrit MSS. in Cambridge and Paris. By E. B. COWELL, M.A. and R. A. NEIL, M.A. Demy 8vo. 18s.

GREEK.

(See also pp. 26, 27.)

Aeschylus. Agamemnon. With a translation in English Rhythm, and Notes Critical and Explanatory. **New Edition, Revised.** By the late B. H. KENNEDY, D.D. Crown 8vo. 6s.

Aeschyli Fabulae.—ΙΚΕΤΙΔΕΣ ΧΟΗΦΟΡΟΙ in libro Mediceo mendose scriptae ex vv. dd. coniecturis emendatius editae cum Scholiis Graecis et brevi adnotatione critica, curante F. A. PALEY, M.A., LL.D. Demy 8vo. 7s. 6d.

Aristophanes. Equites. With Introduction and Notes by R. A. NEIL, M.A. Demy 8vo. *[In the Press.*

Aristotle.—ΠΕΡΙ ΨΥΧΗΣ. Aristotle's Psychology, in Greek and English, with Introduction and Notes, by E. WALLACE, M.A. Demy 8vo. 18s.

Aristotle. The Rhetoric. With a Commentary by the late E. M. COPE, Fellow of Trinity College, Cambridge, revised and edited by J. E. SANDYS, Litt.D. 3 Vols. Demy 8vo. 21s.

London: Cambridge Warehouse, Ave Maria Lane.

GREEK.

Demosthenes against Androtion and against Timocrates, with Introductions and English Commentary by WILLIAM WAYTE, M.A. Crown 8vo. 7s. 6d.

Select Private Orations of Demosthenes with Introductions and English Notes, by F. A. PALEY, M.A., & J. E. SANDYS, Litt.D.

Part I. Contra Phormionem, Lacritum, Pantaenetum, Boeotum de Nomine, de Dote, Dionysodorum. Cr. 8vo. *New Edition.* 6s.

Part II. Pro Phormione, Contra Stephanum I. II.; Nicostratum, Cononem, Calliclem. Crown 8vo. *New Edition.* 7s. 6d.

Demosthenes, Speech of, against the Law of Leptines. With Introduction and Critical and Explanatory Notes, by J. E. SANDYS, Litt.D. Demy 8vo. 9s.

Euripides. Bacchae, with Introduction, Critical Notes, and Archæological Illustrations, by J. E. SANDYS, Litt. D. Third Edition. Crown 8vo. 12s. 6d.

Euripides. Ion. The Greek Text with a Translation into English Verse, Introduction and Notes by A. W. VERRALL, Litt.D. Demy 8vo. 7s. 6d.

The Mimes of Herondas: the text edited with a Commentary by WALTER HEADLAM, M.A., Fellow of King's College. Demy 8vo.
[*In the Press.*

Homer's Odyssey. The text edited in accordance with modern criticism by ARTHUR PLATT, M.A., late Fellow of Trinity College, Cambridge. Crown 8vo. 4s. 6d.

Homer's Iliad. By the same Editor. [*In the Press.*

Pindar. Olympian and Pythian Odes. With Notes Explanatory and Critical, Introductions and Introductory Essays. Edited by C. A. M. FENNELL, Litt. D. Crown 8vo. 9s.

— **The Isthmian and Nemean Odes** by the same Editor. 9s.

Plato's Phædo, literally translated, by the late E. M. COPE, Fellow of Trinity College, Cambridge. Demy Octavo. 5s.

The Theætetus of Plato, with a Translation and Notes by the late B. H. KENNEDY, D.D. Crown 8vo. 7s. 6d.

The Nuptial Number of Plato: its solution and significance, by J. ADAM, M.A., Fellow and Tutor of Emmanuel College, Cambridge. Demy 8vo. 2s. 6d. Net.

Plato's Protagoras. With Introduction and Notes by J. ADAM, M.A., and A. M. ADAM. [*In the Press.*

London: Cambridge Warehouse, Ave Maria Lane.

Sophocles: the Plays and Fragments. With Critical Notes, Commentary, and Translation in English Prose, by R. C. JEBB, Litt. D., LL.D., Regius Professor of Greek in the University of Cambridge.

Part I. Oedipus Tyrannus. Demy 8vo. *Second Edit.* 12s. 6d.

Part II. Oedipus Coloneus. Demy 8vo. *Second Edit.* 12s. 6d.

Part III. Antigone. Demy 8vo. *Second Edit.* 12s. 6d.

Part IV. Philoctetes. Demy 8vo. 12s. 6d.

Part V. Trachiniae. Demy 8vo. 12s. 6d.

Part VI. Electra. *[In the Press.*

Fragments of Zeno and Cleanthes, an Essay which obtained the Hare Prize in the year 1889. By A. C. PEARSON, B.A., Christ's College, Cambridge. Crown 8vo. 10s.

Pronunciation of Ancient Greek translated from the Third German edition of Dr BLASS by W. J. PURTON, B.A. Demy 8vo. 6s.

An Introduction to Greek Epigraphy. Part I. The Archaic Inscriptions and the Greek Alphabet. By E. S. ROBERTS, M.A., Fellow and Tutor of Gonville and Caius College. Demy 8vo. 18s.

LATIN.

(*See also* pp. 27, 28.)

M. Tulli Ciceronis ad M. Brutum Orator. A Revised Text. Edited with Introductory Essays and Critical and Explanatory Notes, by J. E. SANDYS, Litt.D. Demy 8vo. 16s.

M. T. Ciceronis de Finibus Bonorum Libri Quinque. The Text revised and explained by J. S. REID, Litt.D. *[In the Press.*

Vol. III., containing the Translation. Demy 8vo. 8s.

M. T. Ciceronis de Natura Deorum Libri Tres, with Introduction and Commentary by JOSEPH B. MAYOR, M.A. Demy 8vo. Vol. I. 10s. 6d. Vol. II. 12s. 6d. Vol. III. 10s.

M. T. Ciceronis de Officiis Libri Tres with Marginal Analysis, an English Commentary, and Indices. New Edition, revised, by H. A. HOLDEN, LL.D., Crown 8vo. 9s.

M. T. Ciceronis de Officiis Libri Tertius, with Introduction, Analysis and Commentary by H. A. HOLDEN, LL.D. Cr. 8vo. 2s.

London: Cambridge Warehouse, Ave Maria Lane.

LATIN.

M. Tulli Ciceronis pro C. Rabirio [Perduellionis Reo] Oratio ad Quirites. With Notes, Introduction and Appendices. By W. E. HEITLAND, M.A. Demy 8vo. 7s. 6d.

P. Vergili Maronis Opera, cum Prolegomenis et Commentario Critico pro Syndicis Preli Academici edidit BENJAMIN HALL KENNEDY, S.T.P. Extra fcp. 8vo. 3s. 6d.

A Latin-English Dictionary. Printed from the (Incomplete) MS. of the late T. H. KEY, M.A., F.R.S. Demy 4to. £1. 11s. 6d.

Graduated Passages from Greek and Latin Authors for First-Sight Translation. Selected and supplied with short Notes for beginners by H. BENDALL, M.A., Head Master, and C. E. LAURENCE, B.A., Assistant Master, of Blackheath Proprietary School. Crown 8vo. Part I. EASY. 1s. 6d. Part II. MODERATELY EASY. 2s. Part III. MODERATELY DIFFICULT. 2s. Part IV. DIFFICULT. 2s.

CAMBRIDGE PHILOLOGICAL SOCIETY'S PUBLICATIONS.

Transactions. Vol. I. 1872—1880. 15s. Vol. II. 1881—1882. With Index to Vols. I., II. and Proceedings for 1882. 12s. Vol. III. Pt. I. 1886. 3s. 6d. Pt. II. 1889. 2s. Pt. III. 1890. 2s. 6d.

Proceedings. I—III. 2s. 6d. IV—VI. 2s. 6d. VII—IX. 2s. 6d. X—XII. 2s. 6d. XIII—XV. 2s. 6d. XVI—XVIII. 2s. 6d. XIX—XXI. 2s. 6d. XXII—XXIV. 1889. 1s. XXV—XXVII. 1s. net. XXVIII—XXX. With Laws and List of Members for 1892. 1s. net.

Spelling Reform and English Literature by H. SWEET. 2d. PRONUNCIATION OF LATIN in the Augustan Period. 3d.

An Eighth Century Latin-Anglo-Saxon Glossary preserved in the Library of Corpus Christi College, Cambridge, edited by J. H. HESSELS. Demy 8vo. 10s.

FRENCH.

Random Exercises in French Grammar, Homonyms and Synonyms for Advanced Students, by L. BOQUEL, Lecturer at Emmanuel and Newnham Colleges. Crown 8vo. 3s. 6d.

Key to the above by the same. Crown 8vo. 10s. 6d. (net).

Exercises in French Composition for Advanced Students. By the same. Demy 8vo. 5s. 6d. (net).

London: Cambridge Warehouse, Ave Maria Lane.

CELTIC.

A Grammar of the Irish Language. By Prof. WINDISCH. Translated by Dr NORMAN MOORE. Crown 8vo. 7s. 6d.

ENGLISH LITERATURE AND LITERARY HISTORY.

Chapters on English Metre. By Rev. JOSEPH B. MAYOR, M.A. Demy 8vo. 7s. 6d.

Studies in the Literary Relations of England with Germany in the Sixteenth Century. By C. H. HERFORD, M.A. Crown 8vo. 9s.

From Shakespeare to Pope. An Inquiry into the causes and phenomena of the Rise of Classical Poetry in England. By E. GOSSE, M.A. Crown 8vo. 6s.

Gray and his Friends. Letters and Relics in great part hitherto unpublished. Edited by the Rev. D. C. TOVEY, M.A. Crown 8vo. 6s.

THE STANFORD DICTIONARY.

The Stanford Dictionary of Anglicised Words and Phrases. Edited for the Syndics of the University Press by C. A. M. FENNELL, D.Litt., late Fellow of Jesus College, Cambridge, Editor of Pindar. Demy 4to. Half-buckram, 31s. 6d.; half-morocco, 42s.

OTHER MODERN EUROPEAN LITERATURE.

Contributions to the Textual Criticism of the Divina Commedia. Including the complete collation throughout the *Inferno* of all the MSS. at Oxford and Cambridge. By the Rev. E. MOORE, D.D. Demy 8vo. 21s.

The Literature of the French Renaissance. An Introductory Essay. By A. A. TILLEY, M.A. Crown 8vo. 6s.

MATHEMATICS, PHYSICS AND CHEMISTRY.

The Collected Mathematical Papers of ARTHUR CAYLEY, Sc.D., F.R.S. Demy 4to. 10 vols.
Vols. I., II., III., IV. and V. 25s. each. [Vol. VI. *In the Press.*

Mathematical and Physical Papers. By Sir G. G. STOKES, Sc.D., LL.D. Reprinted from the Original Journals and Transactions, with additional Notes by the Author. Vol. I. Demy 8vo. 15s. Vol. II. 15s.
[Vol. III. *In the Press.*

London: Cambridge Warehouse, Ave Maria Lane.

MATHEMATICS, PHYSICS AND CHEMISTRY. 13

Mathematical and Physical Papers. By Lord KELVIN (Sir W. THOMSON), LL.D., F.R.S. Collected from different Scientific Periodicals from May, 1841, to the present time. Demy 8vo. Vol. I. 18s. Vol. II. 15s. Vol. III. 18s.

The Scientific Papers of the late Prof. J. Clerk Maxwell. Edited by W. D. NIVEN, M.A. 2 vols. Royal 4to. £3. 3s. (net.)

Scientific Papers compiled by the Royal Society of London, Catalogue of. Vols. I.—VI., for the years 1800—1863, Demy 4to. cloth (Vol. I. in half-morocco), £4 (net); half-morocco, £5. 5s. (net). Vols. VII.—VIII. for the years 1864—1873, cloth, £1. 11s. 6d. (net); half-morocco, £2. 5s. (net). Single volumes cloth, 20s., or half-morocco, 28s. (net). Vol. IX. New series for the years 1874–1883, cloth, 25s., half-morocco, 32s. (net). [Vol. X. *In the Press.*

A History of the Study of Mathematics at Cambridge. By W. W. ROUSE BALL, M.A. Crown 8vo. 6s.

Diophantos of Alexandria; a Study in the History of Greek Algebra. By T. L. HEATH, M.A. Demy 8vo. 7s. 6d.

A History of the Theory of Elasticity and of the Strength of Materials, from Galilei to the present time. Vol. I. GALILEI TO SAINT-VENANT, 1639–1850. By the late I. TODHUNTER, Sc.D., edited and completed by Prof. KARL PEARSON, M.A. Demy 8vo. 25s. Vol. II. By the same Editor. [*Nearly ready.*

The Elastical Researches of Barre de Saint-Venant (extract from Vol. II. of TODHUNTER'S History of the Theory of Elasticity), edited by Professor KARL PEARSON, M.A. Demy 8vo. 9s.

A Short History of Greek Mathematics. By J. GOW, Litt. D., Fellow of Trinity College. Demy 8vo. 10s. 6d.

A Treatise on Plane Trigonometry. By E. W. HOBSON, Sc.D. Demy 8vo. 12s.

A Treatise on the Theory of Determinants and their Applications in Analysis and Geometry. By R. F. SCOTT, M.A. Demy 8vo. 12s.

Theory of Differential Equations. Part I. Exact Equations and Pfaff's Problem. By A. R. FORSYTH, Sc.D., F.R.S. Demy 8vo. 12s.

A Treatise on the Theory of Functions of a Complex Variable. By A. R. FORSYTH, Sc.D., F.R.S. Royal 8vo. [*In the Press.*

An Elementary Treatise on Quaternions. By P. G. TAIT, M.A. *Second Edition.* Demy 8vo. 14s.

A Treatise on Natural Philosophy. By Lord KELVIN (Sir W. THOMSON), LL.D., and P. G. TAIT, M.A. Part I. Demy 8vo. 16s. Part II. 18s.

Elements of Natural Philosophy. By Lord KELVIN (Sir W. THOMSON), and P. G. TAIT. *Second Edition.* Demy 8vo. 9s.

London: Cambridge Warehouse, Ave Maria Lane.

A Treatise on Analytical Statics. By E. J. ROUTH, Sc.D., F.R.S. Demy 8vo. Vol. I. 14s. Vol. II. 10s.

A Treatise on Dynamics. By S. L. LONEY, M.A. New and Enlarged Edition. Crown 8vo. 7s. 6d.

Solutions of the Examples in a Treatise on Elementary Dynamics. By the same Author. Crown 8vo. 7s. 6d.

A Treatise on Geometrical Optics. By R. S. HEATH, M.A. Demy 8vo. 12s. 6d.

An Elementary Treatise on Geometrical Optics. By R. S. HEATH, M.A. Crown 8vo. 5s.

Hydrodynamics, a Treatise on the Mathematical Theory of Fluid Motion, by HORACE LAMB, M.A. Demy 8vo. 12s.

A Treatise on the Mathematical Theory of Elasticity. By A. E. H. LOVE, M.A., Fellow of St John's College. In Two Volumes. Demy 8vo. Vol. I. 12s.

An attempt to test the Theories of Capillary Action, by F. BASHFORTH, B.D., and the late J. C. ADAMS, M.A. Demy 4to. £1. 1s.

A Revised Account of the Experiments made with the Bashforth Chronograph, to find the resistance of the air to the motion of projectiles. By FRANCIS BASHFORTH, B.D. Demy 8vo. 12s.

Astronomical Observations made at the Observatory of Cambridge from 1846 to 1860, by the late Rev. J. CHALLIS, M.A.

Astronomical Observations from 1861 to 1865. Vol. XXI Royal 4to., 15s. From 1866 to 1869. Vol. XXII. 15s.
[Vol. XXIII. *In the Press.*

The Mathematical Works of Isaac Barrow, D.D. Edited by W. WHEWELL, D.D. Demy Octavo. 7s. 6d.

The Analytical Theory of Heat. By JOSEPH FOURIER. Translated with Notes, by A. FREEMAN, M.A. Demy 8vo. 12s.

Elementary Thermodynamics, by J. PARKER, M.A., Fellow of St John's College, Cambridge. Crown 8vo. 9s.

The Electrical Researches of the Honourable Henry Cavendish, F.R.S. Written between 1771 and 1781. Edited by J. CLERK MAXWELL, F.R.S. Demy 8vo. 18s.

Practical Work at the Cavendish Laboratory. Heat. Edited by W. N. SHAW, M.A. Demy 8vo. 3s.

A Treatise on the General Principles of Chemistry, by M. M. PATTISON MUIR, M.A. Second Edition. Demy 8vo. 15s.

Elementary Chemistry. By M. M. PATTISON MUIR, M.A., and CHARLES SLATER, M.A., M.B. Crown 8vo. 4s. 6d.

London: Cambridge Warehouse, Ave Maria Lane.

Practical Chemistry. A Course of Laboratory Work. By M. M. PATTISON MUIR, M.A., and D. J. CARNEGIE, M.A. Cr. 8vo. 3s.

Notes on Qualitative Analysis. Concise and Explanatory. By H. J. H. FENTON, M.A., F.C.S. New Edit. Crown 4to. 6s.

(*See also p.* 32, *Pitt Press Mathematical Series.*)

BIOLOGY AND GEOLOGY.

Lectures on the Physiology of Plants, by S. H. VINES, Sc.D., Professor of Botany in the University of Oxford. Demy 8vo. 21s.

Studies from the Morphological Laboratory. Edited by ADAM SEDGWICK, M.A., Fellow and Lecturer of Trinity College, Cambridge. Vol. II. Part I. Royal 8vo. 10s. Vol. II. Part II. 7s. 6d. Vol. III. Parts I. and II. 7s. 6d. each. Vol. IV. Part I. 12s. 6d. Vol. IV. Part II. 10s. Vol. IV. Part III. 5s. Vol. V. Part I. 7s. 6d. Vol. V. Part II. 5s.

A Catalogue of Books and Papers on Protozoa, Coelenterates, Worms, etc. published during the years 1861–1883, by D'ARCY W. THOMPSON, M.A. Demy 8vo. 12s. 6d.

A Catalogue of the Collection of Birds formed by the late Hugh EDWIN STRICKLAND, now in the possession of the University of Cambridge. By O. SALVIN, M.A., F.R.S. £1. 1s.

Illustrations of Comparative Anatomy, Vertebrate and Invertebrate. Second Edition. Demy 8vo. 2s. 6d.

Catalogue of Osteological Specimens contained in the Anatomical Museum of the University of Cambridge. Demy 8vo. 2s. 6d.

Catalogue of Type Fossils in the Woodwardian Museum, Cambridge. By H. WOODS, B.A., F.G.S., with Preface by Professor T. M^cKENNY HUGHES. Demy 8vo. 7s. 6d.

A Catalogue of the Collection of Cambrian and Silurian Fossils contained in the Geological Museum of the University of Cambridge, by J. W. SALTER, F.G.S. Royal Quarto. 7s. 6d.

A Catalogue of Australian Fossils. By R. ETHERIDGE, Jun., F.G.S. Demy 8vo. 10s. 6d.

The Fossils and Palæontological Affinities of the Neocomian Deposits of Upware and Brickhill, being the Sedgwick Prize Essay for 1879. By W. KEEPING, M.A. Demy 8vo. 10s. 6d.

The Jurassic Rocks of Cambridge, being the Sedgwick Prize Essay for the year 1886, by the late T. ROBERTS, M.A. Demy 8vo. 3s. 6d.

The Bala Volcanic Series of Caernarvonshire and Associated Rocks, being the Sedgwick Prize Essay for 1888, by A. HARKER, M.A., F.G.S. Demy 8vo. 7s. 6d.

Fossil Plants as Tests of Climate, being the Sedgwick Prize Essay for 1892. By A. C. SEWARD, M.A., St John's College. Demy 8vo.
[*Nearly ready.*

London: Cambridge Warehouse, Ave Maria Lane.

LAW.

Digest XIX. 2. Locati Conducti, with a Translation and Notes by C. H. MONRO, M.A., Fellow of Gonville and Caius College. Crown 8vo. 5s.

An Introduction to the Study of Justinian's Digest. By HENRY JOHN ROBY. Demy 8vo. 9s.

Justinian's Digest. Lib. VII., Tit. I. De Usufructu, with a Legal and Philological Commentary by H. J. ROBY. Demy 8vo. 9s.
The Two Parts complete in One Volume. Demy 8vo. 18s.

Selected Titles from the Digest, by BRYAN WALKER, M.A., LL.D.
Part I. Mandati vel Contra. Digest XVII. 1. Cr. 8vo. 5s.
Part II. De Adquirendo rerum dominio, and De Adquirenda vel amittenda Possessione, Digest XLI. 1 and 2. Crown 8vo. 6s.
Part III. De Condictionibus, Digest XII. 1 and 4—7 and Digest XIII. 1—3. Crown 8vo. 6s.

The Commentaries of Gaius and Rules of Ulpian. Translated and Annotated, by J. T. ABDY, LL.D., and BRYAN WALKER, M.A. LL.D. New Edition by BRYAN WALKER. Crown 8vo. 16s.

The Institutes of Justinian, translated with Notes by J. T. ABDY, LL.D., and BRYAN WALKER, M.A., LL.D. Cr. 8vo. 16s.

The Fragments of the Perpetual Edict of Salvius Julianus, Arranged, and Annotated by the late BRYAN WALKER, LL.D. Cr. 8vo. 6s.

Grotius de Jure Belli et Pacis, with the Notes of Barbeyrac and others; an abridged Translation of the Text, by W. WHEWELL, D.D. Demy 8vo. 12s. The translation separate, 6s.

The Science of International Law. By T. A. WALKER, M.A., LL.M.; of the Middle Temple. Demy 8vo. [*Nearly ready.*

An Analysis of Criminal Liability. By E. C. CLARK, LL.D., Regius Professor of Civil Law. Crown 8vo. 7s. 6d.

Practical Jurisprudence. A comment on AUSTIN. By the same. Crown 8vo. 9s.

The Constitution of Canada. By J. E. C. MUNRO, LL.M. Demy 8vo. 10s.

Elements of the Law of Torts. A Text-book for Students. By MELVILLE M. BIGELOW, Ph.D. Crown 8vo. 10s. 6d.

A Selection of Cases on the English Law of Contract. By GERARD BROWN FINCH, M.A. Royal 8vo. 28s.

Bracton's Note Book. A Collection of Cases decided in the King's Courts during the Reign of Henry the Third, annotated by a Lawyer of that time, seemingly by Henry of Bratton. Edited by F. W. MAITLAND. 3 vols. Demy 8vo. £3. 3s. (net).

London: Cambridge Warehouse, Ave Maria Lane.

LAW. 17

A Selection of the State Trials. By J. W. WILLIS-BUND, M.A.,
LL.B. Crown 8vo. Vols. I. and II. In 3 parts. 30s.

Land in Fetters. Being the Yorke Prize Essay for 1885. By
T. E. SCRUTTON, M.A. Demy 8vo. 7s. 6d.

Commons and Common Fields, or the History and Policy of the
Laws of Commons and Enclosures in England. Being the Yorke Prize
Essay for 1886. By T. E. SCRUTTON, M.A. Demy 8vo. 10s. 6d.

History of the Law of Tithes in England. Being the Yorke Prize
Essay for 1887. By W. EASTERBY, B.A., LL.B. Demy 8vo. 7s. 6d.

History of Land Tenure in Ireland. Being the Yorke Prize Essay
for 1888. By W. E. MONTGOMERY, M.A., LL.M. Demy 8vo. 10s. 6d.

History of Equity as administered in the Court of Chancery. Being
the Yorke Prize Essay for 1889. By D. M^cKENZIE KERLY, M.A., St John's
College. Demy 8vo. 12s. 6d.

The History of the Law of Prescription in England. Being the
Yorke Prize Essay for 1890. By T. A. HERBERT, B.A., LL.B. Demy
8vo. 10s.

The History of the Doctrine of Consideration in English Law.
Being the Yorke Prize Essay for 1891. By E. JENKS, M.A., Fellow of
King's College. Crown 8vo. [*Nearly ready.*]

Tables shewing the Differences between English and Indian Law.
By Sir ROLAND KNYVET WILSON, Bart., M.A., LL.M. Demy 4to. 1s.

HISTORY.

Cambridge Historical Essays.

Political Parties in Athens during the Peloponnesian War,
by L. WHIBLEY, M.A. (Prince Consort Dissertation, 1888.) Second
Edition. Crown 8vo. 2s. 6d.

Pope Gregory the Great and his relations with Gaul, by
F. W. KELLETT, M.A. (Prince Consort Dissertation, 1888.) Crown
8vo. 2s. 6d.

The Constitutional Experiments of the Commonwealth, being
the Thirlwall Prize Essay for 1889, by E. JENKS, M.A., LL.B.
Crown 8vo. 2s. 6d.

On Election by Lot at Athens, by J. W. HEADLAM, M.A.
(Prince Consort Dissertation, 1890.) Crown 8vo. (*Out of print.*)

The Influence and Development of English Gilds. (Thirlwall
Prize Essay, 1891.) By F. AIDAN HIBBERT, B.A. Crown 8vo.
(*Out of print.*)

London: Cambridge Warehouse, Ave Maria Lane.

The Somerset Religious Houses. By W. A. J. ARCHBOLD, B.A., LL.B. (Prince Consort Dissertation, 1890.) Crown 8vo. 10s. 6d.

The Early History of Frisia, with special relation to its Conversion. By W. E. COLLINS, B.A. (Prince Consort Dissertation, 1890.) Cr. 8vo. [*Preparing.*

The Origin of Metallic Currency and Weight Standards. By W. RIDGEWAY, M.A., Professor of Greek, Queen's College, Cork, and late Fellow of Gonville and Caius College. Demy 8vo. 15s. Net.

The Growth of English Industry and Commerce during the Early and Middle Ages. By W. CUNNINGHAM, D.D. Demy 8vo. 16s.

The Growth of English Industry and Commerce in Modern Times. By the same Author. Demy 8vo. 18s.

A History of Epidemics in Britain. From A.D. 664 to the extinction of the Plague in 1666. By CHARLES CREIGHTON, M.D., M.A., formerly Demonstrator of Anatomy in the University of Cambridge. Demy 8vo. 18s.

Two Unfinished Papers by the late HENRY BRADSHAW. 1. The Collectio Canonum Hibernensis. 2. On the Chartres and Tours MSS. of the Hibernensis. (64 pp.) Demy 8vo. 2s. 6d.

Statutes of Lincoln Cathedral. Arranged by the late HENRY BRADSHAW, with illustrative Documents. Edited by Chr. WORDSWORTH, M.A. Part I. containing the complete text of 'Liber Niger' with Mr Bradshaw's Memorandums. Demy 8vo. 12s. 6d.

Ecclesiae Londino-Batavae archivum. TOMVS PRIMVS. ABRAHAMI ORTELII et virorum eruditorum ad eundem et ad JACOBVM COLIVM ORTELIANVM Epistulae, (1524—1628). TOMVS SECVNDVS. EPISTVLAE ET TRACTATVS cum Reformationis tum Ecclesiae Londino-Batavae Historiam Illustrantes 1544—1622. Ex autographis mandante Ecclesia Londino-Batava edidit JOANNES HENRICVS HESSELS. Demy 4to. Each vol., separately, £3. 10s. Taken together £5. 5s. Net.

The Growth of British Policy, by J. R. SEELEY, M.A.
[*In the Press.*

The Despatches of Earl Gower, English Ambassador at the court of Versailles, June 1790 to August 1792, and the Despatches of Mr Lindsay and Mr Monro. By O. BROWNING, M.A. Demy 8vo. 15s.

Life and Times of Stein, or Germany and Prussia in the Napoleonic Age, by J. R. SEELEY, M.A. Portraits and Maps. 3 vols. Demy 8vo. 30s.

Rhodes in Ancient Times. By CECIL TORR, M.A. With six plates. 10s. 6d.

Rhodes in Modern Times. By the same Author. With three plates. Demy 8vo. 8s.

Ancient Ships. By the same Author. With numerous illustrations. [*In the Press.*

London: Cambridge Warehouse, Ave Maria Lane.

Chronological Tables of Greek History. By CARL PETER. Translated from the German by G. CHAWNER, M.A. Demy 4to. 10s.

History of Nepāl, edited with an introductory sketch of the Country and People by Dr D. WRIGHT. Super-royal 8vo. 10s. 6d.

Kinship and Marriage in early Arabia, by W. ROBERTSON SMITH, M.A., LL.D. Crown 8vo. 7s. 6d.

Natural Religion in India. The Rede Lecture, delivered in the Senate-House, Cambridge, on June 17, 1891, by Sir ALFRED LYALL, K.C.B., K.C.I.E. Cloth, 2s. Paper Covers, 1s.

BIOGRAPHY.

Erasmus. The Rede Lecture, delivered in the Senate-House, Cambridge, June 11, 1890, by R. C. JEBB, Litt.D. Cloth, 2s. Paper Covers, 1s.

The Life and Letters of the Reverend Adam Sedgwick, LL.D., F.R.S. (Dedicated, by special permission, to Her Majesty the Queen.) By JOHN WILLIS CLARK, M.A., F.S.A., and THOMAS McKENNY HUGHES, M.A. 2 vols. Demy 8vo. 36s.

Memorials of the Life of George Elwes Corrie, D.D., formerly Master of Jesus College. By M. HOLROYD. Demy 8vo. 12s.

TRAVELS.

Travels in Arabia Deserta in 1876 and 1877. By CHARLES M. DOUGHTY. With Illustrations. Demy 8vo. 2 vols. £3. 3s.

A Journey of Literary and Archæological Research in Nepal and Northern India, 1884—5. By C. BENDALL, M.A. Demy 8vo. 10s.

ART, &c.

Illuminated Manuscripts in Classical and Mediaeval Times, their Art and their Technique, by J. HENRY MIDDLETON, Slade Professor of Fine Art. Royal 8vo. With Illustrations. 21s.

The Engraved Gems of Classical Times with a Catalogue of the Gems in the Fitzwilliam Museum by J. H. MIDDLETON, M.A. Royal 8vo. 12s. 6d.

The Lewis Collection of Gems and Rings, in the possession of Corpus Christi College, Cambridge, with an Introductory Essay on Ancient Gems by J. H. MIDDLETON, M.A. Royal 8vo. 6s.

A Catalogue of Ancient Marbles in Great Britain, by Prof. ADOLF MICHAELIS. Translated by C. A. M. FENNELL, Litt.D. Royal 8vo. Roxburgh (Morocco back). £2. 2s.

Some Interesting Syrian and Palestinian Inscriptions, by J. RENDEL HARRIS, M.A. Royal 8vo. 4s.

London: Cambridge Warehouse, Ave Maria Lane.

The Types of Greek Coins. By PERCY GARDNER, Litt.D., F.S.A. With 16 plates. Impl. 4to. Cloth £1. 11s. 6d. Roxburgh (Morocco back) £2. 2s.

Essays on the Art of Pheidias. By C. WALDSTEIN, Litt.D., Phil.D. Royal 8vo. With Illustrations. Buckram, 30s.

The Woodcutters of the Netherlands during the last quarter of the Fifteenth Century. By W. M. CONWAY. Demy 8vo. 10s. 6d.

The Literary remains of Albrecht Dürer, by W. M. CONWAY. With Transcripts from the British Museum Manuscripts, and Notes upon them by LINA ECKENSTEIN. Royal 8vo. 21s.

The Collected Papers of Henry Bradshaw, including his Memoranda and Communications read before the Cambridge Antiquarian Society. With 13 facsimiles. Edited by F. J. H. JENKINSON, M.A. Demy 8vo. 16s.

MUSIC.

Counterpoint. A practical course of study. By the late Prof. Sir G. A. MACFARREN, Mus. D. 5th Edition, revised. Cr. 4to. 7s. 6d.

EDUCATIONAL SCIENCE, &c.

Eighteen Years of University Extension. By R. D. ROBERTS, M.A., D.Sc., Organizing Secretary for Lectures to the Local Examinations and Lectures Syndicate. With Map and Diagrams. Crown 8vo. 1s.

Occasional Addresses on Educational Subjects. By S. S. LAURIE, M.A., F.R.S.E. Crown 8vo. 5s.

Lectures on Language and Linguistic Method in the School. By S. S. LAURIE, M.A., LL.D. Crown 8vo. 4s.

Lectures on Teaching, delivered in the University of Cambridge. By J. G. FITCH, M.A., LL.D. Cr. 8vo. 5s.

Lectures on the Growth and Training of the Mental Faculty, delivered in the University of Cambridge. By FRANCIS WARNER, M.D., F.R.C.P. Crown 8vo. 4s. 6d.

SHORTHAND.

A Primer of Cursive Shorthand. By H. L. CALLENDAR, M.A. 6d.

Essays from the Spectator in Cursive Shorthand, by H. L. CALLENDAR, M.A. 6d.

Reading Practice in Cursive Shorthand. Easy extracts for Beginners. St Mark, Pt. I. Vicar of Wakefield, Chaps. I.—IV. Alice in Wonderland, Chap. VII. Price 3d. each.

London: Cambridge Warehouse, Ave Maria Lane.

A System of Phonetic Spelling, adapted to English by H. L. CALLENDAR, M.A. Extra Fcap. 8vo. 6d.

A Manual of Orthographic Cursive Shorthand. By H. L. CALLENDAR, M.A. 1s. Supplement to the above. 6d.

A Manual of Cursive Shorthand, by H. L. CALLENDAR, M.A. Extra Fcap. 8vo. 2s.

MISCELLANEOUS.

Town and Gown. Some five years of work in St George's, Camberwell. By J. TETLEY ROWE, M.A., Trinity College Missioner, with a few words of Preface by Rev. H. MONTAGU BUTLER, D.D., Master of Trinity College, Cambridge. Crown 4to. 1s.

CAMBRIDGE.

The Architectural History of the University of Cambridge and of the Colleges of Cambridge and Eton, by the late Professor WILLIS, M.A., F.R.S. Edited with large Additions and a Continuation to the present time by J. W. CLARK, M.A. 4 Vols. Super Royal 8vo. £6. 6s.

Also a limited Edition of the same, consisting of 120 numbered Copies only, large paper Quarto; the woodcuts and steel engravings mounted on India paper; of which 100 copies are now offered for sale, at Twenty-five Guineas net each set.

The University of Cambridge from the Earliest Times to the Royal Injunctions of 1535. By J. B. MULLINGER, M.A. Demy 8vo. 12s.
—— Part II. From the Royal Injunctions of 1535 to the Accession of Charles the First. Demy 8vo. 18s.

Scholae Academicae: some Account of the Studies at the English Universities in the Eighteenth Century. By CHRISTOPHER WORDSWORTH, M.A. Demy 8vo. 10s. 6d.

History of the College of St John the Evangelist, by THOMAS BAKER, B.D., Ejected Fellow. Edited by JOHN E. B. MAYOR, M.A., Fellow of St John's. Two Vols. Demy 8vo. 24s.

Admissions to Gonville and Caius College in the University of Cambridge March 1558—9 to Jan. 1678—9. Edited by J. VENN, Sc.D., and S. C. VENN. Demy 8vo. 10s.

A Chronological List of the Graces, etc. in the University Registry which concern the University Library. 2s. 6d.

Trusts, Statutes and Directions affecting (1) The Professorships of the University. (2) The Scholarships and Prizes. (3) Other Gifts and Endowments. Demy 8vo. 5s.

Graduati Cantabrigienses: sive catalogus exhibens nomina eorum quos gradu quocunque ornavit Academia Cantabrigiensis (1800—1884). Cura H. R. LUARD, S.T.P. Demy 8vo. 12s. 6d.

London: Cambridge Warehouse, Ave Maria Lane.

Letters patent of Elizabeth and James the First, addressed to the University of Cambridge, with other Documents. Edited (with a translation of the letters of Elizabeth) by J. W. CLARK, M.A. Demy 8vo. 2s. 6d.

Statutes for the University of Cambridge and for the Colleges therein, made, published and approved (1878—1882) under the Universities of Oxford and Cambridge Act, 1877. Demy 8vo. 16s.

Statutes of the University of Cambridge. 3s. 6d.

Ordinances of the University of Cambridge. 1892. 7s. 6d.

A Compendium of University Regulations. Demy 8vo. 6d.

Cambridge University Reporter (*Published by authority*). Containing all the Official Notices of the University Reports of Discussions in the Schools, and Proceedings of the Cambridge Philosophical, Antiquarian and Philological Societies. 3d. weekly.

CATALOGUES.

University Library.

A Catalogue of the Manuscripts. Demy 8vo. 5 vols. 10s. each. Index to Catalogue. 10s.

A Catalogue of Adversaria and printed books containing MS. notes. Demy 8vo. 3s. 6d.

Catalogus Bibliothecæ Burckhardtianæ. Demy Quarto. 5s.

A Catalogue of the Hebrew Manuscripts. By the late Dr S. M. SCHILLER-SZINESSY. 9s.

Catalogue of the Buddhist Sanskrit Manuscripts. Edited by C. BENDALL, M.A. 12s.

Bulletin (weekly), containing titles of new books added to the Library. Crown 8vo. 6s. a year, paid in advance.

Catalogue of the collection of books on Logic presented by J. VENN, Sc.D. 2s. 6d.

A Catalogue of the Portsmouth Collection of Books and Papers written by or belonging to SIR ISAAC NEWTON. Demy 8vo. 5s.

The Illuminated Manuscripts in the Library of the Fitzwilliam Museum, Cambridge, by W. G. SEARLE, M.A. 7s. 6d.

A Catalogue of the Egyptian Antiquities in the Fitzwilliam Museum. By E. A. WALLIS BUDGE, Litt.D., F.S.A. [*In the Press.*

A Descriptive Catalogue of the Manuscripts in the Fitzwilliam MUSEUM. Illustrated with Twenty Plates of Photographic Reproductions. By M. R. JAMES, M.A. Royal 8vo. [*In the Press.*

London: Cambridge Warehouse, Ave Maria Lane.

CAMBRIDGE UNIVERSITY EXAMINATION PAPERS.

These Papers are published in occasional numbers every Term, and in volumes for the Academical year.

Vol. XVII. Papers for the year 1887—88. Vol. XVIII. Papers for the year 1888—89. Vol. XIX. Papers for the year 1889—90. Vol. XX. Papers for the year 1890—91. Vol. XXI. Papers for the year 1891—92. 15s. each.

COLLEGE EXAMINATION PAPERS.

Examination Papers for Entrance and Minor Scholarships and Exhibitions in the Colleges of the University of Cambridge. Part I. Mathematics and Science. Part II. Classics, Mediaeval and Modern Languages and History (Michaelmas Term, 1890). Part III. Mathematics and Science. Part IV. Classics, Law and History (Lent Term, 1891). Part V. Mathematics and Science. Part VI. Classics, Mediæval and Modern Languages and History (June 1891—June 1892). 2s. each.

CAMBRIDGE LOCAL EXAMINATIONS.

Examination Papers, for various years, with the Regulations for the Examination. Demy 8vo. 2s. each, or by post 2s. 2d.

Class Lists, for various years. Boys 1s. Girls 6d.

Annual Reports of the Syndicate, with Supplementary Tables showing the success and failure of Candidates. 2s. each, by post 2s. 3d.

CAMBRIDGE HIGHER LOCAL EXAMINATIONS.

Examination Papers, for various years, with the Regulations for the Examination. Demy 8vo. 2s. each, by post 2s. 2d.

Class Lists, for various years. 1s. each. By post 1s. 2d.

Reports of the Syndicate. Demy 8vo. 1s., by post 1s. 2d.

TEACHERS' TRAINING SYNDICATE.

Examination Papers for various years with the Regulations for the Examination. Demy 8vo. 6d., by post 7d.

OXFORD AND CAMBRIDGE SCHOOLS EXAMINATIONS.

Papers set in the Examination for Certificates, July, 1891. 2s.

Papers set in the Examination for Commercial Certificates, July, 1891. 6d.

List of Candidates who obtained Certificates at the Examination held in 1891; and Supplementary Tables. 9d.

Regulations of the Board for 1893. 9d.

Regulations for the Commercial Certificate, 1893. 3d.

Report of the Board for the year ending Oct. 31, 1891. 1s.

London: Cambridge Warehouse, Ave Maria Lane.

The Cambridge Bible for Schools and Colleges.
GENERAL EDITOR: J. J. S. PEROWNE, D.D., BISHOP OF WORCESTER.

"It is difficult to commend too highly this excellent series."—*Guardian.*

Now Ready. Cloth, Extra Fcap. 8vo. With Maps.

Book of Joshua. By Rev. G. F. MACLEAR, D.D. 2s. 6d.
Book of Judges. By Rev. J. J. LIAS, M.A. 3s. 6d.
First Book of Samuel. By Rev. Prof. KIRKPATRICK, D.D. 3s. 6d.
Second Book of Samuel. By Rev. Prof. KIRKPATRICK, D.D. 3s. 6d.
First Book of Kings. By Rev. Prof. LUMBY, D.D. 3s. 6d.
Second Book of Kings. By Rev. Prof. LUMBY, D.D. 3s. 6d.
Book of Job. By Rev. A. B. DAVIDSON, D.D. 5s.
Book of Psalms. Book I. By Rev. Prof. KIRKPATRICK, D.D. 3s. 6d.
Book of Ecclesiastes. By Very Rev. E. H. PLUMPTRE, D.D. 5s.
Book of Jeremiah. By Rev. A. W. STREANE, B.D. 4s. 6d.
Book of Ezekiel. By Rev. A. B. DAVIDSON, D.D. 5s.
Book of Hosea. By Rev. T. K. CHEYNE, M.A., D.D. 3s.
Books of Obadiah and Jonah. By Archd. PEROWNE. 2s. 6d.
Book of Micah. By Rev. T. K. CHEYNE, M.A., D.D. 1s. 6d.
Books of Haggai, Zechariah & Malachi. By Arch. PEROWNE. 3s. 6d.
Book of Malachi. By Archdeacon PEROWNE. 1s.
Gospel according to St Matthew. By Rev. A. CARR, M.A. 2s. 6d.
Gospel according to St Mark. By Rev. G. F. MACLEAR, D.D. 2s. 6d.
Gospel according to St Luke. By Archdeacon FARRAR. 4s. 6d.
Gospel according to St John. By Rev. A. PLUMMER, D.D. 4s. 6d.
Acts of the Apostles. By Prof. LUMBY, D.D. 4s. 6d.
Epistle to the Romans. Rev. H. C. G. MOULE, M.A. 3s. 6d.
First Corinthians. By Rev. J. J. LIAS, M.A. 2s.
Second Corinthians. By Rev. J. J. LIAS, M.A. 2s.
Epistle to the Galatians. By Rev. E. H. PEROWNE, D.D. 1s. 6d.
Epistle to the Ephesians. Rev. H. C. G. MOULE, M.A. 2s. 6d.
Epistle to the Hebrews. By Archdeacon FARRAR, D.D. 3s. 6d.
Epistle to the Philippians. By Rev. H. C. G. MOULE, M.A. 2s. 6d.
Epistles to the Thessalonians. By Rev. G. G. FINDLAY, B.A. 2s.
General Epistle of St James. By Very Rev. E. H. PLUMPTRE. 1s. 6d.
Epistles of St Peter and St Jude. By the same Editor. 2s. 6d.
Epistles of St John. By Rev. A. PLUMMER, M.A., D.D. 3s. 6d.
Book of Revelation. By Rev. W. H. SIMCOX, M.A. 3s.

London: Cambridge Warehouse, Ave Maria Lane.

BIBLE FOR SCHOOLS AND COLLEGES.

Preparing.

Book of Genesis. By the Bishop of Worcester.
Books of Exodus, Numbers and Deuteronomy. By Rev. C. D. Ginsburg, LL.D.
First and Second Books of Chronicles. By Very Rev. Dean Spence, D.D.
Books of Ezra and Nehemiah. By Rev. Prof. Ryle, B.D.
Book of Isaiah. By Prof. W. Robertson Smith, M.A.
Epistles to Colossians & Philemon. By Rev. H. C. G. Moule, M.A.
Epistles to Timothy and Titus. By Rev. A. E. Humphreys, M.A.

The Smaller Cambridge Bible for Schools.

"The notes elucidate every possible difficulty with scholarly brevity and clearness."—*Saturday Review.*

"We can cordially recommend this series of text-books, not only to those for whom it is primarily intended, but also to the clergy and other workers for use in Bible-classes."—*Church Review.*

"Accurate scholarship is obviously a characteristic of their productions, and the work of simplification and condensation appears to have been judiciously and skilfully performed."—*Guardian.*

Now ready. Price 1s. each.

Book of Joshua. By J. S. Black, M.A.
Book of Judges. By J. S. Black, M.A.
First and Second Books of Samuel. By Prof. Kirkpatrick, D.D.
First and Second Books of Kings. By Rev. Prof. Lumby, D.D.
Gospel according to St Matthew. By Rev. A. Carr, M.A.
Gospel according to St Mark. By Rev. G. F. Maclear, D.D.
Gospel according to St Luke. By Archdeacon Farrar, D.D.
Gospel according to St John. By Rev. A. Plummer, D.D.
Acts of the Apostles. By Professor Lumby, D.D.

THE CAMBRIDGE GREEK TESTAMENT
FOR SCHOOLS AND COLLEGES
with a Revised Text, based on the most recent critical authorities, and English Notes.

Gospel according to St Matthew. By Rev. A. Carr, M.A. 4s. 6d.
Gospel according to St Mark. By Rev. G. F. Maclear, D.D. 4s. 6d.
Gospel according to St Luke. By Archdeacon Farrar. 6s.
Gospel according to St John. By Rev. A. Plummer, D.D. 6s.
Acts of the Apostles. By Prof. Lumby, D.D. 4 Maps. 6s.
First Corinthians. By Rev. J. J. Lias, M.A. 3s.
Second Corinthians. By Rev. J. J. Lias, M.A. 3s.
Epistle to the Hebrews. By Archdeacon Farrar, D.D. 3s. 6d.
Epistles of St John. By Rev. A. Plummer, M.A., D.D. 4s.
Book of Revelation. By Rev. W. H. Simcox, M.A. [*In the Press.*

London: Cambridge Warehouse, Ave Maria Lane.

THE PITT PRESS SERIES.

* *Copies of the Pitt Press Series may generally be obtained in two volumes, Text and Notes separately.*

I. GREEK.

Aristophanes. Aves—Plutus—Ranae. By W. C. GREEN, M.A., late Assistant Master at Rugby School. 3s. 6d. each.

Aristophanes. Vespae. By C. E. GRAVES, M.A. [*In the Press.*

Euripides. Heracleidæ. By E. A. BECK, M.A. 3s. 6d.

Euripides. Hercules Furens. By A. GRAY, M.A., and J. T. HUTCHINSON, M.A. 2s.

Euripides. Hippolytus. By W. S. HADLEY, M.A. 2s.

Euripides. Iphigeneia in Aulis. By C. E. S. HEADLAM, M.A. 2s. 6d.

Herodotus. Book V. By E. S. SHUCKBURGH, M.A. 3s.

Herodotus. Book VI. By the same Editor. 4s.

Herodotus. Books VIII., IX. By the same Editor. 4s. each.
[*Nearly ready.*

Herodotus. Book VIII., Ch. 1—90. Book IX., Ch. 1—89. By the same Editor. 3s. 6d. each.

Homer. Odyssey, Book IX. Book X. By G. M. EDWARDS, M.A. 2s. 6d. each.

Homer. Odyssey, Book XXI. By the same Editor. 2s.

Homer. Iliad. Book VI. By the same Editor. 2s.

Homer. Iliad. Books XXII., XXIII. By the same Editor. 2s. each.

Luciani Somnium Charon Piscator et De Luctu. By W. E. HEITLAND, M.A., Fellow of St John's College, Cambridge. 3s. 6d.

Lucian. Menippus and Timon. By E. C. MACKIE, B.A. 3s. 6d.

Platonis Apologia Socratis. By J. ADAM, M.A. 3s. 6d.

—— **Crito.** By the same Editor. 2s. 6d.

—— **Euthyphro.** By the same Editor. 2s. 6d.

London: Cambridge Warehouse, Ave Maria Lane.

Plutarch's Lives of the Gracchi—Sulla—Timoleon. By H. A. HOLDEN, M.A., LL.D. 6*s.* each.

Plutarch's Life of Nicias. By the same Editor. 5*s.*

Plutarch's Life of Demosthenes. By the same Editor.
[*Nearly ready.*]

Sophocles.—Oedipus Tyrannus. School Edition. By R. C. JEBB, Litt.D., LL.D. 4*s.* 6*d.*

Thucydides. Book VII. By Rev. H. A. HOLDEN, M.A., LL.D. 5*s.*

Xenophon.—Agesilaus. By H. HAILSTONE, M.A. 2*s.* 6*d.*

Xenophon.—Anabasis. By A. PRETOR, M.A. Two vols. 7*s.* 6*d.*

—— —— Books I. III. IV. and V. By the same Editor. *Price* 2*s.* each. Books II. VI. and VII. 2*s.* 6*d.* each.

Xenophon.—Cyropaedeia. Books I. II. By Rev. H. A. HOLDEN, M.A., LL.D. 2 vols. 6*s.*

—— —— Books III. IV. and V. By the same Editor. 5*s.*

—— —— Books VI. VII. and VIII. By the same Editor. 5*s.*

II. LATIN.

Beda's Ecclesiastical History, Books III., IV. Edited by J. E. B. MAYOR, M.A., and J. R. LUMBY, D.D. Revised Edit. 7*s.* 6*d.*

—— —— Books I. II. [*In the Press.*

Caesar. De Bello Gallico Comment. I. By A. G. PESKETT, M.A. 1*s.* 6*d.* Com. II. III. 2*s.*

—— Comment. I. II. III. 3*s.* Com. IV. V. 1*s.* 6*d.* Com. VI. and Com. VIII. 1*s.* 6*d.* each. Com. VII. 2*s.*

—— De Bello Civili. Comment. I. By the same Editor. 3*s.*

M. T. Ciceronis de Amicitia.—de Senectute.—pro Sulla Oratio. By J. S. REID, Litt.D., Fellow of Gonville and Caius College. 3*s.* 6*d.* each.

M. T. Ciceronis Oratio pro Archia Poeta. By the same. 2*s.*

M. T. Ciceronis pro Balbo Oratio. By the same. 1*s.* 6*d.*

M. T. Ciceronis in Gaium Verrem Actio Prima. By H. COWIE, M.A., Fellow of St John's College. 1*s.* 6*d.*

M. T. Ciceronis in Q. Caecilium Divinatio et in C. Verrem Actio. By W. E. HEITLAND, M.A., and H. COWIE, M.A. 3*s.*

M. T. Ciceronis Oratio pro Tito Annio Milone. By JOHN SMYTH PURTON, B.D. 2*s.* 6*d.*

London: Cambridge Warehouse, Ave Maria Lane.

M. T. Ciceronis Oratio pro L. Murena. By W. E. HEITLAND, M.A. 3*s*.

M. T. Ciceronis pro Cn. Plancio Oratio, by H. A. HOLDEN, LL.D. Third Edition. 4*s*. 6*d*.

M. Tulli Ciceronis Oratio Philippica Secunda. By A. G. PESKETT, M.A. 3*s*. 6*d*.

M. T. Ciceronis Somnium Scipionis. By W. D. PEARMAN, M.A. 2*s*.

Horace. Epistles, Book I. By E. S. SHUCKBURGH, M.A. 2*s*. 6*d*.

Livy. Books IV., VI., IX. By H. M. STEPHENSON, M.A. 2*s*. 6*d*. ea.

—— **Book V.** By L. WHIBLEY, M.A. 2*s*. 6*d*.

—— **Books XXI., XXII.** By M. S. DIMSDALE, M.A. 2*s*. 6*d*. each.

—— **Book XXVII.** By H. M. STEPHENSON, M.A. 2*s*. 6*d*.

M. Annaei Lucani Pharsaliae Liber Primus. By W. E. HEITLAND, M.A., and C. E. HASKINS, M.A. 1*s*. 6*d*.

Lucretius, Book V. By J. D. DUFF, M.A., Fellow of Trinity College. *Price* 2*s*.

P. Ovidii Nasonis Fastorum Liber VI. By A. SIDGWICK, M.A. 1*s*. 6*d*.

Ovidii Nasonis Metamorphoseon Liber I. By L. D. DOWDALL, LL.B., B.D. 1*s*. 6*d*.

Quintus Curtius. A Portion of the History (Alexander in India). By W. E. HEITLAND, M.A. and T. E. RAVEN, B.A. 3*s*. 6*d*.

Vergil. The Complete Works. By A. SIDGWICK, M.A. Two Vols. Vol. I. Introduction and Text. 3*s*. 6*d*. Vol. II. Notes. 4*s*. 6*d*.

P. Vergili Maronis Aeneidos Libri I.—XII. By the same Editor. 1*s*. 6*d*. each.

P. Vergili Maronis Bucolica. By the same Editor. 1*s*. 6*d*.

P. Vergili Maronis Georgicon Libri I. II. By the same Editor. 2*s*. **Libri III. IV.** By the same Editor. 2*s*.

III. FRENCH.

Bataille de Dames. By SCRIBE and LEGOUVÉ. By Rev. H. A. BULL, M.A. 2*s*.

Dix Années d'Exil. Livre II. Chapitres 1—8. Par MADAME LA BARONNE DE STAËL-HOLSTEIN. By the late G. MASSON, B.A. and G. W. PROTHERO, M.A. New Edition, enlarged. 2*s*.

Histoire du Siècle de Louis XIV, par Voltaire. Chaps. I.—XIII. By GUSTAVE MASSON, B.A. and G. W. PROTHERO, M.A. 2*s*. 6*d*. Chaps. XIV.—XXIV. 2*s*. 6*d*. Chap. XXV. to end. 2*s*. 6*d*.

London: Cambridge Warehouse, Ave Maria Lane.

Frédegonde et Brunehaut. A Tragedy in Five Acts, by N. LE-MERCIER. By GUSTAVE MASSON, B.A. 2s.

Jeanne D'Arc. By A. DE LAMARTINE. By Rev. A. C. CLAPIN, M.A. Revised Edition by A. R. ROPES, M.A. 1s. 6d.

La Canne de Jonc. By A. DE VIGNY. By H. W. EVE, M.A. 1s. 6d.

La Jeune Sibérienne. Le Lépreux de la Cité D'Aoste. Tales by COUNT XAVIER DE MAISTRE. By GUSTAVE MASSON, B.A. 1s. 6d.

La Picciola. By X. B. SAINTINE. By Rev. A. C. CLAPIN, M.A. 2s.

La Guerre. By MM. ERCKMANN-CHATRIAN. By the same Editor. 3s.

La Métromanie. A Comedy, by PIRON. By G. MASSON, B.A. 2s.

Lascaris ou Les Grecs du XVE Siècle, Nouvelle Historique, par A. F. VILLEMAIN. By the same. 2s.

La Suite du Menteur. A Comedy by P. CORNEILLE. By the same. 2s.

Lazare Hoche—Par EMILE DE BONNECHOSE. With Four Maps. By C. COLBECK, M.A. 2s.

Le Bourgeois Gentilhomme, Comédie-Ballet en Cinq Actes. Par J.-B. Poquelin de Molière (1670). By Rev. A. C. CLAPIN, M.A. 1s. 6d.

Le Directoire. (Considérations sur la Révolution Française. Troisième et quatrième parties.) Revised and enlarged. By G. MASSON, B.A. and G. W. PROTHERO, M.A. 2s.

Les Plaideurs. RACINE. By E. G. W. BRAUNHOLTZ, M.A., Ph.D. 2s.

—— —— (Abridged Edition.) 1s.

Les Précieuses Ridicules. MOLIÈRE. By E. G. W. BRAUNHOLTZ, M.A., Ph.D. 2s.

—— —— (Abridged Edition.) 1s.

L'École des Femmes. MOLIÈRE. By GEORGE SAINTSBURY, M.A. 2s. 6d.

Le Philosophe sans le savoir. Sedaine. By H. A. BULL, M.A., late Master at Wellington College. 2s.

Lettres sur l'histoire de France (XIII—XXIV). Par AUGUSTIN THIERRY. By G. MASSON, B.A. and G. W. PROTHERO. 2s. 6d.

Le Verre d'Eau. A Comedy, by SCRIBE. Edited by C. COLBECK, M.A. 2s.

Le Vieux Célibataire. A Comedy, by COLLIN D'HARLEVILLE. With Notes, by G. MASSON, B.A. 2s.

London: Cambridge Warehouse, Ave Maria Lane.

M. Daru, par M. C. A. SAINTE-BEUVE (Causeries du Lundi, Vol. IX.). By G. MASSON, B.A. Univ. Gallic. 2s.

Polyeucte. By CORNEILLE. By E. G. W. BRAUNHOLTZ, M.A. [*Nearly ready.*

Recits des Temps Merovingiens I—III. THIERRY. By the late G. MASSON, B.A. and A. R. ROPES, M.A. Map. 3s.

IV. GERMAN.

A Book of Ballads on German History. By W. WAGNER, Ph.D. 2s.

A Book of German Dactylic Poetry. By W. WAGNER, Ph.D. 3s.

Benedix. Doctor Wespe. Lustspiel in fünf Aufzügen. By KARL HERMANN BREUL, M.A., Ph.D. 3s.

Culturgeschichtliche Novellen, von W. H. RIEHL. By H. J WOLSTENHOLME, B.A. (Lond.). 3s. 6d.

Das Jahr 1813 (THE YEAR 1813), by F. KOHLRAUSCH. By WILHELM WAGNER, Ph.D. 2s.

Der erste Kreuzzug (1095—1099) nach FRIEDRICH VON RAUMER. THE FIRST CRUSADE. By W. WAGNER, Ph.D. 2s,

Der Oberhof. A Tale of Westphalian Life, by KARL IMMERMANN. By WILHELM WAGNER, Ph.D. 3s.

Der Staat Friedrichs des Grossen. By G. FREYTAG. By WILHELM WAGNER, PH.D. 2s.

Die Karavane, von WILHELM HAUFF. By A. SCHLOTTMANN, Ph.D. 3s.

Goethe's Hermann and Dorothea. By W. WAGNER, Ph.D. Revised edition by J. W. CARTMELL. 3s. 6d.

Goethe's Knabenjahre. (1749—1761.) **Goethe's Boyhood.** By W. WAGNER, Ph.D. Revised edition by J. W. CARTMELL, M.A. 2s.

Hauff, Das Bild des Kaisers. By KARL HERMANN BREUL, M.A., Ph.D. 3s.

Hauff, Das Wirthshaus im Spessart. By A. SCHLOTTMANN, Ph.D., late Assistant Master at Uppingham School. 3s. 6d.

Mendelssohn's Letters. Selections from. By JAMES SIME, M.A. 3s.

Schiller. Wilhelm Tell. By KARL HERMANN BREUL, M.A., Ph.D. 2s. 6d.

—— —— (Abridged Edition.) 1s. 6d.

—— **Geschichte des Dreissigjährigen Kriegs.** By the same Editor. 3s.

London: Cambridge Warehouse, Ave Maria Lane.

Selected Fables. Lessing and Gellert. By KARL HERMANN
BREUL, M.A., Ph.D. 3s.

Uhland. Ernst, Herzog von Schwaben. By H. J. WOLSTEN-
HOLME, B.A. (Lond.). 3s. 6d.

Zopf und Schwert. Lustspiel in fünf Aufzügen von KARL GUTZ
KOW. By H. J. WOLSTENHOLME, B.A. (Lond.). 3s. 6d.

V. ENGLISH.

An Apologie for Poetrie by Sir PHILIP SIDNEY. By E. S. SHUCK-
BURGH, M.A. The text is a revision of that of the first edition of 1595. 3s.

A Discourse of the Commonwealf of thys Realme of Englande.
First printed in 1581, and commonly attributed to W. S. Edited from
the MSS. by the late ELIZABETH LAMOND. [In the Press.

An Elementary Commercial Geography. A Sketch of the Com-
modities and Countries of the World. By H. R. MILL, Sc. D., F.R.S.E. 1s.

An Atlas of Commercial Geography. (Companion to the above.)
By J. G. BARTHOLOMEW, F.R.G.S. With an Introduction by Dr H. R.
MILL. 3s.

Ancient Philosophy from Thales to Cicero, A Sketch of, by
JOSEPH B. MAYOR, M.A. 3s. 6d.

Bacon's History of the Reign of King Henry VII. By the Rev.
Professor LUMBY, D.D. 3s.

British India, a Short History of. By Rev. E. S. CARLOS, M.A. 1s.

Cowley's Essays. By Prof. LUMBY, D.D. 4s.

General Aims of the Teacher, and Form Management. Two Lectures by F. W. FARRAR, D.D. and R. B. POOLE, B.D. 1s. 6d.

John Amos Comenius, Bishop of the Moravians. His Life and
Educational Works, by S. S. LAURIE, A.M., F.R.S.E. 3s. 6d.

Locke on Education. By the Rev. R. H. QUICK, M.A. 3s. 6d.

Milton's Arcades and Comus. By A. W. VERITY, M.A. 3s.

Milton's Ode on the Morning of Christ's Nativity, L'Allegro, Il Pen-
seroso, and Lycidas. By the same Editor. 2s. 6d.

Milton's Samson Agonistes. By the same Editor. 2s. 6d.

Milton's Paradise Lost. Books I., II. By the same Editor.
[In the Press.

Milton's Paradise Lost. Books V., VI. By the same Editor. 2s.

Milton's Paradise Lost. Books XI., XII. By the same Editor. 2s.

London: Cambridge Warehouse, Ave Maria Lane.

Milton's Tractate on Education. A facsimile reprint from the Edition of 1673. Edited by O. BROWNING, M.A. 2s.

More's History of King Richard III. By J. RAWSON LUMBY, D.D. 3s. 6d.

On Stimulus. A Lecture delivered for the Teachers' Training Syndicate at Cambridge, May 1882, by A. SIDGWICK, M.A. New Ed. 1s.

Outlines of the Philosophy of Aristotle. Compiled by EDWIN WALLACE, M.A., LL.D. Third Edition, Enlarged. 4s. 6d.

Sir Thomas More's Utopia. By Prof. LUMBY, D.D. 3s. 6d.

Theory and Practice of Teaching. By E. THRING, M.A. 4s. 6d.

Teaching of Modern Languages in Theory and Practice. By C. COLBECK, M.A. 2s.

Two Noble Kinsmen. By Professor SKEAT, Litt.D. 3s. 6d.

Three Lectures on the Practice of Education. I. On Marking, by H. W. EVE, M.A. II. On Stimulus, by A. SIDGWICK, M.A. III. On the Teaching of Latin Verse Composition, by E. A. ABBOTT, D.D. 2s.

VI. MATHEMATICS.

Arithmetic for Schools. By C. SMITH, M.A., Master of Sidney Sussex College, Cambridge. 3s. 6d.

Elementary Algebra (with Answers to the Examples). By W. W. ROUSE BALL, M.A. 4s. 6d.

Euclid's Elements of Geometry, Books I.—IV. By H. M. TAYLOR, M.A. 3s. Books I. and II. 1s. 6d. Books III. and IV. 1s. 6d. Books V. and VI. [In the Press.

Solutions to the Exercises in Euclid, Books I.—IV. By W. W. TAYLOR, M.A. [Nearly ready.

Elements of Statics and Dynamics. By S. L. LONEY, M.A. 7s. 6d. Or in Two Parts. Part I. Elements of Statics. 4s. 6d. Part II. Elements of Dynamics. 3s. 6d.

Mechanics and Hydrostatics for Beginners. By S. L. LONEY, M.A. [In the Press.

Elementary Treatise on Plane Trigonometry. By E. W. HOBSON, Sc.D., and C. M. JESSOP, M.A. 4s. 6d.

London: C. J. CLAY AND SONS,
CAMBRIDGE WAREHOUSE, AVE MARIA LANE.
Glasgow: 263, ARGYLE STREET.
Cambridge: DEIGHTON, BELL AND CO. **Leipzig:** F. A. BROCKHAUS.
New York: MACMILLAN AND CO.

CAMBRIDGE: PRINTED BY C. J. CLAY, M.A. & SONS, AT THE UNIVERSITY PRESS.

www.ingramcontent.com/pod-product-compliance
Lightning Source LLC
Chambersburg PA
CBHW032223230426

43666CB00033B/1077